NEW YORK GIANTS

YESTERDAY & TODAY ™

Marty Strasen

WEST
SIDE
PUBLISHING

Marty Strasen is an editor at *The Tampa Tribune* and TBO.com in Tampa, Florida—second home to many a New Yorker—and a former assistant editor for *Football News* who covered the Giants in their Super Bowl XXXV appearance. A University of Notre Dame graduate, he also authored *Notre Dame Football: Yesterday & Today,* and he has contributed to numerous other books as author, contributing writer, and editor.

Factual verification by Ed Maloney

Special thanks to collectors Chris Champy of GiantsRUs, Michael Moran, and Pat Nester.

Front cover, clockwise from left: Eli Manning; Mel Triplett (No. 33) carries the ball in the 1958 title game past the Colts' Gino Marchetti (No. 89); Frank Gifford; Phil Simms; Lawrence Taylor.

Back cover, from left: Roosevelt Brown, Gene Filipski, and Don Chandler watch the action from the bench; Y. A. Tittle; Fran Tarkenton; David Tyree makes "Catch 42" in Super Bowl XLII.

Picture credits:

Front cover: © **Corbis** Bettmann (top right); **Getty Images** (top left); *Sports Illustrated* (top center & bottom right); NFL (bottom left)

Back cover: **Getty Images** (left, left center & right); NFL (right center)

AP Images: 18 (right), 27 (top), 29, 30 (left), 31, 36, 38, 44, 47, 70 (top), 76 (bottom), 82 (top center), 90 (top), 91, 92, 93 (left), 99 (top), 102 (right), 103 (top), 105 (bottom), 107 (bottom left), 111 (bottom), 113 (top right), 116 (left), 117 (bottom), 134, 135 (bottom), 140 (bottom), 144 (top right); **Chris Champy Collection:** contents, 7 (right), 25 (top), 32 (top left), 34, 59 (bottom right), 69 (bottom right), 74 (bottom left), 75 (top left & bottom right), 82 (top right & bottom right), 83 (left, bottom center & bottom right), 86 (top left & bottom right), 87 (top left & top right), 96 (top center & bottom), 106 (top left), 113 (top left), 114 (left), 117 (top), 118 (top center & bottom left), 119 (top left, top center & bottom right), 120, 130 (top right & bottom right), 131 (bottom right), 135 (top), 136 (left, top center & top right), 137 (top left & bottom left), 144 (top left), 146 (bottom left & bottom right), 147 (top right & bottom right), 150 (top & bottom left), 151; © **Corbis:** David Bergman, 123; Bettmann, design element backgrounds, 8–9, 10, 11, 12, 14, 15 (left), 16–17, 19, 23, 26 (left), 28 (bottom), 40 (right), 43, 57 (bottom), 60–61, 62 (top), 64 (right), 65 (top), 99 (bottom); Anthony J. Causi/Icon SMI, 141, 148 (right); Peter Foley/epa, 138 (top); Darren Hauck/epa, 142; Hulton-Deutsch Collection, 12; Tony Kurdzuk/*The Star-Ledger*, 139; Jim Leary/Icon SMI, 125 (bottom); Tannen Maury/epa, 145; Reuters, 133 (top); Charles E. Rotkin, 80; Underwood & Underwood, 22 (top); **Diamond Images:** 42 (left), 46, 50 (left), 52; **Getty Images:** contents, design element backgrounds, 3, 13 (top), 34–35, 37 (top), 42 (right), 55, 57 (top), 65 (bottom), 76 (top), 78 (left), 81 (bottom), 94, 95 (right), 98, 101 (right), 108, 109, 111 (top), 114 (right), 115 (bottom), 116 (right), 120–121, 124 (right), 126 (right), 127 (right), 128 (left), 129 (top), 132, 133 (bottom), 138 (bottom), 140 (top), 144 (bottom), 149 (bottom); AFP, 115 (top), 122, 129 (bottom), 143 (right); Focus on Sport, 53 (bottom), 54 (bottom); *Sports Illustrated*, 39, 41, 45, 50 (right), 51 (left), 70 (bottom), 85, 90 (bottom), 95 (left), 104 (bottom), 105 (top), 106 (bottom right), 113 (bottom center & bottom right), 118 (top left), 119 (top right), 124 (left), 125 (top), 137 (top right), 143 (left), 146 (top left), 148 (left); Time Life Pictures, 62 (bottom), 73 (top); **Michael Moran:** 25 (bottom right); **NFL:** endsheets, design element backgrounds, 6, 7 (left), 15 (right), 16, 18 (left), 20 (right), 21 (top), 27 (bottom), 40 (left), 51 (right), 53 (top), 56 (bottom), 63 (left), 66 (bottom), 67, 71, 72, 73 (bottom), 77 (right), 78 (right), 79, 81 (top), 84, 88–89, 100 (right), 101 (left), 103 (bottom), 110, 127 (left); **Naval History and Heritage Command:** NH 103901, 30 (bottom right); **The Nester Collection:** 8, 20 (left); **PIL Collection:** contents, 13 (bottom), 21 (bottom), 22 (bottom), 24, 25 (bottom left & bottom center), 26 (right), 28 (top), 30 (top right), 32 (bottom left, top right & bottom right), 33, 37 (bottom), 46, 48, 49, 54 (top), 56 (top), 58, 59 (top, bottom left & bottom center), 60, 63 (right), 64 (left), 66 (top), 68, 69 (top left, top right, bottom left & bottom center), 74 (top, right & bottom center), 75 (top center, top right & bottom left), 77 (left), 82 (top left & bottom left), 83 (top), 86 (top right & bottom left), 87 (top center, bottom left & bottom right), 88, 93 (right), 96 (top left & top right), 97, 100 (left), 102 (left), 104 (top), 106 (top right, bottom center & bottom left), 107 (top left, top right & bottom right), 112, 113 (bottom left), 118 (top right & bottom right), 119 (bottom left), 126 (left), 128 (right), 130 (top left, left center, right center & bottom left), 131 (top left, top center & top right), 136 (bottom right), 137 (bottom right), 146 (top right), 147 (top left & bottom left), 149 (top), 150 (bottom right)

Memorabilia photography: Thomas Kelly – Kelly/Mooney; PDR Productions Inc./Peter Rossi

The Giants celebrate their epic upset over the New England Patriots in Super Bowl XLII.

Contents

Wellington Mara

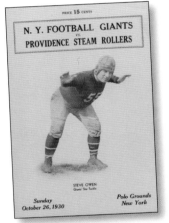

1930 game program

Frank Gifford

Mid-1960s souvenir pin

CHAPTER FOUR
The Dead Zone

CHAPTER FIVE
Return to Glory

1980s Lawrence Taylor pennant

CHAPTER SIX
Giants of Today

CHAPTER SEVEN

Harry Carson

Phil Simms '91 novelty football

David Tyree's "Catch 42"

Dedication to Wellington Mara

Almost everything about Wellington Mara would qualify as "old school." He was named after the Duke of Wellington, an Irish soldier and statesman born in the 18th Century. A staunch Irish Catholic, he fathered 11 children and attended Mass daily. In a thick New York accent, he espoused old-fashioned virtues such as patience, hard work, and humility.

Even as times changed and tattoos, hip-hop, and wild touchdown celebrations became the norm, Mara's players continued to revere him as much as they had several decades ago.

Seven busloads of players, from past and present, walked with heavy hearts to the site of Mara's funeral in October 2005 to honor the 89-year-old patriarch whose father had purchased the team when "Well" was 9.

"Well Mara was a perfect friend," said Y. A. Tittle, who quarterbacked the Giants in the 1960s. "He was a friend of all the players."

When Mara was a young boy, he would shine the players' shoes as a way to win their affection and be part of the team. As a teenager, he prepared scouting reports on opponents and potential Giants draft picks—long before the NFL had scouting services and experts who made a living at the trade.

As team owner during the NFL's formative and modern decades, Mara made the moves he felt necessary to put the team in championship contention, but he was fiercely loyal to those who wore the Giants' red, white, and blue. He considered everyone his family—from water boys to players to

Wellington Mara celebrates with the 1963 Giants in the locker room.

coaches to fellow executives—and that's how he treated them. His concern for each individual in his organization was rare and legendary.

Mara took troubled players such as Lawrence Taylor and Jeremy Shockey under his wing, getting involved in their personal lives and befriending them when they felt the rest of the world was against them. He absorbed criticism for being perhaps *too* loyal to players and coaches who had worn out their welcome with fans. That, however, was Mara's way. It became the Giants' way.

"You don't appreciate it until you quit," said former Giants quarterback Phil Simms, "but there is no such thing as ex-Giants. There are just old Giants."

Even in his eighties, Mara could make a room of players or fellow owners fall silent when he stood up to speak. Sure, there were stories to tell—stories of football from the leather-helmet days, of how the NFL grew to become America's most popular professional sports league, and of how ball control and defense would win championships, as they did for Mara's New York Giants.

However, Mara could usually be found squarely in the present, keeping his eye on the proverbial ball, working toward making the Giants and the NFL even better in the years to come. The wisdom he dispensed led to some of the greatest developments in the booming growth of the league, from television contracts to new stadiums to expansion teams.

"Wellington Mara represented the heart and soul of the National Football League," longtime friend and former NFL commissioner Paul Tagliabue said.

"I wanted him to write a book," recalled former Giants coach Dan Reeves. "Of course, he was so humble, he said, 'I don't need to write one. I don't deserve one.'"

The Mara family's ownership sets the Giants apart from almost every other professional sports franchise. In an era

DAILY SPORTS NEWS

A TRUE GIANT

Wellington Mara
1916-2005

Mara walks the field of Giants Stadium, one of his lasting achievements that made him, as the Daily News *reported (above right), "a true Giant."*

when billion-dollar corporations buy and sell sports teams like so many commodities, the Giants have retained a family-run tradition. Old-fashioned, sure. Just as Mara wanted it.

When he supported the salary cap—the reason the NFL serves as the model for parity in pro sports—Mara insisted that a league is only as strong as its weakest link.

The Giants, because of Mara, grew to be as strong as their strongest link—the man who linked past Giants with present ones and top executives with passionate fans. Once you were a Giant under Wellington Mara, you were always a Giant.

And among Giants, he was the greatest of them all.

Marty Strasen

CHAPTER ONE

The $500 Franchise

1925–1929

> *"Any sports franchise for New York ought to be worth $500. Even football."*

TIM MARA IN 1925, WHEN PRO FOOTBALL WAS NOT ON THE NATIONAL SPORTS MAP

Above: *This program comes from the New York Giants initial season, 1925, when drawing fans proved difficult save for one game.* Right: *The New York Giants were at risk of folding in their inaugural 1925 season before Red Grange and the Chicago Bears saved the day by drawing 70,000-plus fans to the Polo Grounds.*

Tim Mara's Giant Gamble

Bookmaking was legal and boxing huge in 1925 New York City. That's why a tall Irishman named Tim Mara had his sights set squarely on heavyweight Gene Tunney.

Mara—a successful bookie, businessman, and promoter who had gotten Tunney a few big fights—was interested in upping his investment in the up-and-coming pugilist. Mara had a keen eye for talent, and Tunney was a "find" who went on to beat Jack Dempsey twice and earn the heavyweight championship.

However, the 38-year-old Mara was sidetracked from backing Tunney's career, so later in 1925, Tim said (in the presence of his young sons), "I'm gonna try to put pro football over in New York today." The cost of a franchise was $500 (though some peg the figure at $2,500).

It was a bold move, purchasing a team for even $500 at the time. The NFL was made up of 18 teams in cities including Racine, Wisconsin; Hammond, Indiana; Rock Island, Illinois; and Duluth, Minnesota. Two teams played in Chicago—the Bears and the Cardinals—but the league longed for a franchise in New York City that could bring its game to the masses.

It was "all in the family" for the New York Giants from the day Tim Mara purchased the franchise for $500 in 1925. The Maras have owned the club ever since.

When he was approached with the offer to buy in for $500, Mara had never seen a pro football game. Still, the entrepreneur in him saw opportunity, even if American sports fans preferred the college game. "Any sports franchise for New York," Mara predicted, "ought to be worth $500. Even football."

It seemed for a while as though that statement might be a stretch. Fans in New York were unaccustomed to the game, and Mara knew it would take a big-name player to win them over. He signed 37-year-old Jim Thorpe—former Olympic decathlon gold medalist and the first true pro football superstar—to a unique $250-per-half contract, understanding that the aging icon would not be able to play a full game. Mara also inked top collegians such as Century Milstead of Yale, Hinkey Haines of Penn State, and Jack McBride of Syracuse.

None of those talents, old or young, was big enough to keep the fledgling franchise from suffering the economic pains of an era when a ticket to a game at the Polo Grounds could be had for as little as 50 cents. Nor were they enough to keep the Giants from struggling, at least initially, against more seasoned clubs.

They lost their first regular-season game at Providence on October 11, 1925, by a 14–0 score. They got on the scoreboard in their second game six days later but lost at Frankford—in north Philadelphia—5–3 on a safety. In the first Giants home game the very next day, Frankford rolled to a 14–0 win at the Polo Grounds. It was Thorpe's last game with the Giants, due to age and a knee injury, and he collected his $250 despite not making it through an entire half.

The Giants actually fared better without him, winning seven straight games and eight of their final nine after his release. The one loss in that stretch, however, might have been the most important game of New York's initial season.

All-time great Jim Thorpe shows his form as a 37-year-old back for the 1925 Giants. He was never expected to play more than a half.

If the Giants struggled to stop Chicago's Red Grange (shown passing) in 1925, at least they benefited from the visibility Grange gave pro football in its infancy—and the 70,000 New Yorkers who bought tickets.

Entering the second half of the season, Mara's costs were exceeding his revenue. Without a known headliner like Thorpe to attract fans, he decided to go after the biggest name in football—Harold "Red" Grange. The Illinois All-American routinely drew sellout crowds to the biggest stadiums in the country during his college career, so Mara called on Grange, trying to convince him to launch his pro career in a Giants uniform.

Mara returned with good news and bad. "He'll be playing in the Giants-Bears game," he told his sons, Wellington and Jack, "only he'll be playing for the Bears." The game, played December 6 at the Polo Grounds, was one of the most anticipated spectacles in New York sports history. More than 70,000 fans, the largest pro football crowd in history at the time, crammed into a stadium that seated 65,000.

Grange returned an interception 35 yards for a late touchdown in the Bears' 19–7 win, but the afternoon was a clear victory for Mara. Grange, under the terms of a generous contract from Bears boss George Halas, cleared about $30,000 of the gate for himself. However, Mara saw his deficit of some $40,000 for the season erased, becoming a reported $18,000 profit.

That one game might have saved the Giants. All of a sudden, Mara's $500 investment was looking like a Gene Tunney knockout.

Giants Crowned Champs in Third Season

New York in 1927 could truly be called "the city of champions." Months after Babe Ruth, Lou Gehrig, and the '27 Yankees made claim to being baseball's best team ever with a 110–44 record and a World Series title, the New York Giants became NFL champions in just their third season. Six years before the league staged a championship game, the Giants were crowned after compiling an 11–1–1 record, tops among the 12 teams.

Under Bob Folwell, the 1925 Giants overcame losses in their first three games to finish 8–4 in their NFL debut. Doc Alexander coached in 1926 and led the team to an 8–4–1 mark. In both seasons, former Syracuse fullback Jack McBride led a power-running offense and paced the team in scoring.

Entering 1927, Dr. Harry March—secretary and later president of the team—had a feeling it was defense that could put the Giants over the top. To that end, with Earl Potteiger now coaching and playing running back, March signed lineman Cal Hubbard (who played at tiny Centenary College and Geneva College) to solidify a defensive line that included such standouts as Steve Owen and Al Nesser. The opposition could not move the ball.

There were few signs of a title run when the Giants opened the season with an 8–0 victory at Providence and a scoreless tie at Cleveland, however. In the first home game, a struggling New York attack sputtered and Cleveland posted a 6–0 win, dropping the Giants to 2–1–1.

Then McBride and the offense found their stride, reeling off at least 13 points in each remaining game,

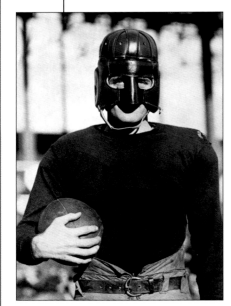

Hinkey Haines, an explosive Penn State product, models an early leather helmet designed to protect the entire face. Haines helped the Giants to a title in 1927 and was their top scorer in '28.

garnering nine straight wins. McBride again finished with the team scoring lead (57 points), followed by Hinkey Haines and Mule Wilson (36 points each).

March's defensive upgrades paid dividends, as the Giants kept their opponents from scoring a point in seven of those remaining nine games. New York pitched 10 shutouts and racked up a 197–20 scoring advantage.

Owen called a November 27 win over George Halas and the visiting Chicago Bears the toughest game he ever played. Owen and his teammates fought to keep the Bears from overcoming a 13–0 deficit at the Polo Grounds. Chicago managed a second-half touchdown to make it 13–7, but the Giants held on by that margin.

The Bears finished 9–3–2, behind the second-place Green Bay Packers (7–2–1). The Giants and Packers did not square off, but suffice it to say Green Bay would have needed its best to have found the end zone against the 1927 champions.

Jack McBride—upended here while carrying the ball in a 1928 game at the Polo Grounds—led the Giants in scoring in each of their first three seasons.

Benny Brings in Fans, Bumps Bears

What Red Grange was to running the football, Benny Friedman was to throwing it. Like Grange, Friedman—the former Michigan star—could do much more than pass. He ran, kicked, blocked, tackled, and drew fans by the thousands. The way he spiraled the ball to his teammates, however, put him light-years beyond any other quarterback of the era.

Those skills did not help the Giants in 1928. That year, Friedman was—remarkably—leading the NFL in both rushing scores and touchdown passes for the Detroit Wolverines. The Giants, meanwhile, were struggling to a dreary four-win season on the heels of their '27 championship. What's worse, they lost somewhere in the vicinity of $40,000.

Owner Tim Mara decided to make a bold move. He wanted Friedman and was not about to let him get away, as Grange had when he signed with the Bears over the Giants in 1925.

To land Friedman, Mara bought the entire Wolverines franchise. The most expensive piece was Friedman, who signed for $10,000, which might have been the richest contract in the NFL

Chicago's Red Grange (left) and New York's Benny Friedman traded 12–0 decisions in 1930, a season in which Friedman led the Giants in scoring and also coached the team in two games—both wins.

at the time. "It was a bargain," wrote football historian Bob Carroll, noting that the team quickly returned to profitability.

During an era when touchdown passes were rarely thrown, Friedman tossed 20 in 1929, including *four* in a 34–0 November 17 shutout of the Bears. Both stood as NFL records for years. The Giants, as a result, turned their fortunes around under new coach Roy Andrews, finishing second in the league with a 13–1–1 record.

Friedman led the NFL in touchdown passes for four straight years. He became player-coach for the Giants and was enshrined in the Pro Football Hall of Fame in 2005.

This 2005 Goal Line card celebrates Friedman's enshrinement in the Pro Football Hall of Fame.

Cal Hubbard: Two-Sport Hall of Famer

Making the Hall of Fame in one's sport is an athlete's highest honor.

The sports fan who visits Canton, Ohio, can read about football star Cal Hubbard; make a trip to Cooperstown, New York, and read the plaque of Cal Hubbard, Hall of Fame baseball umpire; then travel to the College Football Hall of Fame to learn about—you guessed it—Cal Hubbard.

Hubbard is the only man in both the Pro Football Hall of Fame and the Baseball Hall of Fame. The most feared lineman of his day at 250 pounds (very large for that era), Hubbard possessed a rare combination of size and speed. He began his career with the Giants in 1927 and '28, anchoring the defense that shut out 10 opponents to win the 1927 championship.

Ownership: All in the Family

In October 1929, the New York Giants were in the middle of a fine 13–1–1 season when, across town on Wall Street, widespread panic hit. The stock market crash that brought on the Great Depression took its toll on most of America. Even the wealthy were not immune.

Truth is, even when the Giants were winning, running a pro football team in the NFL's early years was not always a profitable endeavor. Tim Mara was determined to make a go of it, but he was up against it in 1930. He had suffered significant losses on Wall Street, the club was fighting to stay in the black, and he was involved in an expensive lawsuit against boxing champion Gene Tunney and his manager, Billy Gibson, over money Mara felt was owed him.

Fearing a legal outcome that might force him to lose the Giants, Mara shifted ownership of the franchise to the biggest fans he knew—sons Jack, 22, and Wellington ("Well"), 14. The youngest owner in professional sports, Wellington Mara proved to be ahead of his time both then and throughout his lifelong leadership of the team.

While Jack handled most of the business matters, Well was perfectly in tune with the personnel. As a teen who looked up to the players, he wowed them by providing scouting reports of opponents that were remarkably accurate and that helped the Giants become consistent winners. Young Wellington advocated for paying top players good salaries, while Jack kept a more watchful eye on the bottom line. Father Tim fell closer to his younger son's outlook.

The Giants knocked down Ernie Nevers (with ball) and the Chicago Cardinals, 24–21, at the Polo Grounds en route to a 13–1–1 record and second-place finish in 1929.

Wellington (left) and Jack Mara (right) were not shy about going after talent they felt would help the Giants, including the 1946 signing of quarterback Frank Filchock (seated).

"Jack would say, 'Suppose we have a bad year?'" Wellington once recalled of the early years. "And my father would say, 'How can we have a bad year?' Jack was pretty conservative, and my father and I both wanted to take a chance."

That dynamic worked, well, *dynamically* for the Mara ownership triumvirate. Wellington, involved in the operation of the Giants for eight decades until his death in 2005, made most of the club's football decisions through 1973. The team played in six NFL championship games between 1956 and '63, thanks largely to trades Well orchestrated for players like Y. A. Tittle, Andy Robustelli, Pat Summerall, Joe Walton, Dick Lynch, and a long list of others.

After Tim Mara's death in 1959, Jack and Wellington continued to thrive as co-owners. Jack died in 1965—two years after his father was enshrined in the Pro Football Hall of Fame—passing his ownership share to his son, Tim, in the continuation of the family tradition. Wellington took over Jack's team president role at that time.

In addition to shaping the success of the Giants—leading the team to 21 first-place finishes, 27 playoff trips, and six NFL championships—Wellington was instrumental in the growth of the NFL as a force on the American sports scene. He helped craft the league's first national television deal in the 1960s, and he chaired or served on several ownership committees.

"He was such a dignified and in some ways regal character," former Giants running back Tiki Barber said, "who always respected the game and respected what this league is all about."

As with most families, things were not always smooth between the Maras over the years. During lean times from 1964 to 1980, Wellington and nephew Tim had disputes over stadium issues, personnel questions, and financial decisions. Ultimately, however, they were onboard as the Giants won two Super Bowls, in 1986 and '90.

Right after that second Super Bowl title, Tim Mara sold his 50 percent share in the Giants to business magnate Robert Tisch, the chairman and director of Loews, one of the most successful financial companies in America. It marked the first time since the team's 1925 inception that ownership extended beyond the Mara family. It did not, however, keep the Giants from continuing to operate as a family business of sorts.

No man in club history was more influential than Wellington Mara, who served the Giants in some capacity for almost 80 years, beginning the day his father purchased the franchise in 1925.

Wellington Mara, who died October 25, 2005, at 89, has three sons—John, Chris, and Frank—serving prominent front-office roles in leading the Giants. And Tisch, who died of brain cancer at 79 just three weeks after Mara, has son Steve serving as chairman, executive vice president, and co-owner of a franchise that became a Super Bowl champion for the third time in 2007.

Steve Owen and the Early Giants

1930–1953

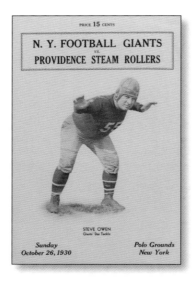

"A fellow like Steve comes along so rarely. I knocked heads with him when we both were players, and I knocked heads with him when we both were coaches. Every time, he gained my hearty respect."

GEORGE "PAPA BEAR" HALAS, ON LONGTIME GIANTS COACH STEVE OWEN

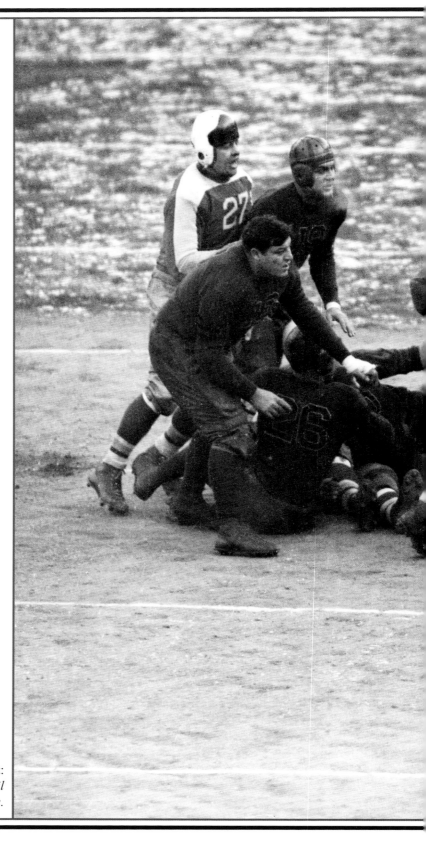

Above: *This program from 1930 features Owen, who was one of the best linemen of his day.* Right: *Bronko Nagurski (with ball) and the Bears had the edge in the 1934 NFL championship game until the Giants changed into sneakers for the second half of their 30–13 win at the Polo Grounds.*

Steve Owen: Giant Among Giants

Steve Owen was born to homesteaders in the Cherokee Strip area of the Oklahoma Territory in 1898, almost a decade before Oklahoma became a state. His ambition: to become a jockey.

Somewhere along the way to 260 pounds, Owen realized that sitting atop a horse was not in his future. Instead, he took up football as a lineman, and it carried "Stout Steve" to almost 30 years of success in the Big Apple—a far cry from his hometown of Cleo Springs, Oklahoma, which had fewer than 300 residents.

During Owen's playing days, scouts did not routinely make their way to Oklahoma. So after his career at Phillips University in tiny Enid, Owen latched on with semi-pro teams and dominated the line of scrimmage. His first NFL job paid $50 per game with Kansas City. It also exposed his talents to the Mara family. In 1926, the Giants owners bought his rights for $500.

Owen captained the 1927 Giants to their first NFL championship. He anchored a defense that allowed just 20 points all season, and he would make a career out of his demand for defensive excellence.

After LeRoy Andrews was fired as coach in 1930, and after star quarterback Benny Friedman said he would not take a player/coach position alone, the Maras asked Owen—almost as an afterthought—to join Friedman as co-coach with two games left in the season. New York won both, and in 1931 Owen took sole command of a job he would hold through 1953.

During his coaching tenure, Owen steered the Giants to two NFL championships and eight division titles. The NFL instituted a title game in 1933, and Owen led the Giants to the title game each year from 1933 to 1935. As manager Joe McCarthy created

The first great coach in Giants history, Steve Owen was an innovator responsible for the A formation offense and umbrella defense. He won two NFL championships and eight divisional titles over 24 seasons.

the "Yankee image" for that club, wrote Pulitzer Prize-winning *New York Times* sportswriter Arthur Daley, "Steve Owen created an even stronger 'Giant image' in football, a spiritual quality of sorts that gave his team a matchless esprit de corps. He was sound and he was solid. So were his teams."

Owen *was* Giants football. He was the innovator who put his 1934 team in sneakers on an icy field to upset the Bears for the NFL championship. He was the visionary who designed the "umbrella defense" to stop the 1950s Cleveland Browns' passing game with coverage rather than quarterback pressure—a concept that lives on today in "nickel" and "dime" secondary packages.

"Stout Steve" Owen (left), coach of the Giants, shares congratulations with his players after their December 12, 1943, win in Washington forced a playoff with the Redskins the following week.

Coach Steve Owen watches his Giants warm up for a workout at their new Bear Mountain training camp in New York in August 1944.

Owen for not spending time developing the Giants' offense to the same high standard, the Maras were so comfortable with their head coach that they never offered him a written contract. Owen worked for more than 20 years under the annual terms of a preseason handshake.

For a time, Owen was in fact known for offensive expertise. He invented the A formation, a version of the single wing where the line was strong on one side and the backfield strong on the other. With center Mel Hein up front, he used it in the 1930s and '40s to deceive opponents, as Hein could snap the ball to any of three backs on each play. Defenses eventually caught on, however, and Owen turned to the more conventional T formation.

Owen's all-time record of 153 Giants victories nearly double the 77 of No. 2 Bill Parcells. Steve Owen was generally well-liked by his players in good times and lean years alike. It may have had something to do with his early embrace of two-platoon football, which gave players an occasional breather rather than relying on top stars

Owen would order four, five, or even six defensive backs to line up in an arc-like formation, working together like spokes on an umbrella, and charge them with anticipating passes before they were thrown. It gave Cleveland's Otto Graham and other top passing quarterbacks fits.

Owen knew defense better than anyone, and the Mara family was keen enough to know that defense wins. While some criticized

to log a full 60 minutes.

It was with heavy hearts that the Maras decided to end his tenure after 1953. Late in his life, they welcomed him back as a scout.

"It's quite possible," wrote Daley after Owen's death in 1964, "that no professional coach ever inspired more love, devotion, and admiration among his players than did Steve."

Bears Drop Giants in First Title Game

The New York Giants did not emerge victorious in the NFL's first championship game. But professional football did.

The Chicago Bears won the game, held on December 17, 1933, and were crowned champs on the strength of a 23–21, come-from-behind win over the Giants at Wrigley Field. The real winner, though, was the young league.

Marred by low scoring and numerous ties, the 1932 season ended with a dilemma. The Bears and Portsmouth had tied atop the standings, so a tiebreaker game was hastily scheduled and played indoors, on an 80-yard dirt field in Chicago Stadium, which the Bears won 9–0. The NFL took steps to ensure such circumstances would never be repeated.

The league was split into two divisions, with the winner of each advancing to a championship game that would be played outdoors, on a regulation field. To increase scoring, the rules were changed to allow forward passes from any position behind the line of scrimmage, and the goalposts were moved up to the goal line. As a result, the number of successful field goals doubled and there were only half as many ties in 1933.

The NFL had high hopes for its first title game, pitting the Eastern champion Giants and Western champion Bears, and those hopes materialized on Chicago's North Side.

"The game was a thrilling combat of forward passing skill, desperate line plunging and gridiron strategy that kept the chilled spectators on their feet in constant excitement," noted *The New York Times*.

An estimated 26,000 fans witnessed a back-and-forth battle that featured long runs and expert passing. The Bears took the lead on two field goals by "Automatic Jack" Landers, but the

An estimated 26,000 attended the first title game, where they could purchase this program.

After catching a jump pass from Bronko Nagurski, Chicago end Bill Hewitt laterals the ball to Bill Karr for the winning touchdown in the 23–21 Bears win over the Giants in the first-ever NFL title game in 1933.

Giants unleashed the passing attack that helped them lead the league with 244 points.

It started with Mel Hein, in just the third season of his 15-year, Hall of Fame career. With the sturdy lineman keeping Chicago's defense at bay, quarterback Harry Newman put on a passing clinic, resulting in two touchdown passes, one to top receiver Red Badgro in the second quarter and one to Ken Strong in the fourth. Each TD toss overcame a Bears lead, as did Max Krause's third-quarter scoring plunge.

However, the Bears overcame a 21–16 deficit in the final minutes to win on a dazzling play. Bronko Nagurski connected on a 13-yard pass to Bill Hewitt, who tossed a long lateral to Billy Karr. Karr slipped two defenders on his way to the end zone.

Victory, NFL.

Giants Boot Bears with Rubber Soles

More than 50 years before Nike's "It's Gotta Be the Shoes" campaign, it was, indeed, the shoes…basketball shoes, to be exact.

The setting was the 1934 NFL championship game on December 9 at the Polo Grounds. More than 35,000 fans braved conditions better suited to hockey than football. Frost blanketed New York that morning, and sleet fell. The field was literally a sheet of ice as the teams skated onto it.

The weather was not the only daunting sight for the Giants, who had finished the regular season with a modest 8–5 record. The Chicago Bears, featuring the power running of Bronko Nagurski, were riding an 18-game winning string and had downed the Giants twice that year. How, New York coach Steve Owen wondered, could Chicago be stopped?

A change of shoes gave the Giants a huge second-half advantage over the Chicago Bears on a frozen field in the 1934 NFL title clash. New York scored 27 unanswered points in the final quarter for a 30–13 win.

Team captain Ray Flaherty offered the answer: "Basketball shoes."

Flaherty's Gonzaga team had once worn rubber-soled sneakers instead of cleats on a frozen field in a college game against Montana. The shoes had given them better traction.

One problem: This was Sunday, and stores were closed. So Owen sent Abe Cohen, a pint-size tailor who helped the Giants' equipment manager, on a city-wide mission to find sneakers.

With both teams in cleats to start the game, the Bears were superior. They took a 10–3 halftime lead that could have been wider. Then Cohen returned with nine pairs of shoes he borrowed from Manhattan College's athletic program. The Giants scrambled into them and began running circles around their stronger foes in the second half.

New York scored 27 points in the fourth quarter, pounding the Bears 30–13 to win the championship in one of the greatest turnarounds in sports history. Nike could not have scripted a commercial any better.

One Strong Performance

Ken Strong was a four-time All-Pro and led the NFL in scoring in '33. Yet it was one game that put this NYU All-American (as seen in this '55 Topps card) in the record books.

KEN STRONG — Halfback — ALL AMERICAN

The 17 points Strong scored in the 1934 "Sneakers Game" stood for nearly three decades as an NFL championship record. He opened the scoring on a 38-yard field goal, and it looked like the Giants might be held to those three points.

In the fourth quarter, though, Strong scored on 42- and 11-yard touchdown runs and added two extra-point kicks, as the Giants, wearing sneakers, raced past the Bears 30–13.

Strong starred for eight seasons with the Giants and was enshrined in the Pro Football Hall of Fame in 1967.

Lions Humble Giants for 1935 Championship

If Detroit's automobile industry was struggling during the Great Depression, its sports teams were having no such troubles in 1935.

In October, the Tigers won their first World Series. And in December, the Western Division champion Lions welcomed the Eastern champion Giants for Detroit's first appearance in the NFL championship game.

New York, 9–3, arrived in Michigan to find the 7–3–2 Lions slightly favored by the oddsmakers, though the Giants were playing in their third consecutive title game and featured the top defense in the league.

Giants quarterback Ed Danowski had completed more than half his passes during the season and had a league-high 10 touchdown tosses. With standouts like Bill Morgan up front, New York usually dominated the scrimmage line. And fullback Kink Richards led the league with 153 carries and rushed for four scores—tied for second in the NFL behind the six scored by Detroit's Ernie Caddel.

Harry Newman (No. 12) smiles as he eludes Giants teammate Tod Goodwin during a 1935 practice at the Polo Grounds.

Tuffy Leemans: One "Tuff" Runner

Young Wellington Mara, then in high school, saw George Washington's Alphonse Leemans running through Alabama during a mid-1930s college game. The son of Giants owner Tim Mara turned this love-at-first-sight moment into the start of a Hall of Fame NFL career for "Tuffy."

A second-round pick in the first NFL draft in 1936, Leemans (shown on this '89 Goal Line card) led the NFL with 830 rushing yards as a rookie and made the first or second All-NFL team every year through '42. A workhorse who starred as a halfback, fullback, defender, and return man, Leemans ran for 17 touchdowns, caught three TD passes, and passed for 25 scores in his career.

Cold rain and heavy snow on December 15 kept all but 15,000 fans from the University of Detroit Stadium, but they had plenty to cheer. Four different Lions, including Caddel, ran for touchdowns in their 26–7 rout. Detroit marched 61 yards for their first TD in the opening minutes, added a second one before the end of the first quarter for a 13–0 lead, and kept motoring over the Giants throughout the game. New York's only score came on a 42-yard, second-quarter pass from Danowski to Ken Strong.

"Despite the fact that the game was played under the most miserable conditions," stated *The New York Times,* "the Lions moved along to their objective with an ease and degree of perfection that stunned their foes from the East."

Despite the loss, with Danowski at the controls, Steve Owen's Giants were churning out Eastern titles and championship game appearances like an auto assembly line.

Giants Rally Past Pack for '38 Title

After further review…the 1938 NFL championship might have benefited from instant replay. Because the league was almost 50 years away from using "moving pictures" to review official calls, it had to settle for a little controversy in one of its most exciting title clashes.

"It just isn't fair for us to lose a game on account of incompetent officiating," Green Bay coach Curly Lambeau said after the Giants overtook his Packers on a third-quarter touchdown to snare a 23–17 triumph December 11 at the Polo Grounds.

Two plays irked Lambeau. On a second-quarter drive that ended on a 21-yard Ed Danowski-to-Hap Barnard pass, the Green Bay coach claimed the Giants were awarded a completion for a play on which the receiver never had possession of the ball. And on a Packers drive that stalled in the scoreless fourth quarter, Lambeau objected to an ineligible receiver penalty that negated a substantial gain.

Still, the record preserves this game as a classic. While coach Steve Owen had most of the players from the 1935 team back in 1936 and '37, he wasn't quite able to drive them to the championship game. But in 1938, with the leadership of NFL MVP Mel Hein, Owen was able to get the G-Men back to the championship, and what a game it was.

Tuffy Leemans ran six yards for a first-quarter touchdown that gave the Giants a 9–0 lead. The Packers grabbed their first lead, 17–16, on a field goal in the third quarter, but New York answered by marching 62 yards for the winning score. From the Green Bay 23, Danowski fired a pass to Hank Soar, who dragged defender Clarke Hinkle into the end zone.

A then-playoff record 48,120 fans at the Polo Grounds saw fierce blocking, a few punches, and one of the hardest-hitting games ever staged. The Giants capped an 8–2–1 season with their third NFL championship.

"This was a struggle of such magnificent stature that words seem such feeble tools for describing it," wrote Arthur Daley in *The New York Times*.

Veteran official Tom Thorpe said it was the "best-played and most exciting game I have ever worked in or seen," Lambeau's critique notwithstanding.

The normally reliable Don Hutson of the Packers bobbles a pass from Arnie Herber during the 1938 NFL title game at the Polo Grounds. The Giants defeated Green Bay 23–17 for the championship.

As *The New York Times* notes, basketball shoes helped the Giants take the title from the Bears in the 1934 title game.

Former Giant Benny Friedman wrote in this 1934 issue of *Liberty* magazine that of all the coaches in football, Knute Rockne was the best.

Harry Newman, on a 1955 Topps card, was an All-American at Michigan before landing on the Giants.

Red Badgro waited 45 years from his final game, in 1936, until his election to the Pro Football Hall of Fame, in 1981. He is shown on a Hall of Fame Gold card.

The 1925 Giants squad, 8-4 on the season, was stocked mostly with rookies, and only a few veterans were sprinkled in.

N. Y. FOOTBALL GIANTS
vs.
CLEVELAND BULLDOGS

PRICE, 10 CENTS

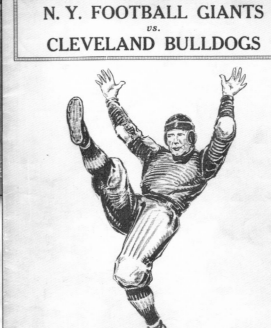

Sunday
November 1, 1925

Polo Grounds
New York

This '52 Bowman card celebrates coach Steve Owen, considered by many to be the heart and soul of the Giants in the early years.

Ed Danowski

Ed Danowski, a Giants quarterback in the '30s, autographed this 1977 Touchdown card.

This program is from 1925, when the Cleveland Bulldogs were the defending NFL champs. It was the Giants, however, who won, 19-0.

Giants of the Early Era

Steve Owen coached some of the greatest players in pro football history between 1930 and 1953, particularly early in his Giants tenure. Some of those greats have been introduced or featured on previous and following pages. Other introductions follow.

Leland Shaffer, Back (1935–45): A blocking back in the New York single wing during the 1938 NFL championship season, Shaffer was a Pro Bowler that year and caught two touchdown passes during the regular season. It was his best campaign, but others came close.

A member of five Eastern division-winning clubs and that '38 NFL championship team, Shaffer ran and caught the ball as a wingback and fullback, and he was an outstanding defensive player as well. He made six career interceptions, including four in 1940, and scored offensive touchdowns as a runner and receiver in a versatile Giants offense.

The 1937 Giants lined up with (backfield, from left) Kink Richards, Ed Danowski, Dale Burnett, and Red Corzine, along with (line, from left) Bill Walls, Len Grant, John Dell Isola, Art White, Mel Hein, Jack Haden, and Jim Poole.

Ox Parry, Tackle (1937–39): Though he played only three seasons, all with the Giants, this 6'4", 230-pound Texan powered some of the NFL's most dominant lines. Behind the Baylor product, the Giants ran and passed their way to two Eastern championships and the 1938 NFL title with one of the most productive attacks in the league.

Hank Soar, Running Back/Defensive Back (1937–46): Catching the winning touchdown pass in the 1938 NFL championship game was just the start of Soar's great career. Owen called Soar his favorite player for his spirit, will to win, easygoing personality, and knack for delivering in the clutch. Soar accounted for touchdowns rushing, passing, receiving, and on interception returns during his 10-year career, all with the Giants.

After hanging up his football cleats, the Rhode Island native coached professional basketball's Providence Steamrollers and served as a longtime American League baseball umpire. Soar was working first base when the Yankees' Don Larsen pitched a perfect game against Brooklyn in the 1956 World Series.

Ed Widseth, Tackle (1937–40): Like Parry, Widseth helped anchor pro football's most dominant line during the late 1930s. In 1938, the Minnesota native pushed the Giants to their third NFL title, leading an offense that could move the ball just as readily through the air as on the ground.

Widseth led the University of Minnesota to national championships in

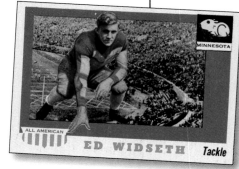

Ed Widseth (shown on this 1955 Topps card) helped the Minnesota win three national titles.

each of his three seasons, losing just once in 24 games. He later coached St. Thomas College and was inducted into the College Football Hall of Fame in 1954.

Ward Cuff, Kicker/Running Back (1937–47): Playing the first 9 of his 11 seasons for the Giants, Cuff was one of the most

Paving the way for the Giants' 1938 championship squad were linemen (from left) Jim Lee Howell, Jack Haden, John Dell Isola, Mel Hein, Orville Tuttle, Ed Widseth, and Jim Poole.

complete athletes of his day. He led New York in scoring each year from 1937 through 1942, thanks to his ability to run, catch, and kick. The three-time All-Pro was also a terrific defensive back whose skills were not limited to the football field. While playing college ball at Marquette, Cuff doubled as the school's heavyweight boxing champion and javelin record-holder.

Jim Lee Howell, Wide Receiver/Defensive Back (1937–47): Before taking over as Owen's head coaching successor, Howell was a standout two-way end who helped the Giants to four NFL championship games, including their 1938 title. At 6′5″, he had captained Arkansas's basketball team as a collegian but opted for football as a pro. With the Giants, his rare combination of size, speed, and athleticism served him well on both sides of the ball.

Howell caught two touchdown passes during the '38 championship season and two in each of the next two years as well. While playing, he also served in the Arkansas Legislature in his home state.

Arnie Weinmeister, Defensive Tackle (1948–53): So dominant was this rugged Canadian that he was elected to the Pro Football Hall of Fame after a career that lasted just six seasons, including four (1950–53) with the Giants.

Weinmeister was big, strong, and fast. He sniffed out plays before they developed and used his strength, speed, and agility to get to the ball carrier. Once there, he made hits that caused crowds to gasp. A great pass rusher, Weinmeister was All-Pro in each of his Giants seasons and co-captained the team in '53.

Arnie Weinmeister played just six seasons of pro football, but he redefined the defensive tackle position as one of the most dominant linemen the game had ever seen.

Giants Rule East but Not League

While the Bears, Packers, and Lions battled for Western Division supremacy in the 1930s, there was no doubt about who ruled the East. Steve Owen's Giants won the Eastern Division and played for the NFL championship six times between 1933 and 1941.

The 1939 Giants were among the best of those teams. They outscored their regular-season foes 168–85 with a stifling defense. Going 9–1–1, the Giants scored their final win with a 9–7 thriller over Washington in the game that decided the Eastern crown. The Redskins began celebrating what they thought was the winning field goal before 62,500 fans at the Polo Grounds, but referee Bill Halloran signaled that the last-minute kick was wide, sending New York to another title game and the visitors into a fury. To this day, no one knows for sure whether the kick went through the uprights.

The Packers hosted the championship game but moved it from Green Bay to State Fair Park in Milwaukee to take advantage of a larger gate—32,279 turned out. December 10 was a bitter and windy day in Wisconsin, and the Giants offense was as cold as the weather. New York managed just 164 yards of offense and was intercepted six times in a 27–0 loss, the first shutout in NFL championship game history.

The NFL did not have to wait long for its second title game shutout, and it was a doozy. In 1940, the Bears hammered the Redskins 73–0 while the Giants settled for third place in the East

at 6–4–1. By 1941, however, New York was poised to resume its top spot.

Tackle John Mellus, a rookie on the 1938 championship team, was now a veteran up front. Tuffy Leemans passed for four touchdowns and ran for four others during an 8–3 regular season. Howie Yeager, Jim Poole, and Ward Cuff had each caught multiple touchdown passes for a Giants team that could beat you on the ground or through the air.

Football was not foremost in anyone's mind when the powerful Bears hosted the Giants at Wrigley Field on December 21, 1941. Two weeks after the Japanese attack on Pearl Harbor, only 13,341 fans came out to watch Chicago cruise to a 37–9 win. George Franck caught a 31-yard TD pass from Leemans to give New York an early 6–3 lead, but Chicago took over from there.

Two players who appeared in the game, the Giants' Jack Lummus and the Bears' Young Bussey, would be killed in action during World War II.

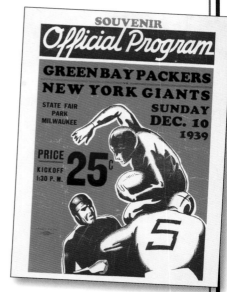

The 1939 title game was moved to Milwaukee's State Fair Park to accomodate a larger crowd, where they sold this program.

Tuffy Leemans of the Giants gains six yards in the fourth quarter against the Packers, but Green Bay was too much for New York, defeating the Giants 27–0 at Wisconsin's State Fair Park in the 1939 NFL title game.

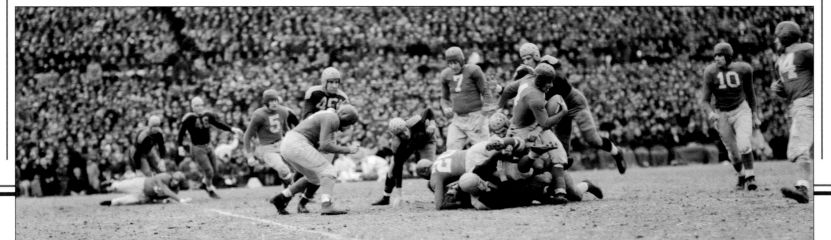

Giants Come Up Short in 1944 Title Loss

Some called Bill Paschal "Bazooka," and he certainly arrived in the NFL as if shot from one. As a rookie in 1943, he led the league in rushing with 572 yards and in touchdowns with 10. Bazooka was even better in 1944.

The Giants, looking to regain their 1930s dominance of the East, rode the powerful legs of Paschal to an 8–1–1 record. Their star fullback became the first man in NFL history to win back-to-back rushing titles, steamrolling defenses for 737 yards and again topping the league in TDs, with nine.

Paschal was not a one-man show, of course. His 34-year-old backfield mate, Arnie Herber, threw six touchdown passes and provided veteran leadership. Jack-of-all-trades Len Younce anchored the offensive line as a guard, intercepted three passes from his linebacker position, and gave the Giants one of the NFL's best kicking games. Howie Livingston led the league with nine interceptions. He returned them for 172 yards, running one back for a score.

Still, as Paschal went, so went the Giants. So when the second-year star injured his ankle in the regular-season finale, a 31–0 rout of Washington, speculation turned to his availability for the December 17 championship game against powerful Green Bay at the Polo Grounds.

Initial fears that the ankle was broken were quelled by an X-ray showing it was a sprain, but Paschal was unable to put in a full practice in the days leading up to the game. Though he tried to play through it, the injury forced him out early in the second half of the title game.

Their weaknesses exposed by the injury to Paschal and the subsequent lack of a running game, the Giants struggled. They failed to advance beyond their own 35-yard line until late in the third quarter. By then, the Packers had taken a 14–0 lead on two touchdowns scored by Ted Fritsch.

New York made it 14–7 when Ward Cuff plowed in from the 1-yard line on the first play of the fourth quarter, but Green Bay's

Ward Cuff (center) outleaps a crowd for an interception during New York's 1944 victory at Washington. The 31–0 rout sent Cuff's Giants to the NFL championship game.

defense held firm after that. The Packers' Joe Laws set a playoff record with three interceptions, and the Packers picked off four New York aerials. Without Paschal, the Giants racked up more penalty yards (90) than rushing yards (70).

New York fought gamely under trying circumstances, scribes from both cities agreed, but most of the crowd of 46,016 went home disappointed in the outcome.

Mel Hein: An Original Hall of Famer

Mel Hein's 50-yard return of an interception against the Packers during the Giants' 1938 NFL championship season accounted for the lone score of his 15-year career as a star center and linebacker. It was not, however, the most significant interception of his career, as far as the Giants were concerned.

That came when he managed to intercept a contract he had signed to play for Providence for $125 a week after his college career at Washington State. After he mailed the signed deal, he got a better offer from the Giants—for $150 a week, good money for a lineman in those days. Hein managed to get a telegram to the postmaster in Providence and had the first contract returned before delivery.

Hein had written letters to pitch his services to NFL teams before receiving those offers, and he delivered time and time

Hall of Fame center Mel Hein signed with the Giants for $150 per game in 1931 and wound up being a 60-minute regular over 15 seasons. He was injured only once and never missed a game.

again for the Giants. He played all 60 minutes of most games, called timeout only once in his career—to have a broken nose repaired in 1941—and served as team captain for 10 years. Teammates said he never made a bad snap, and the techniques he mastered at center set a standard that was followed for years to come.

"Mel was one of the greatest football players who ever lived," said Raiders owner Al Davis, who once hired Hein as supervisor of American Football League officials.

A mobile 225-pounder, Hein in 1938 became the only offensive lineman ever named NFL Most Valuable Player. He led the Giants to seven Eastern Division titles and two NFL championships.

Elected to the College Football Hall of Fame in 1954, Hein became a charter member of the Pro Football Hall of Fame nine years later.

As shown on this '55 Topps card, Mel Hein was an All-American center at Washington State.

Giants of Honor

One New York Giant received an honor far more prestigious than any NFL award in 1946. Unfortunately for his teammates, family, and friends, Jack Lummus received his Medal of Honor posthumously. Lummus and teammate Al Blozis were killed in World War II combat.

Lummus was one of the first American assault troops to land at Iwo Jima during the invasion in 1945. Two weeks later, he lost his legs when he stepped on a mine and famously told his doctor before passing, "The New York Giants lost a mighty good end today."

The Giants lost a good tackle, too, when Blozis—a former discus and shot put champ who could throw a grenade a country mile—was killed in the Vosges Mountains during the Battle of the Bulge.

First Lieutenant Jack Lummus, USMC

From Wartime to Controversy

At the end of World War II, in 1945, the Giants had their worst season, a 3–6–1 campaign that marked the end of Hall of Fame Mel Hein's career. New Yorkers were clamoring for a return to the top. They almost got their wish the following season, when the Giants returned to the NFL championship game amid the league's first big scandal.

With the All-America Football Conference having launched to compete with the NFL and the crosstown football Yankees playing at Yankee Stadium, the Giants wasted no time reestablishing themselves as an Eastern power. They opened with consecutive road wins over Boston and Pittsburgh, put themselves in position to clinch the East in the regular-season finale, and took that game decisively, avenging an earlier setback to Washington in front of 60,000-plus at the Polo Grounds.

A big reason for the Giants' 7–3–1 resurgence was the arrival of Frank Filchock, one of the NFL's top passers, from Washington. The club had struggled to move the ball through the air since the Ed Danowski days, but Filchock changed that immediately.

Filchock was also involved in the scandal. Fullback Merle Hapes admitted before the title game that he had been offered $2,500 from Alvin J. Paris to assure that the Giants lost to the Chicago Bears by more than the 10-point spread. Commissioner Bert Bell banned Hapes from playing. Filchock, who was intercepted six times in the game, said afterward that he too had been offered—but declined—a bribe to fix the outcome.

No one pointed fingers at any of the Giants after their 24–14 loss, which drew a championship game-record 58,346 fans to the Polo Grounds. Playing without four of their top backs after Frank Reagan broke his nose in the second quarter, the Giants fought valiantly against George Halas's Bears. Filchock suffered his own broken nose to accompany bruises and a blood-stained uniform.

The winning margin was a "push"—falling exactly on the point spread, a victory for neither those who bet the favored Bears or the underdog Giants. The Bears' Sid Luckman starred,

Giants quarterback Frank Filchock and coach Steve Owen watch helplessly from the sideline as the Bears break a 14-all tie in the fourth quarter of the 1946 NFL title game en route to a 24–14 decision.

throwing a touchdown pass and breaking a 14–14 tie on a 19-yard bootleg in the fourth quarter.

Neither Hapes nor Filchock was accused of accepting a bribe. However, Hapes never played again, and Filchock played just one more game in his career, in 1950 for Baltimore after a stint in Canada. The Giants did not fare much better in the aftermath, beginning a run of two straight losing seasons and a decade-long absence from the NFL championship game.

This pennant dates from the 1940s, a decade that saw the Giants make it to three championship games, only to lose all three.

Elected to the Hall of Fame in 1984, Arnie Weinmeister is shown on a '51 Bowman card.

This program is from the first of three straight games between the Giants and the Redskins that closed the 1943 season for New York.

Frank Gifford makes an appearance on this Ohio Blue Tip matchbook cover, a collectible from the 1950s.

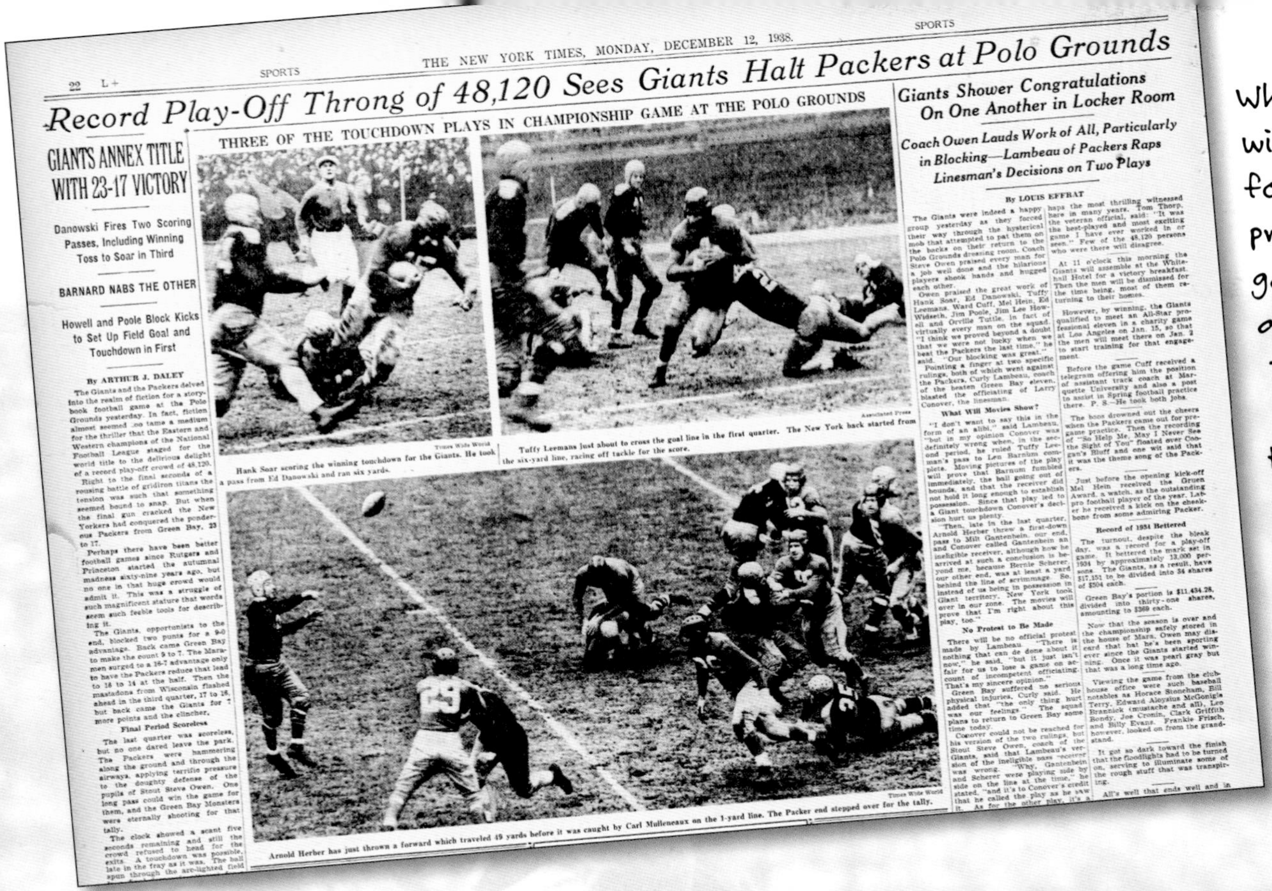

22 L+ SPORTS THE NEW YORK TIMES, MONDAY, DECEMBER 12, 1938. SPORTS

Record Play-Off Throng of 48,120 Sees Giants Halt Packers at Polo Grounds

GIANTS ANNEX TITLE WITH 23-17 VICTORY

Danowski Fires Two Scoring Passes, Including Winning Toss to Soar in Third

BARNARD NABS THE OTHER

Howell and Poole Block Kicks to Set Up Field Goal and Touchdown in First

By ARTHUR J. DALEY

The Giants and the Packers delved into the realm of fiction for a storybook football game at the Polo Grounds yesterday. In fact, fiction almost seemed too tame a medium for the thriller that the Eastern and Western champions of the National Football League staged for the world title to the delirious delight of a record play-off crowd of 48,120.

Right to the final seconds of a rousing battle of gridiron titans the tension was such that something seemed bound to snap. But when the final gun cracked the New Yorkers had conquered the ponderous Packers from Green Bay, 23 to 17.

THREE OF THE TOUCHDOWN PLAYS IN CHAMPIONSHIP GAME AT THE POLO GROUNDS

Hank Soar scoring the winning touchdown for the Giants. He took a pass from Ed Danowski and ran six yards.

Tuffy Leemans just about to cross the goal line in the first quarter. The New York back started from the six-yard line, racing off tackle for the score.

Arnold Herber has just thrown a forward which traveled 49 yards before it was caught by Carl Mulleneaux on the 1-yard line. The Packer end stepped over for the tally.

Giants Shower Congratulations On One Another in Locker Room

Coach Owen Lauds Work of All, Particularly in Blocking—Lambeau of Packers Raps Linesman's Decisions on Two Plays

By LOUIS EFFRAT

While not on par with college football, the pro game was gaining an audience. *The New York Times* notes that more than 48,000 saw the 1938 title game.

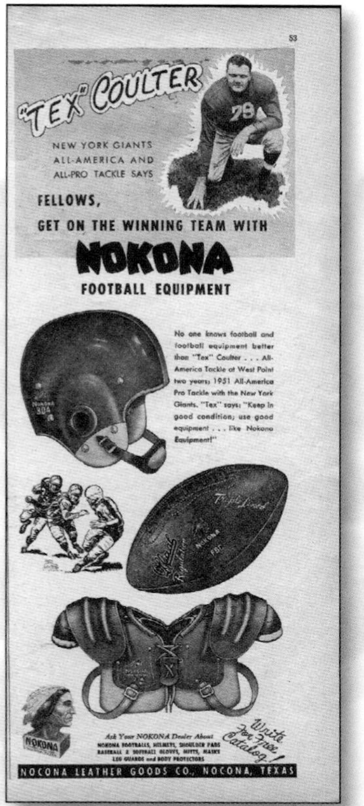
"TEX" COULTER
NEW YORK GIANTS ALL-AMERICA AND ALL-PRO TACKLE SAYS
FELLOWS, GET ON THE WINNING TEAM WITH
NOKONA
FOOTBALL EQUIPMENT
No one knows football and football equipment better than "Tex" Coulter . . . All-America Tackle at West Point two years; 1951 All-America Pro Tackle with the New York Giants. "Tex" says: "Keep in good condition; use good equipment . . . like Nokona Equipment!"
NOCONA LEATHER GOODS CO., NOCONA, TEXAS

This magazine ad features Tex Coulter, who was an All-Pro left tackle for the Giants after a stellar career at West Point.

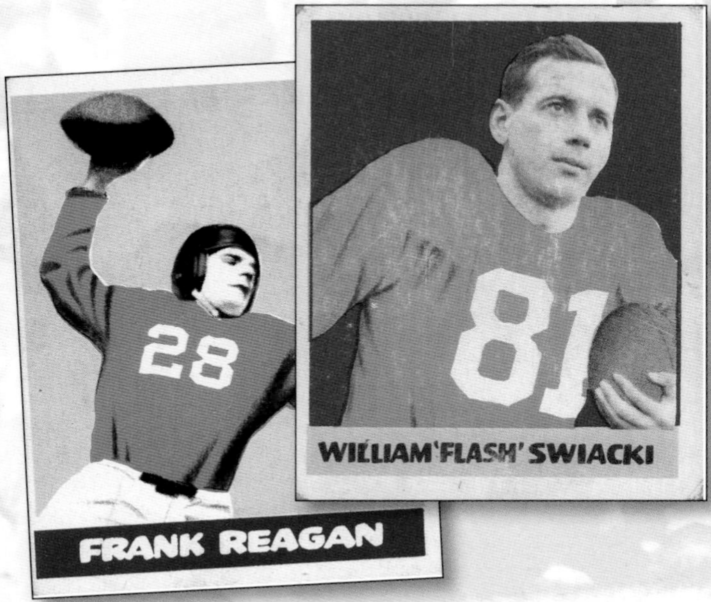
WILLIAM 'FLASH' SWIACKI
FRANK REAGAN

These nifty 1948 Leaf cards feature two colorful Giants, quarterback/kicker Frank Reagan and end Bill Swiacki.

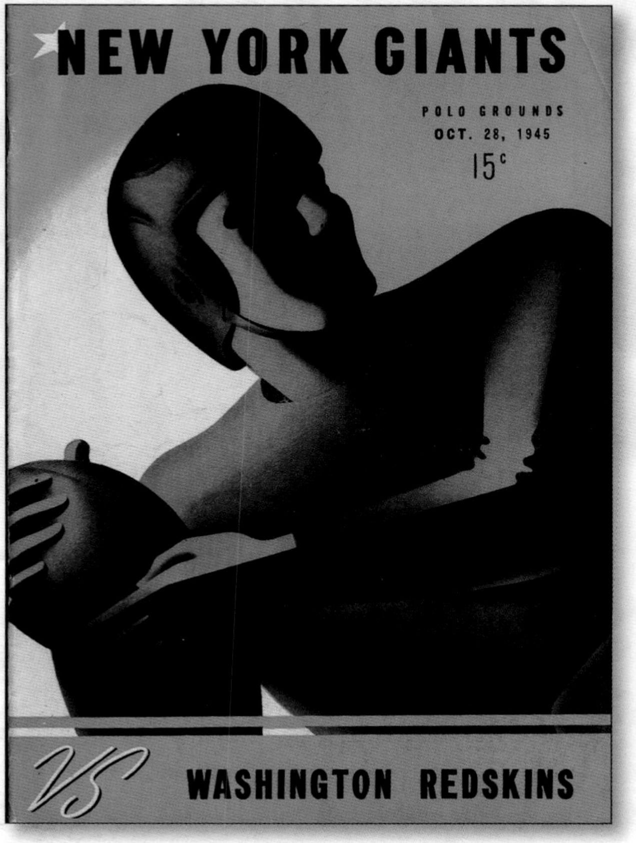
NEW YORK GIANTS
POLO GROUNDS
OCT. 28, 1945
15¢
VS
WASHINGTON REDSKINS

This program is from 1945, when, due to the war, the Giants fielded such oldsters as Mel Hein (age 36) and Arnie Herber (age 35).

CHAPTER THREE

Toasts of the Town

1954–1964

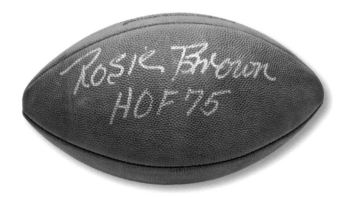

> *"We liked our work, and we liked the people we worked*
> *for. We liked knowing we were playing for a first-*
> *class organization—no, a first-class family."*

FRANK GIFFORD

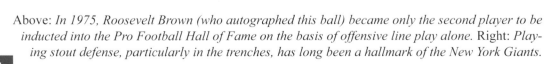

Above: *In 1975, Roosevelt Brown (who autographed this ball) became only the second player to be inducted into the Pro Football Hall of Fame on the basis of offensive line play alone.* Right: *Playing stout defense, particularly in the trenches, has long been a hallmark of the New York Giants.*

Howell Takes Charge

Jim Lee Howell used to describe the secret to his success as Giants coach thusly: "I'll just blow up the footballs and keep order."

Managers of all kinds could have learned a thing or two about delegation from Howell, who mastered the art better than perhaps anyone in coaching or in the business world. Of course, when your offensive coordinator is Vince Lombardi and your defensive coordinator is Tom Landry, you can attain remarkable success simply by clearing out of the way.

Those who knew Howell, though, understood that his leadership extended far beyond that. The former Arkansas basketball captain played for and coached under Giants coach Steve Owen, where he learned to settle for nothing short of victory. As a player, Howell made four trips to the NFL championship game.

Howell's coaching style was also shaped by his experience as a Marine company commander in World War II. "He ran the team as if we were all members of his unit," offered Andy Robustelli,

Lombardi, Landry: What an Assist!

Prepping for a game was said to have gone like this for the 1950s Giants: offensive coach and his players in one room; defensive coach and his players in another room; head coach Jim Lee Howell in a third room, reading a newspaper.

Perhaps that's a mild exaggeration. But with an offensive coordinator named Vince Lombardi and a defensive coordinator named Tom Landry, Howell had a luxury of Hall of Fame proportions.

Howell gave Lombardi his first NFL coaching job in 1954. Two years later, Landry took over the defense and the Giants whipped the Bears for the 1956 NFL crown. They reached the title game again in '58, after which Lombardi took Green Bay's head coaching job.

Landry turned the Giants into one of the NFL's best defensive teams from 1956 through '59, and the following year he became the first head coach of the Dallas Cowboys.

Coach Jim Lee Howell gives his Giants a pep talk before their 1956 NFL title clash against the Bears at Yankee Stadium. Whatever he said worked, as New York rolled to a 47–7 blowout.

one of several Hall of Famers coached by Howell. "While he may not have known all the technical secrets of football, he certainly tolerated nothing less than a full effort, and he was absolutely bearish on anyone making mistakes."

Under Howell's authority from 1954 to 1960, New York never had a losing season. His 53–27–4 record (.663) is better than that of any Giants coach of similar tenure, and his teams competed in three NFL championship games. They routed the Bears 47–7 for the 1956 title and lost in overtime to Baltimore in '58 in what some still call the greatest game ever played.

From the Trombone to Canton

Roosevelt Brown was a 13-year-old trombone player in his high school band when the football coach noticed that Rosey was bigger than many of his players. Brown was turned into a two-way tackle who made it to Morgan State at the age of 16.

The Giants selected Brown with the 321st pick in the 1953 NFL Draft. Scouting then was not nearly what it is today, and the Giants had almost run out of ideas when their turn came to pick in the 27th round. Fortunately, someone in the front office had seen *The Pittsburgh Courier,* a black newspaper, and noticed a little-known lineman had been named to a 1952 Black All-American Team.

"We had nothing to lose," Giants owner Wellington Mara said of the selection of Brown, a 6′3″, 225-pound tackle who arrived in camp wearing his only suit. It turned out Mara's Giants had everything to gain.

Brown, only 21 as a rookie, had to be taught the proper stance for his position. Brown signed for $2,700, a great bargain for the Giants, thanks to an array of skills and intangibles Brown possessed that cannot be taught.

Brown was remarkably nimble and athletic for his size, which grew to 255 pounds with weight training despite a slim waist that made his torso look like a triangle. The Giants' defense was one of the best in the NFL, so scrimmaging against the likes of Arnie Weinmeister prepared Brown for his debut. The first game

New York Giants (from left) Roosevelt Brown, Gene Filipski, and Don Chandler keep warm while watching the action from the bench in a 1956 game.

he played in was the first pro football game Brown had ever seen.

Brown not only made the team but won a starting tackle job as a rookie and held it for 13 years, until phlebitis ended his career after 1965. Opening gaping holes on running plays, using his agility to keep pass rushers at bay, and racing to the front of plays like no other tackle of his era, Brown excelled in every aspect of line play.

"What made him so great," recalled coach Allie Sherman, "was the fact that there are only two moves a defensive lineman can put on you when you pass block, and Rosey had different answers for both."

Brown was named NFL Lineman of the Year in 1956, when he began a run of eight consecutive All-Pro seasons. He played in nine Pro Bowls and led the Giants to six divisional crowns and one NFL championship during an eight-year stretch. Of a possible 166 regular-season games, Brown missed just four.

In 1975, Brown became just the second player elected to the Pro Football Hall of Fame based solely on offensive line play. The Colts' Jim Parker was the first.

ROOSEVELT BROWN
TACKLE   NEW YORK GIANTS

Brown, shown on this 1959 Topps card, was a nine-time Pro Bowl player.

Gifford Turns Heads On and Off the Field

If Frank Gifford looked more Hollywood than New York City when he arrived to play for the Giants as a No. 1 draft pick in 1952, it's because he was. Having grown up and starred as a high school and college football hero in Southern California, Gifford already had four film titles on his acting résumé by the time he finished his All-America career at USC. The fact that he was a heartthrob was not lost on his new coaches and teammates.

Giants coach Steve Owen, for one, considered Gifford's running style a bit too flashy for the rough and tough pro game, so he converted "Giff" to defensive back. It did not take long for the Giants, and their opponents, to learn that Frank's substance matched his considerable style.

Gifford quickly earned All-Pro honors in the defensive secondary. When he was moved back to halfback, he became an All-Pro there, too. In an era when platoon football was the norm, Owen used Gifford to run, pass, kick, play defense, and return punts and kickoffs. Wellington Mara called Gifford the most versatile player in franchise history.

The multitalented Frank Gifford races through a big hole for a touchdown that helped the Giants post a 48–7 rout of the Cleveland Browns in 1959.

A four-time All-Pro who played in seven Pro Bowls at three different positions, including defensive back, Gifford dominated in every way in 1956. He was the team's leading scorer, rusher, and receiver that season, won NFL Player of the Year honors, and led the Giants to their first NFL championship since 1938. He topped the club in rushing and receiving from 1956 to '59, four of the team's greatest seasons.

"Frank was the body and soul of our team," said Giants coach Jim Lee Howell, who was known to razz Gifford by calling him "Mr. Hollywood" during a practice session or two. "He was the player we went to in the clutch."

Though Gifford was the All-American boy who made good, his career was not without adversity. He was on the wrong end of one of the hardest hits in NFL history during a 1960 game, when Eagles linebacker Chuck Bednarik leveled him. Gifford suffered a severe head injury that appeared to signal the end of his career. Eighteen months later, he came back.

Gifford came out of retirement in 1962 at a new position, flanker, and became one of the NFL's best pass-catching threats. He made the Pro Bowl as a receiver, and he caught seven touch-down passes in both 1962 and '63. In three years of catching passes from Y. A. Tittle, Gifford helped the Giants win two Eastern Conference championships while proving once again to be among the most versatile athletes in sports.

When he announced his retirement for good, to join CBS Sports in 1965, team president John Mara said he hoped the next generation of Giants would "have a little of the spark of Frank

Whether running the football, catching it, throwing it, or returning kicks, Gifford gave the Giants a weapon few teams could match during a career that landed him in the Pro Football Hall of Fame.

Gifford the Broadcaster

Frank Gifford became almost as famous with a microphone as he did running with, catching, throwing, and kicking footballs. That's because upon his retirement, he joined the television broadcast booth at a time when football was taking off on the tube.

Gifford, one of the most versatile players in NFL history, was a TV chameleon, too. He announced everything from the Olympics to Evel Knievel motorcycle jumps to skiing. But it was his commentary on ABC's *Monday Night Football* with the likes of Howard Cosell and "Dandy" Don Meredith from 1971 to 1997 that introduced Americans born after his Hall of Fame playing career to Gifford.

In 1995, Gifford received the Pete Rozelle Award from the Pro Football Hall of Fame for his outstanding work in the TV broadcast booth with CBS and ABC.

His wife, Kathie Lee, is also a famous TV talk-show host, putting Gifford's family life in the public eye like that of few retired athletes in history.

Gifford," whose combination of athletic skills, intelligence, and leadership set him apart.

"In their 40 years, the Giants have had many outstanding players," John Mara added. "Once in a long while one comes along who stands out." Mara said that Gifford was always a credit to the organization off the field as well as on the field.

With nearly 10,000 combined yards and 484 points in his career, Gifford was enshrined in the Pro Football Hall of Fame in 1977. By then, he was already well on his way to extending his fame from the big screen and gridiron to the broadcast booth.

One Good Gem Deserves Another

If Yankee Stadium could speak, oh the stories it would tell about the final three months of 1956.

On October 8, the Yankees' Don Larsen pitched a perfect game against the Dodgers in Game 5 of the World Series. More than 50 years later, it remains the only no-hitter in World Series history.

Larsen's gem was the last baseball game played at Yankee Stadium that year, as the Bronx Bombers wrapped up the championship in Brooklyn. It left the Giants with a tough act to follow as they prepared to play their first football game at Yankee Stadium less than two weeks later, having abandoned their previous home at the Polo Grounds.

The Giants did not come up with a perfect game, or even a perfect season, but their fans would agree that the 1956 championship team did Yankee Stadium proud in the wake of one of its most memorable moments.

"I'll always believe," noted Giants star Frank Gifford, "that '56 [championship] game and how it opened everyone's eyes to the excitement of pro football was the key to the development of the NFL today.... We became heroes in New York."

The Giants' Yankee Stadium opener was a laugher—a 38–10 rout of the struggling Pittsburgh Steelers. It brought the Giants' record to 3–1, the only blemish being a 35–27 road loss to the Chicago Cardinals. Coach Jim Lee Howell had predicted 9–3 would be enough to secure the team's first Eastern title in a decade. It turned out 8–3–1 sufficed. The Giants avenged the loss to the Cardinals to finish one-and-a-half games ahead of them in the standings.

With one Chicago team dispatched, another awaited. The Bears and Giants had fought to a 17-all tie on November 25 at Yankee

Stadium, where the rematch would be played in frigid weather on December 30 for the NFL championship.

Some argue that the Giants' 47–7 shellacking of the Bears in that rematch helped pro football supplant baseball as the favorite American spectator sport. That's open for debate. What's not is that the following season, the Giants began selling many more tickets to their games—even regular-season contests.

If football did overtake baseball on this day, it was in basketball shoes that it happened. The Giants, as they had in the famous 1934 "Sneakers Game," donned rubber-soled shoes for better

The official program for the 1956 NFL championship game cost 35 cents—less than a penny for each point the Giants scored in their 47–7 win against the Chicago Bears in the contest.

With Rote, Fortune Smiled on Giants

In 1951, Coach Steve Owen reached into a hat and grabbed a ticket that earned the Giants the right to choose a college player in advance of that year's regular draft process. They chose Kyle Rote, a Heisman Trophy runner-up from SMU who became an 11-year offensive force and a four-time Pro Bowler.

"He made some great moves on people," noted Giants owner Wellington Mara of Rote, who at the time of his retirement owned club records for career receptions (300), receiving yards (4,795), and touchdown catches (48). "We had many pictures of him going one way and the defender going the other way."

A heralded runner in college who once rushed for 115 yards and passed for 146 in a game against Notre Dame, Rote switched to end after suffering early injuries as a pro. He led New York to four NFL championship games, including a 1956 victory over the Bears.

Rote was the first elected president of the NFL Players Association, which he helped found in the 1950s.

Alex Webster reaches the end zone for a touchdown during the Giants' 47–7 shellacking of the Bears in the 1956 NFL championship game at Yankee Stadium.

traction on an icy field. The new "kicks"—48 pairs, sizes 9 to 13—were ordered a week earlier by All-Pro defensive end Andy Robustelli, who owned a sporting goods store on the side.

As Gifford recalled, it wasn't talent that decided the game, but the choice of footwear. On New York's first possession, Gifford said, "I was flanked out on second down and long. J. C. Caroline was playing me man-to-man. I faked an inside move and broke it out. He fell right on his [rear]. I knew we had them then." The game itself was no contest—the second-most lopsided NFL

championship game since the Bears' 73–0 whitewashing of the Redskins in 1940—as the Giants won their first NFL title since 1938. Gifford caught four passes for 131 yards and a touchdown, halfback Alex Webster scored twice, and the Giants sprinted to a 34–7 halftime lead. Charlie Conerly threw two second-half touchdown passes to complete the rout.

"The Bears were no more than a good practice opponent," reported the *Chicago Tribune,* "for a resolute Giant team that romped recklessly over a frozen gridiron in basketball shoes."

The Men Behind the Microphone

Through 50 years of blood-stained, mud-caked, and sweat-soaked New York Giants football, a gentlemanly voice boomed from the stadium loudspeakers.

Bob Sheppard has been called "The Voice of God." A professor and poet turned sports announcer, Sheppard began announcing Giants games in 1956 and did so through 2006. Whether at Yankee Stadium, the Yale Bowl, or Giants Stadium, he always began in a precise and proper diction that New York sports fans can hear in their sleep: "Good afternoon... ladies and gentlemen... and welcome...." Even more famous were his baseball calls at Yankee Stadium, which began on Opening Day 1951.

Sheppard, who does not reveal his age, played football and baseball at St. John's College in Brooklyn between 1928 and 1932. Suffice it to say his relaxed and soothing voice never got old. Year after year, it only resonated more.

Sheppard might be the only Giants announcer to have his microphone encased at the Baseball Hall of Fame in Cooperstown and a Monument Park plaque honoring him as "The Voice of Yankee Stadium," but he is not the only famous voice who has called Giants football games. Here's a look at some of the others.

Bob Papa: The current radio voice of the Giants, Papa started with the team as pre- and post-game host in 1988 and took over as play-by-play man five years later.

The classy voice of public-address announcer Bob Sheppard became synonymous with Giants home football games and those of the New York Yankees baseball club.

After attaining great success on the field, Carl Banks began applying his football expertise and communications skills to his job as a radio analyst for his former team.

Jim Gordon: Most famous for his "No good!" call after Scott Norwood's missed field goal in Super Bowl XXV, Gordon started in New York radio in 1954 and was the Giants' radio play-by-play man from 1977 to 1994.

Chris Schenkel: Schenkel's baritone began accompanying televised Giants games in 1952. In addition to his prominent work covering several sports, including bowling, the late Hall of Famer handled New York football duties for 13 seasons.

Carl Banks: A linebacker on two Giants Super Bowl championship teams, Banks has done work for Sirius NFL Radio and New York's WFAN. In 2007, he joined the radio broadcast team as color commentator.

Karl Nelson: Nelson played tackle on the Giants' 1986 championship team but had his career cut short battling Hodgkin's disease. He stayed on as a radio analyst from 1989 through 1994.

Dave Jennings: Jennings served as color commentator for both teams he played for, the Jets and Giants. He joined the latter in 2002 and worked in the radio booth until 2006.

Tunnell Breaks Ground and Many a Gameplan

No black player had ever suited up for the Giants before 1948. Emlen Tunnell changed history simply by asking if he could.

There's much more to the Tunnell story than that. After playing basketball at Toledo and serving in the Coast Guard during World War II, he was a very good collegian who was expected to return to Iowa for his senior season in 1948. But the Bryn Mawr, Pennsylvania, native, then 23 years old, instead hitched a ride to New York City and asked Giants owner Tim Mara for a tryout. Tunnell was given one, launching a 14-year career with the Giants and Packers in which he set an NFL record with 79 interceptions.

Tunnell was given the all-important top, or back, spot in the Giants' famed "umbrella" defense, which was the first modern zone defense, used to stop the more sophisticated passing attacks coming into vogue. Tunnell used it to redefine the safety position as the quarterback of the defense. There, he became known as "offense on defense," thanks to his ability to turn opponents' possessions into Giants points.

One of the NFL's first great return men, Tunnell in 1952 gained more yards on interception and kick returns (924) than the league's top rusher managed on the ground. He amassed 4,706 career yards on interception, punt, and kick returns; made nine Pro Bowls; and was a six-time All-Pro.

"Emlen changed the theory of defensive safeties," said Giants coach Jim Lee Howell. "He would have been too big for the job earlier, and they'd have made him a lineman. But he had such strength, such speed, and such quickness, I'm convinced he was the best safety ever to play."

Tunnell broke more ground in 1967. Eight years before his death at age 50, he became the first African-American inducted into the Pro Football Hall of Fame.

Emlen Tunnell of the Giants eyes a loose fumble during New York's home loss to Cleveland in November 1954.

Giants Beat Browns on Back-to-Back Weeks

The "greatest game in NFL history" would never have been played if not for a frenetic 1958 finish from the Giants—two wins in as many weeks against Cleveland and the great Jim Brown.

Needing a win against the Browns in the season finale to force an Eastern playoff between the same clubs, New York survived Brown's 65-yard touchdown run on Cleveland's first possession to claim a 13–10 thriller at Yankee Stadium. They did it on Pat Summerall's improbable 49-yard field goal in the snow—a kick few could believe he was asked to try.

One week later, again at Yankee Stadium, New York's defense stifled Brown and his teammates for a 10–0 decision, setting up a memorable championship game between the Giants and Colts.

"The Greatest Game Ever Played"

"The Greatest Game Ever Played," in most respects, was not the greatest game ever played, at least artistically speaking. It was not a particularly compelling game for the first three quarters. It included missed field goals, six lost fumbles, and play-calling that was conservative even by the standards of the era.

For the New York Giants, the historic 1958 NFL championship game against the Baltimore Colts was not the greatest game ever played for another reason: the scoreboard.

"It wasn't great for me because we lost," said defensive end Andy Robustelli of New York's 23–17 overtime setback. "All that we accomplished that season didn't mean too much to me when I walked out of Yankee Stadium an hour after Alan Ameche scored the winning touchdown in the fifth quarter of that game."

After back-to-back, do-or-die wins over the Browns to get there, the Giants' offense looked lethargic against the Colts' sturdy defense. After Pat Summerall got New York on the board first with a 36-yard field goal late in the first quarter, the Giants were held scoreless for the remainder of the half. Baltimore took advantage of two Frank Gifford fumbles to score a pair of second-quarter touchdowns for a 14–3 advantage.

The Colts were one yard away from turning the game into a rout early in the third quarter. They reached New York's 1-yard line, but Ameche was stuffed for no gain on third down and tackled for a four-yard loss on fourth, as the Giants took over on downs.

One of the most famous photos in NFL history depicts one of the most famous touchdowns in NFL history—that of the Colts' Alan Ameche in overtime of the 1958 title game against the Giants.

Ninety-five yards later, New York was back in the game. The big play on a 95-yard Giants touchdown drive was an 86-yard play that saw Kyle Rote catch a Charlie Conerly pass and run 62 yards before fumbling. Teammate Alex Webster scooped up the ball and rumbled to the 1, setting up a Mel Triplett touchdown that whittled the deficit to 14–10.

Gifford caught a 15-yard touchdown pass in the fourth quarter to put the Giants on top for the first time, 17–14, and with less than three minutes to go he had a chance to put the game out of reach. The Giants had the ball on their own 40, with a chance to run out the clock if they could convert on third-and-four. Gifford ran a sweep, covered the first three yards easily, and lunged forward as he was tackled.

On the ground, he heard screams from the Colts' Gino Marchetti, who broke his leg on the play. By the time the pile had been cleared and a stretcher summoned, the ball had been spotted a few inches short of a first down. Giants coach Jim Lee Howell opted to punt.

"I still feel to this day," Gifford said, "and will always feel, that I got the first down that would have let us run out the clock. And given us the title."

Instead, Johnny Unitas added to his legend and put this game in the "unforgettable" category. There was a minute and 56 sec-

As the Yankee Stadium clock wound down to zero in regulation play of the 1958 NFL championship tilt, some of the players started to head to the locker room.

onds left in the game. Unitas's first clutch play was hitting Lenny Moore with an 11-yard pass in a third-and-ten situation. Then Johnny U hit Raymond Berry with three precise passes totaling 62 yards, driving his Colts to a tying, chip-shot field goal with seven seconds left, at which point overtime was required to settle the outcome—a first in the history of a league that was accustomed to tie games.

"We had no idea you went into sudden death," Colts defensive back Lenny Lyles said. Indeed, many of the players on both sides of the field started heading to the locker rooms at the end of regulation play, only to be told by game officials that there would be a sudden-death overtime period. The Giants won the coin toss but went three-and-out. Unitas then took the Colts 80 yards on 13 plays, including a pass to Berry that was Berry's championship-game record 12th reception that day. The drive was capped by Ameche's winning touchdown. The black-and-white photo of that score is a staple of the NFL archives.

It remains iconic everywhere, except, perhaps, in New York.

Baltimore fans celebrate as a referee signals Alan Ameche's winning touchdown in overtime of the 1958 NFL championship game at Yankee Stadium.

Was the 1958 Title Game "The Greatest"?

There have been many games in NFL history that were considered to be the best ever played. There was "The Ice Bowl" (Packers-Cowboys, December 1967), "The Catch" (49ers-Cowboys, January 1982), and "The Drive" (Broncos-Browns, January 1987). There was San Diego's Kellen Winslow breaking the hearts of the 1981 Dolphins in a 41–38, overtime classic, and Buffalo erasing an impossible 35–3 deficit against Houston to win the 1992 AFC wild-card game by the same score.

So was Baltimore's 23–17 overtime victory over the Giants in 1958 truly the greatest game in NFL history?

Judging by the seven turnovers and squandered opportunities by both teams to clinch victory in regulation time, certainly not. However, taking the game's impact on the NFL into account, it is not a stretch to call December 28, 1958, a milestone day for pro football.

It was the game that showed Madison Avenue that pro football was a game made for television. Roone Arledge, the man who later created the ready-for-primetime *Monday Night Football,* said of the 1958 championship game, "All of a sudden, the networks woke up and saw that they had to have football."

It has been estimated that 45 million television viewers watched the game, which still would rank it pretty highly as a most-watched TV event. And the game was blacked out in New York City. Played at Yankee Stadium in New York, the game didn't start until 2:00 P.M. on Sunday, December 28. So the game lasted longer than anticipated, and the end of the game was shown in the evening, so more casual fans had the occasion to watch pro football for the first time.

Kyle Rote made the cover of Life *magazine in 1950. He was one of the more recognizable stars in the Giants' galaxy.*

Longtime Giants quarterback Charlie Conerly executes a "jump pass" during the 1958 NFL championship game against the Baltimore Colts.

The NFL grew up that day, taking a big stride forward in its climb past horse racing and baseball on the American popularity scale. It did so at a time when players worked summer jobs to pay the bills, with a championship game that featured 17 future Hall of Famers.

"When I think about the men on that field that day, some of them remembered among the best football players who ever played the game, I picture guys whose talent was all the more remarkable considering how humble their roots had been," said the Giants' Frank Gifford.

Rematch of "Greatest Game" No Classic

The nation's sports pages were predicting great things from the 1959 NFL championship game, a rematch of the 1958 "Greatest Game" contest between the Colts and the Giants. It was said to be the biggest "betting game" in years, though there was no way of verifying such a claim. It would be witnessed by a packed house at Baltimore's Memorial Stadium, viewed on national television, and listened to on radios by families across the land.

The hype stemmed from the previous year's title game between the same Colts and Giants—a 23–17 overtime win by Baltimore that still had football fans buzzing. The rematch, conventional wisdom held, had every chance to be as tight as the original.

"I look for another close contest," Giants coach Jim Lee Howell said. "We're good enough to win it, but whether we will win it is another matter."

The rematch of Eastern and Western champs was also a rematch of quarterbacks, each of whom had won a Player of the Year Award in 1959.

Charlie Conerly had been named the NFL's best by the players after completing 58 percent of his passes and averaging a league-best 8.79 yards per throw during the regular season. He led New York to a 10–2 record, the only blemishes coming at the hands of Philadelphia and Pittsburgh.

His counterpart, Johnny Unitas, had thrown a remarkable 32 touchdown passes to earn the writers' vote as Player of the Year. His Colts were 9–3 as defending champs and were installed as a slight favorite in their bid to repeat.

For all the focus on the quarterbacks, though, the game turned into a defensive battle. After Baltimore struck first on a 60-yard touchdown pass from Unitas to Lenny Moore, the Giants kept the high-powered Colts off the scoreboard until the fourth quarter. Meanwhile, Pat Summerall connected on field goals of 23, 37, and 22 yards to give the Giants a 9–7 lead.

New York appeared to be on a path to victory until the Colts came alive in the fourth quarter. Unitas ran four yards for the go-ahead score, and then hit Jerry Richardson with a 12-yard touchdown pass. The Giants' remaining hopes disappeared when Conerly threw an interception that was returned 42 yards for a score by Johnny Sample. A late Conerly-to-Bob Schnelker TD toss set the final score at 31–16.

New York did not play well, particularly offensively, in the final. But Howell said he didn't know if a good New York game, "would have been good enough to beat Baltimore."

Baltimore's John Sample races to the end zone with an interception as the Giants' Ray Wietecha pursues during the 1959 NFL championship game. The Colts defeated the Giants for the title for the second straight year.

GIANTS GALLERY

OFFICIAL PROGRAM · 50 CENTS

YANKEE STADIUM

N.Y. **GIANTS** VS. PHILADELPHIA **EAGLES**

NOVEMBER 30, 1958

Behind backup quarterback Don Heinrich's two TD passes, the Giants beat the Eagles 24–10 on November 30, 1958, the date this program was issued.

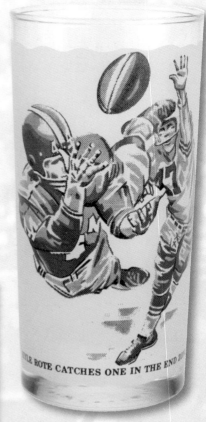

KYLE ROTE CATCHES ONE IN THE END ZONE

This promotional glass was sold at gas stations in the New York area. Kyle Rote had 48 TD receptions in his career.

N.Y. GIANTS STAR LINEBACKER

SAM HUFF
—Indestructible

—except when he shaves!

My razor's unnecessary roughness threw me for a loss—until I used new

afta
AFTER SHAVE LOTION
by MENNEN

Especially made to condition, heal, protect dry sensitive skin
NO STING · NO BURN MENNEN afta

MENNEN **afta**
AFTER SHAVE SKIN CONDITIONER

IN HANDY NEW SQUEEZE FLASK!
Also available in Canada

One of the toughest hitters in the NFL, Sam Huff, in this '63 ad, was able to cash in on his fame, like so many of that era's Giants.

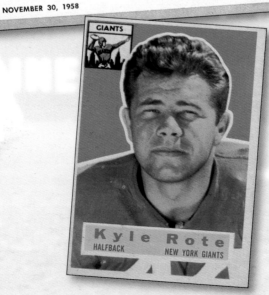

GIANTS

Kyle Rote
HALFBACK   NEW YORK GIANTS

Making the last of his four Pro Bowl appearances in 1956, when this card was issued, Kyle Rote was a top offensive force during the decade.

Frank Gifford made the first team All-Pro squad at halfback in 1956, the year this card was produced. In 1953, he made the Pro Bowl as a defensive back.

THE NEW YORK TIMES, MONDAY, DECEMBER 31, 1956.

Giants Crush Bears at Stadium and Take First Pro Football Title Since 1938

56,836 FANS SEE CHICAGO BOW, 47-7

Giants' Early Drive Decides Play-Off Game—Webster's Two Tallies Set Pace

By LOUIS EFFRAT

GIANTS CELEBRATE BEFORE AND AFTER

Pre-Game Levity Astounds Coach, but it Seems His Men Weren't Worried

By GORDON S. WHITE Jr.

Sports of The Times
By ARTHUR DALEY

Flatter Than a Bear-Rug

Fashion Note

This Mechanical Age

Hands in Gloves

The Varsity G

Mixed emotions on Bear bench yesterday

ON HIS WAY: Giants' Alex Webster off on a long run after taking a pass from Chuck Conerly in yesterday's championship game. Fred Williams, left, of Bears finally caught him.

ALL ALONE: Kyle Rote, Giants' end, snares another Conerly pass to score in third period

The New York Times reports that after many close calls, the Giants in 1956 finally won an NFL title, beating the Bears 47-7.

NEW YORK GIANTS

EMLEN TUNNEL HALFBACK

A nine-time Pro Bowler, Emlen Tunnell (shown on this '55 Bowman as "Tunnel") was able to use his size and quickness to shut down opposing receivers.

HIGHLAND CAPTURES HORSE SHOW AWARD

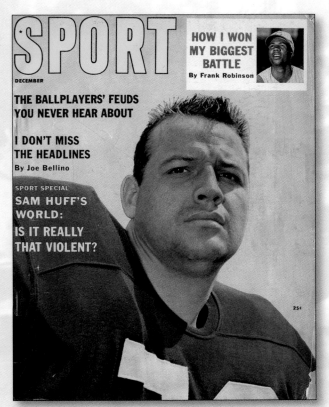

SPORT

DECEMBER

HOW I WON MY BIGGEST BATTLE
By Frank Robinson

THE BALLPLAYERS' FEUDS YOU NEVER HEAR ABOUT

I DON'T MISS THE HEADLINES
By Joe Bellino

SPORT SPECIAL
SAM HUFF'S WORLD:
IS IT REALLY THAT VIOLENT?

25c

Sam Huff's fame was such that he was featured in *The Violent World of Sam Huff,* a 1960 CBS special. *Sport* magazine later examined the truth behind the claim.

Bednarik Flattens Gifford in Famous Tackle

Folks called Chuck Bednarik "Concrete Charlie" because he sold concrete in the off-season. Forgive Frank Gifford if he felt the nickname derived from the Philadelphia linebacker's rock-solid tackles, particularly the most famous one in NFL history.

Gifford, cutting across the middle, caught a pass from Charlie Conerly with his team trailing 17–10 in the last minutes of a key November 20, 1960, game. The All-Pro momentarily took his eyes off Bednarik to look at oncoming safety Don Burroughs and did not look back in time to see what happened next—a clean but punishing shot from Bednarik, one of the nastiest hitters in the game. Bednarik caught the defenseless Gifford just under the chin with his shoulder, knocking the ball loose and sending Gifford to his back, arms sprawled. The Eagles' Chuck Weber recovered the fumble, and Bednarik stood over Gifford pumping his fist, and yelling, "This [expletive] game is over."

"I didn't even know Gifford had not gotten up at the time," said Bednarik, whose jubilation—captured in one of the most recognizable photos in sports history—made him a villain in New York. He said he was just happy. "I knew we had the game won, because we had the ball. That's why I was jumping around."

The hit gave Gifford a severe concussion that kept him sidelined all of 1961, and he didn't return to action until 1962. The hit also added fuel to an already hot rivalry between the Eagles and Giants. The teams became accustomed to fierce battles for Eastern supremacy, and their fans came to despise each other.

Gifford showed no long-term effects after returning, making another Pro Bowl in 1963. In '77, he joined Bednarik in the Pro Football Hall of Fame, never having held the crushing hit against the Philadelphia linebacker who was inducted ten years earlier.

"It was perfectly legal," Gifford said. "If I'd had the chance, I'd have done the same thing Chuck did."

Bednarik and Gifford have since joked about the hit, the latter claiming to have made the former famous by absorbing such a blow. Bednarik called it a shot that defensive players dream about.

"If you go down the field, doing a down and in, and you're coming across, you have to look at that quarterback throwing the ball, and at the same time I'm coming straight across," he offered. "That's dangerous. That's like a Volkswagen going down a one-way street and a Mack truck is coming the opposite way."

A Mack truck made of concrete.

Eagles defender Chuck Bednarik knocks Frank Gifford off his feet—and out, literally—with one of the most legendary hits in football history. The shot sidelined Gifford for the rest of the 1960 season and all of 1961.

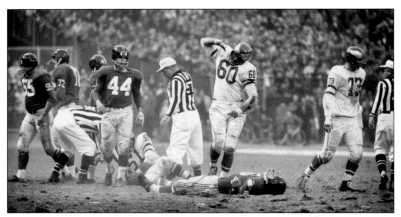

Chuck Bednarik insists he was not celebrating the injury to Frank Gifford that kept Gifford out of football for more than a year, but simply a big stop that clinched the 1960 contest for the Eagles.

These Giants Could Air It Out

Offensive football was vastly different 50 years ago. In 1958 and '59, for instance, half of the NFL's 12 teams did not throw for even 2,000 yards. That's a half-season's work for several modern NFL clubs.

The Giants, however, were consistently among NFL passing leaders in the 1950s thanks to "Chuck'n" Charlie Conerly, a slew of talented offensive weapons, and an offensive coordinator named Vince Lombardi. In an era when the pass took a backseat to the run in most pro offenses, Conerly's ability to throw, run, and think on his feet gave New York one of the league's most versatile and unpredictable attacks.

Charlie Conerly, Quarterback (1948–61): Giants owner Wellington Mara often called Conerly "the best player who is not in the Pro Football Hall of Fame." Conerly does have a place in the College Football Hall. In 1947, the single-wing tailback and World War II veteran led the nation in pass completions, threw for 18 touchdowns and ran for nine, and led Ole Miss to its first SEC championship.

As a pro, he converted to a T formation quarterback and began his assault on the Giants record book. He led the team to the 1956 NFL championship and was named MVP in '59. In 14 years, the QB with rugged good looks (he was one of the models to pose as the "Marlboro Man") set Giants records for career attempts, completions, passing yards, and touchdown tosses.

Bob Schnelker, End (1953–61): While Frank Gifford gave Conerly his top pass-catching option out of the backfield, Schnelker was the team's best end in the '50s. Schnelker's breakthrough '54 season included 30 receptions, including eight that went for touchdowns.

The Bowling Green product averaged 33 catches per year between 1958 and 1960, his last three seasons with the Giants,

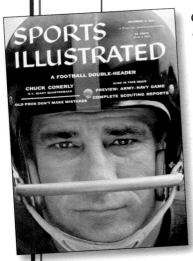

Conerly, on the cover of this 1956 Sports Illustrated, led the Giants to the title that year.

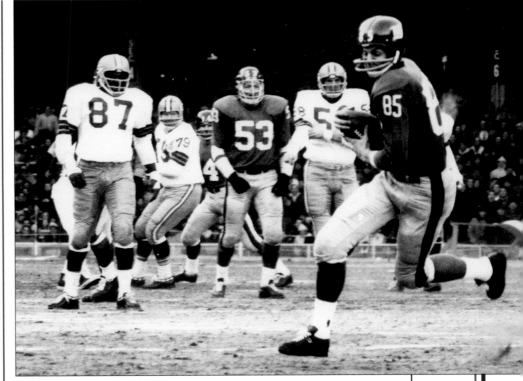

End Del Shofner finds daylight after catching a pass during the 1962 NFL championship game against the Green Bay Packers at Yankee Stadium.

making the Pro Bowl in '58 and '59. He went on to become an assistant coach with the Packers and Vikings.

Del Shofner, End (1957–67): When Allie Sherman took over as Giants head coach in 1961, one of his top priorities was finding a speedy receiver to replace Schnelker. He found his man in Shofner, who had led the NFL with 1,097 receiving yards with the Rams in '58.

Shofner, a Texan who starred at Baylor and could also punt, made three of his five career Pro Bowl trips between 1961 and '63. He caught 68, 53, and 64 passes during those seasons, amassing 32 total touchdown receptions and topping 1,000 receiving yards in each of those years.

"Dee-Fense! Dee-Fense!"

It was at Yankee Stadium during the 1950s that the first chants of "Dee-fense! Dee-fense!" were heard in pro football. Fans loved watching their Giants stuff opponents and were blessed with several defensive stalwarts to cheer.

Sam Huff, Linebacker (1956–69): The Giants' fierce middle linebacker and defensive captain, Huff was one of the most popular and publicized defenders of his era. He made *Time* magazine's cover at age 24 and was the subject of a TV special, *The Violent World of Sam Huff.* Setting the tone with his speed, nose for the football, and punishing hits, Huff played in five Pro Bowls and six NFL championship games. He made 30 career interceptions on his way to the Pro Football Hall of Fame.

New York's defensive line got down and dirty in a 19–14 win over the Eagles in 1962. Pictured are (from left) Andy Robustelli, Dick Modzelewski, Jim Katcavage, and Rosey Grier.

Andy Robustelli, Defensive End (1951–64): A 19th-round choice out of little-known Arnold College, Robustelli began his career with the Rams and was traded to the Giants for a first-round pick in 1956. That year, his remarkable pass rushing and great leadership helped New York earn an NFL championship. Robustelli was a seven-time All-Pro who won the 1962 Maxwell Club Player of the Year Award and entered the Pro Football Hall of Fame in 1971.

Rosey Grier, Defensive Tackle (1955–66): The "Gentle Giant," Grier sparked New York's front four between 1955 and 1962, making two Pro Bowl trips before joining the Rams. His post-NFL career has been equally impressive. He was a bodyguard for Robert F. Kennedy, wresting the gun away from assassin Sirhan Sirhan in 1968. Grier made several TV and movie appearances, wrote several books (including one on needlepoint, a passion of his), and delivered motivational speeches.

Dick Modzelewski, Defensive Tackle (1953–66): A College Football Hall of Famer and 1952 Outland Trophy winner at Maryland, Modzelewski's NFL career was marked by dependability. Though undersized for his position (6'0", 250 lbs.), he never missed a game in 14 seasons, setting a record with 180 consecutive contests. He played in six NFL championship games in eight seasons with the Giants.

Jim Katcavage, Defensive End (1956–68): A three-time All-Pro in 13 seasons (all with the Giants), Katcavage was a rookie standout on the 1956 NFL championship club who totaled three safeties in his career. In 1963, long before the NFL kept statistics for sacks, Jim wrapped up 25 quarterbacks behind the line of scrimmage.

Jim Patton, Defensive Back (1955–66): Patton could cover receivers and deliver hits with equal skill. He spent his entire career with the Giants and made five Pro Bowl trips. In 1958, he led the NFL with 11 interceptions. He picked off 52 career passes, returning two for touchdowns.

Y. A. Wins 'Em Over

One of the most famous names in pro football was not so much a name at all, but two initials: Yelberton Abraham "Y. A." Tittle had taken passing to new levels in three years with Baltimore and ten with San Francisco when he was traded to the Giants for guard Lou Cordileone in 1961, one of the most one-sided deals in NFL history.

Despite his accomplishments, "The Bald Eagle" did not arrive in New York City a popular man. After all, he was taking playing time away from fan favorite Charlie Conerly on a veteran team that had been accustomed to ruling the East.

Tittle, 35, and the 40-year-old Conerly shared signal-calling duties in 1961, before it became clear that Y. A. was the man for the job.

Tittle passed for 3,224 yards and 33 touchdowns in 1962. The following year, he threw 36 TD passes—an NFL record that lasted more than two decades—while leading the league with a 60-percent completion rate. He became the first man in NFL history to pass for 30 touchdowns in consecutive seasons. The Giants made the NFL championship game in each of his first three years with the club.

Tittle played one more season, a forgettable 1964 campaign in which his productivity slipped and the Giants nosedived to 2–10–2. But by the time he retired, he had won over teammates, fans, and everyone who knew him with his right arm and classy leadership.

"He brought the team together with his spirit, viable because he formed no cliques and ran with none," teammate and fellow Hall of Famer Andy Robustelli wrote. Tittle "had as much time for the defensive players as he had for his offensive teammates, and he treated the stars of the team no differently from the last guy on the bench."

A battered and bloodied Y. A. Tittle kneels dejected in Pittsburgh after absorbing a big hit against the Steelers in a 1964 game. It was Tittle's final season with the Giants.

The arrival of Y. A. Tittle in 1961 gave the Giants a Hall of Fame-bound quarterback to direct the offense. He passed for 33 touchdowns in 1962 and 36 more in '63.

Pitching the Pigskin In Style

It was rare for an NFL quarterback to pass for as many as 400 yards in a game when Y. A. Tittle dissected Washington for 505 yards and seven touchdowns on October 28, 1962, at Yankee Stadium. The seven TD tosses tied an NFL record, and Tittle's Giants teammates wanted him to add an eighth late in their 49–34 victory. Tittle refused.

"It would have been bad taste," said the modest quarterback after a 27-of-39 performance that, to this day, ranks among the greatest passing performances of all time.

Tittle did not throw an interception. His longest completion was a 63-yard TD pass to Frank Gifford. Receiver Del Shofner had a career day, matching Gifford's team record with 11 receptions that covered 269 yards—another club mark.

The "Amazing" Alex Webster

If Frank Gifford was the Giants' clean-cut cover boy during the 1950s and '60s, backfield-mate Alex Webster gained popularity via a different route altogether.

Gifford said Webster was a tough guy. "He was always amazing to me. He was always in the worst shape of anyone who ever played, probably. He smoke and drank, not to excess, and then he'd come out and play a whole game and run over people."

Webster, a New Jersey native who loved the New York City nightlife, scored big touchdowns in some of the Giants' biggest games. "Big Red" crossed the goal line twice in New York's 47–7 rout of the Bears for the 1956 NFL championship.

Webster also returned a fumble on an 86-yard play in an overtime loss to the Colts in the classic 1958 title clash, setting up a 1-yard touchdown run by Mel Triplett. Some thought Webster got into the end zone on that play, but the ball was spotted just short. "If only I had a little more speed, I'd have made it easily," Webster said.

At 6'4" and 230 pounds, Webster was 100-percent bruiser and zero-percent burner. He trampled defenders for more than 1,200 total yards in 1961 and '62, coming within 72 yards of a 1,000-yard rushing season in the former campaign. He made two Pro Bowls and finished among the NFL's top 10 in rushing yards and rushing touchdowns four times in his career. Webster amassed 56 career TDs—39 rushing and 17 receiving.

Originally drafted by the Redskins, Webster starred for two seasons in the Canadian Football League before playing his entire NFL career with the Giants. He worked as a radio commentator and assisted coach Allie Sherman after his playing career and was eventually promoted to head coach after Sherman's ouster before the 1969 season.

It was a popular move in New York. Giants' fans who had vocally run Sherman out of town were thrilled that one of their favorites would be leading the charge back to the top. After going 6–8 in his debut, Webster won UPI NFC Coach of the Year honors for steering the Giants to a 9–5 record in 1970, their first winning season in seven years.

The Giants, however, finished a disappointing 4–10 in 1971. Webster did post one more winning campaign (8–6) in 1972, but he resigned after a 2–11–1 collapse in '73.

Alex Webster, shown on this '54 Topps card, played in two Pro Bowls.

Giants running back Alex Webster follows his blockers during a 1963 game. Though the Giants did much of their damage through the air, Webster rushed for four touchdowns that season.

Game Day: Yankee Stadium

Yankee Stadium, "The House That Ruth Built," was never meant to host pro football. Still, Yankee Stadium was the setting for not only the Bronx Bombers' baseball glory days but for the rise of the New York Football Giants to a prominent place in the hearts of New York sports fans.

For decades, baseball, boxing, and horse racing dominated the sports pages, particularly in the Big Apple. Pro football was merely filler. Yankee Stadium had hosted some great college games—Notre Dame's "Win one for the Gipper" victory over Army in 1928 and a scoreless tie between the same schools in 1946—and terrific boxing matches, including traded heavyweight wins between Joe Louis and Max Schmeling. When the Giants moved to Yankee Stadium from the Polo Grounds in 1956, no one would have dared predict their appeal would rival that of the venue's primary tenants.

Then a funny thing happened on the way to shared residency. The Giants won the NFL championship in 1956, on their new home field no less. The following year, season ticket sales soared from 6,000 to 11,000—a sign that the team had taken up residency not only at a baseball stadium, but in Big Apple hearts.

Since the Giants' glory years in the late 1950s and early '60s coincided with their move to the Bronx, it's no wonder fans turned out in droves. Crowds in excess of 50,000 became common, and tailgating became a ritual practice outside the stadium. Inside the stadium, a large, white "NY" was painted in each end zone, flanked by white painted footballs.

Going to a Giants game became a family ritual in many New York homes, as fans flocked in from suburbs and neighboring boroughs. Others crowded around TVs and radios to follow the action. When home games were "blacked out" locally starting in the 1950s, fans gathered at motels that advertised the ability to pick up out-of-state TV broadcasts with powerful antennas.

Longtime Giants fan Phil Derrico and his friends in Massachusetts heard that they could pick up a game on a Connecticut

Giants games at Yankee Stadium were big events in the 1950s, as men dressed in jackets and ties. Confetti filled the air when New York defeated an opponent, as was the case in this 1958 contest.

station if they had a high enough antenna during that era, so they sent up a weather balloon with as much wire as they could afford. It worked, for a while.

"We didn't know it was in the flight path for LaGuardia Airport," Derrico said. "The police came and made us take it down. It wasn't high enough to disrupt any flights, but pilots get fidgety. I don't think we even got through the first quarter."

Back-to-Back-to-Back Heartbreak

There was no denying New York's superiority in the Eastern Conference from 1961 to '63. With Y. A. Tittle directing the offense, the Giants were capable of scoring from virtually anywhere on the field. They racked up more points than any team in the East in each of those three seasons, compiling records of 10–3–1, 12–2, and 11–3 over the newly expanded 14-game schedule to secure three straight berths in the NFL championship game.

Yes, the Giants were unquestioned beasts of the East. Their title game trips, however, produced three straight tame performances against Western champs from Green Bay and Chicago.

December 31, 1961: New Year's Eve in Green Bay brought 21-degree temperatures and an even colder Giants offense. It appeared the visitors might strike first, but Kyle Rote dropped a certain touchdown pass from Tittle in the first quarter and, wide open, was overthrown on a halfback option play from Bob

Gaiters in the second. Those squandered chances wound up haunting the Giants.

The Packers used a Paul Hornung touchdown run, a Hornung field goal, and two Bart Starr touchdown passes to score 24 second-quarter points on the way to a 37–0 rout. Starr added a third touchdown pass and Hornung two more field goals in the second half.

Green Bay racked up 345 yards against a Giants defense that had allowed the fewest points in the NFL. Meanwhile, the Packers held the Giants to 130 yards before 39,029 bundled-up fans at a stadium that would come to be known as Lambeau Field.

December 30, 1962: A championship rematch between the Giants and Packers figured to be a better game than the previous year's whitewashing. New York had cruised to a 12–2 record while throwing a league-high 35 touchdown passes—21 better than the ground-chewing Packers.

"I thought we were the best team in the history of football that year," said Tittle of the 1962 Giants, who had rattled off 12 wins in 13 games after a season-opening loss to the Browns and gained more than 5,000 yards that year. "We scored so many points, just blowing everyone away."

After sitting out the previous year with a concussion, Frank Gifford was back in the lineup as a receiver, giving Tittle yet another weapon. The quarterback delivered 33 touchdown passes.

Vince Lombardi's Packers were also stronger than their previous squad, having lost once in 14 games. They entered the title clash at Yankee Stadium as the league's highest-scoring team, poised to dominate the 1960s.

Again, bad weather played a part. A kickoff temperature in the teens and 35-mile-per-hour winds whipping through Yankee

This program is from the Giants-Steelers game on October 14, 1962.

New York's Sam Huff (No. 70) and Rosey Grier (No. 76) could not stop Hall of Fame running back Jim Taylor of the Packers on this scoring romp in the 1962 NFL championship game.

Green Bay by a half-game in the West, while New York's 11–3 record was one game better than the Browns in the East.

Chicago's Wrigley Field was the setting, under even colder conditions, 9 degrees, than the Giants' previous two title losses. New York grabbed a 7–0 lead on a 14-yard Tittle-to-Gifford scoring strike in the first quarter. Del Shofner dropped a ball in the end zone that could have made it a 14–0 game, and Chicago's Larry Morris intercepted a Tittle pass on the next play, setting up a tying score for the Bears.

Tittle, who had thrown for an NFL-record 36 touchdowns in the regular season, injured his left knee on an early shot from Morris. Tittle missed two series in the second quarter and was never the same. New York took a 10–7 lead on a short field goal by Don Chandler in the second quarter, but the Bears surrendered virtually nothing after that.

An interception set up the winning touchdown for Chicago, a 1-yard run by Bill Wade. As the final seconds ticked off the clock, cameras captured an injured, devastated, and parka-wrapped Tittle on his knees on the sideline, weeping. It would be almost two decades before the Giants returned to the playoffs.

The wind kicks up a cloud of dust as the Packers await the huddling Giants during the 1962 NFL championship game at Yankee Stadium. Green Bay prevailed 16–7.

Stadium were sure to cripple both aerial attacks, a clear edge for the Packers. No points were scored via the pass.

Jerry Kramer kicked a short field goal, and Jim Taylor ran for a touchdown as Green Bay silenced the crowd of 64,892 by scoring all 10 first-half points. For the second straight year, the Giants offense failed to score against Ray Nitschke and the Packers defense. New York's only points in a 16–7 loss came when Erich Barnes blocked a Green Bay punt and Jim Collier recovered in the end zone.

December 29, 1963: This time, it was the Bears blocking the Packers' way to a championship. At 11–1–2, they had edged

Doug Atkins of the Bears pressures Giants backup quarterback Glynn Griffing into throwing an incomplete pass during Chicago's 14–10 win in the 1963 NFL title game at Soldier Field.

GIANTS GALLERY

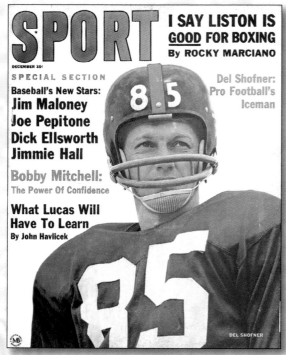
Del Shofner, on *Sport* in '63, was a first-team All-Pro in five different seasons in his NFL career.

This photo, signed by Y. A. Tittle, shows him in a familiar setting: letting her fly.

This 1959 Topps card is from the last year that Charlie Conerly, then 39 years old, was the full-time starter for the Giants, who were 10–2 and conference champs.

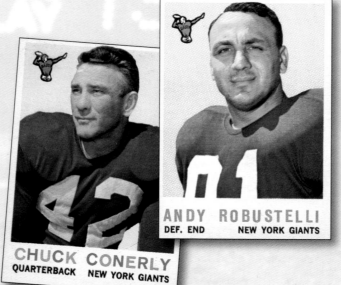

CHUCK CONERLY
QUARTERBACK NEW YORK GIANTS

ANDY ROBUSTELLI
DEF. END NEW YORK GIANTS

One of the all-time NFL greats, Andy Robustelli (also on a '59 Topps) received the Bert Bell Award as the league MVP in 1962.

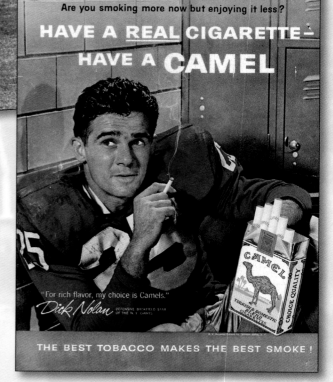
The Giants of the 1950s were Madison Avenue darlings. Dick Nolan (later a long-time NFL head coach) appears in this magazine ad.

The Colts' Alan Ameche scores an overtime touch-down in the 1958 championship game, making front page news for *The New York Times*.

"All the News That's Fit to Print"

The New York Times.

VOL. CVIII....No. 36,864.

THE NEW YORK TIMES, MONDAY, DECEMBER 29, 1958.

LATE CITY EDITION

U. S. Weather Bureau Report (Page 30) forecast: Mild, chance of rain today; partly cloudy, colder tonight and tomorrow. Temp. range: 45—38. Yesterday: 49.3—32.5.

10c beyond 100-mile zone from New York City. Higher in air delivery cities.

FIVE CENTS

DE GAULLE URGES BELT-TIGHTENING TO REVIVE NATION

Outlines in Talk to People Sacrifices Needed to Lift France to Greatness

ALTERNATIVE HELD DIRE

Tax Rise, Cut in Subsidies and Increased Prices for Imports Are in Store

By ROBERT C. DOTY
Special to The New York Times.

PARIS, Dec. 28—Premier Charles de Gaulle told the French people tonight that the price of salvation and national greatness was sacrifice.

The Premier and Finance Minister Antoine Pinay, in radio-television addresses, then outlined the degree of austerity demanded by the 17.55 per cent devaluation of the franc and other stringent financial measures announced...

Colts Beat Giants, Win in Overtime

23-17 Game Tied With 7 Seconds Left in Regulation Time

By LOUIS EFFRAT

Time and fortune finally ran out on professional football's Cinderella team, the New York Giants, yesterday at the Yankee Stadium. And so it was that the Baltimore Colts, with a 23-17 victory, won the championship of the National Football League.

With a couple of minutes to go in the fourth period, the Giants seemed to have the triumph in their grasp. But with seven seconds to go, Baltimore tied the score at 17—17 on a field goal.

Then, in a sudden-death overtime period, the Baltimore team coached by Weeb Ewbank fashioned the winning touchdown after 8 minutes 15 seconds.

The excitement generated by football's longest game left most of the 64,185 spectators limp. Aside from an experimental exhibition contest, it was the first sudden-death game (with victory going instantly to the first team to score) in the league.

Alan (The Horse) Ameche, who had...

Alan Ameche storms across the Giants' goal line for the winning touchdown as his teammates open a wide gap in the New York line during overtime period at Yankee Stadium.

Associated Press

U.S. MAY SPONSOR A WIDENED ROLE FOR WORLD COURT

President Is Studying a Bid in State of Union Message —Senate Action Needed

By JAMES RESTON
Special to The New York Times.

WASHINGTON, Dec. 28—The Eisenhower Administration is actively considering an appeal to all nations to widen the scope and authority of the International Court of Justice at The Hague.

It is understood that a draft of such a proposal is now before President Eisenhower for inclusion in his forthcoming State of the Union message.

This draft—not finally approved by the President—contains a recommendation to the new Congress that the United States lead the way in offering to be more liberal in accepting the jurisdiction of the World Court over international legal disputes involving the United States.

PAPERS RESUME AS DELIVERYMEN END 19-DAY TIE-UP

NEW PACT IS VOTED

Union Accepts 2-Year Terms, 2,091 to 537 —Walkout Costly

To Our Readers

The New York Times, which has been shut down for seventeen days by the strike of the Newspaper and Mail Deliverers Union, resumes publication today.

The texts of statements on strike are on Page 18.

By RUSSELL PORTER

A nineteen-day deliverers' union strike that had closed...

NY GIANTS VS. CLEVELAND BROWNS

YANKEE STADIUM   OFFICIAL PROGRAM · 50 CENTS

DECEMBER 18, 1960

This program is from the final regular season game in 1960, when the Browns beat the Giants. The Eagles behind Norm Van Brocklin, though, were conference champs.

REDSKINS

giants

NOVEMBER 25, 1962 · TAX INCLUDED 50c

In the early 1960s, the Giants' offense was really humming. This 1962 program was sold when they crushed their rivals, the Redskins, 42–24.

NEW YORK FOOTBALL

GIANTS

1963

PRICE: $1.00

19

This is the first "yearbook" produced by the New York Giants, in 1963. As such, it is a collector's item.

CHAPTER FOUR

The Dead Zone
1965–1978

NEW YORK GIANTS
FOOTBALL TEAM

NFL

"We've played in strange places since I've been here, in some strange surroundings. It'll be good to have a home."

GIANTS COACH BILL ARNSPARGER BEFORE
THE 1976 MOVE TO GIANTS STADIUM

Above: *This card shows the '67 Giants, who rebounded from a 1–12–1 record in 1966 to a 7–7 mark after adding quarterback Fran Tarkenton. Right: There were some lean times for the Giants in the 1960s and '70s, but stars like Tarkenton did give fans of the club plenty to cheer about.*

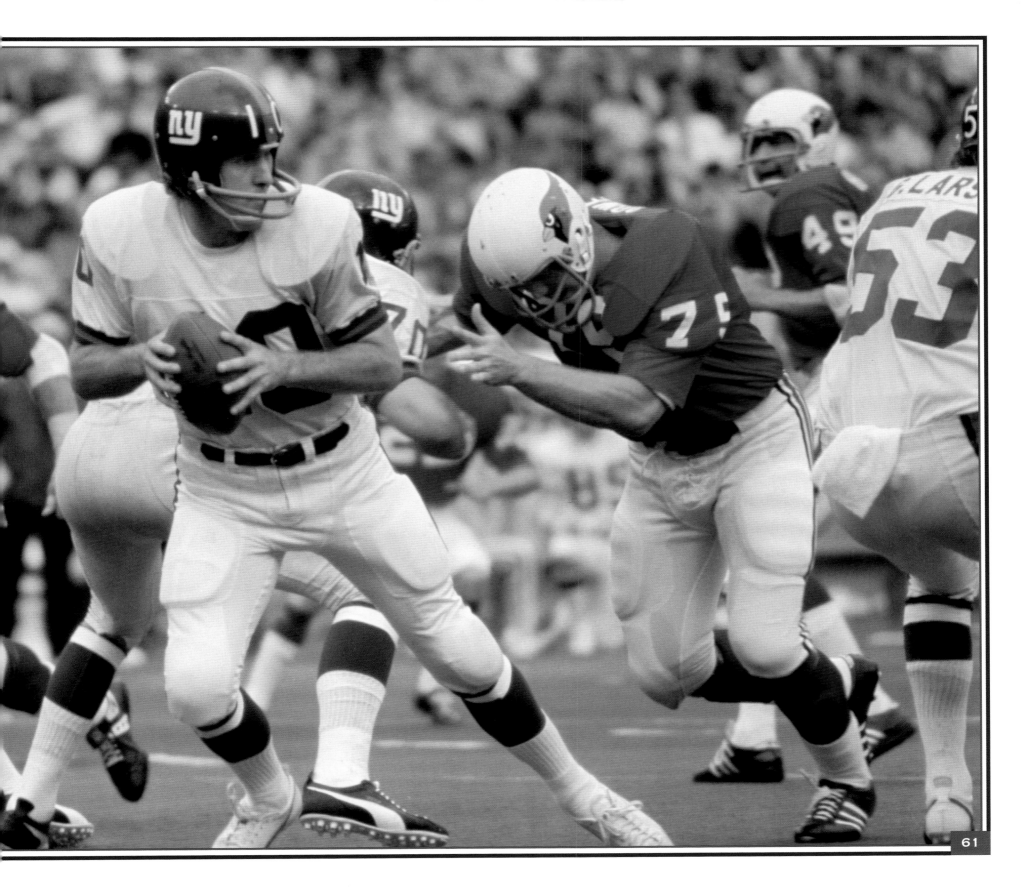

Highs and Lows: Allie Sherman

The song still rings in the ears of Giants fans who heard it, or sang it, during Allie Sherman's coaching tenure: "Goodbye, Allie. Goodbye, Allie. Goodbye, Allie, we hate to see you go." In a 1969 exhibition loss in Montreal, Canadian fans even sang it to the Giants coach in French.

It was a harsh exit for a man whose head coaching career began with such promise—three consecutive trips to the NFL championship game, from 1961 to '63. Allie Sherman earned NFL Coach of the Year accolades in the first two of those seasons, the first time a coach had ever been so honored in back-to-back years.

Sherman was respected for his intelligence. He captained the football team at prestigious Brooklyn College, played as a scrawny quarterback for Philadelphia, and learned Xs and Os from legendary Eagles coach Greasy Neale. Sherman coached in the Canadian Football League, long before those Canadian fans sang for his ouster, and assisted with the Giants offense under Jim Lee Howell. When Howell retired after the 1960 season, Sherman was promoted to head coach, and he steered the Giants to within one win of an NFL championship in each of his first three years.

Despite disappointing losses in those three title games, the Giants appeared to be on the verge of greatness. Then, inexplicably, Sherman found himself commanding a sinking ship. After going 33–8–1 in his first three seasons, he never enjoyed another winning campaign.

The 1964 Giants fell out of contention for their fourth straight Eastern title before the weather turned cold, finishing 2–10–2. A 7–7 campaign followed, but Sherman's 1966 club managed just

Allie Sherman coached the Giants to only 24 wins from 1964 through 1968, and he was unable to overcome a 0–5 start in 1969.

Giants coach Allie Sherman squats in front of a Giants team he led to three straight NFL title game qualifiers from 1961 to '63. He failed to maintain that level of success over the remainder of his tenure.

one win in 14 games. Two more 7–7 seasons followed, but by the time the Giants replaced him with Alex Webster after going 0–5 in the '69 exhibition season, fans were celebrating the dismissal of a man they felt "ran off" too many good players.

"There was no reason in the world to trade me for two guys who never did produce for the Giants," said Hall of Fame linebacker Sam Huff, explaining his bitterness at Sherman over a trade following the 1963 season—a departure that coincided with the Giants' downfall.

"Oh, my heavens," exclaimed longtime fan Mrs. Bernard E. O'Connor when informed by a *New York Times* reporter of Sherman's ouster. "Wait till I tell Bernie when he gets home. This is going to be one of the happiest days of his life."

The Looney Bin

It was likely no coincidence that the aptly named Joe Don Looney came along in 1964, the first year of the Giants' downfall. Though he never made it to a regular-season game with the team, his antics epitomized a tumultuous era in Giants football.

Following is a look at Looney and two other characters of this era—short-lived Giants and longtime Raiders star Ben Davidson and "innovator" Homer Jones.

Looney Tunes: Looney dropped out of Texas, was kicked out of TCU, and had been kicked off the Oklahoma football team for fighting with an assistant coach before the Giants made him their first-round pick in the 1964 NFL Draft. They took a chance based on Looney's sprinter's speed and 230-pound running back frame. "Joe Don Looney had all the God-given talent in the world to play football," explained ex-Giants and Redskins linebacker Sam Huff. "But it was wasted talent on him."

Looney refused to talk to reporters as a rookie in training camp, saying he would let his play do the talking. Problem was, he seemed to have little interest in playing. Looney refused coach Allie Sherman's orders on details like taping ankles and making curfew, and Looney was shipped to Baltimore before the regular season. He "played" for five teams in four seasons.

Coach Don Shula once said he was afraid to put Looney in the game to punt, "because I didn't know if he would punt. He might do anything."

Bad Ben: The Giants did not know what they had in 1961 fourth-round pick Ben Davidson. The big defensive lineman got off to a rocky start with coach Allie Sherman and was traded during camp to Green Bay. He would eventually land in Oakland, where he became an All-Pro.

Sherman knew exactly where he stood with Davidson, however. Shortly after the trade, the rookie intercepted a pass against the Giants during an exhibition game and, as he ran down the sideline past the Giants coach, flipped Sherman a gesture with his middle finger.

Homer Jones: If the Giants did not win many games during his era, Jones at least gave them a claim to fame. After scoring his first touchdown in 1965, he wound up and slammed the football hard into the turf, a celebration he dubbed "the spike." Jones went on to lead the NFL with 13 TD receptions in 1967 and was a two-time Pro Bowler. And more than 40 years later, NFL players still use his maneuver—in addition to dances, leaps, and a variety of other innovations—to celebrate scores.

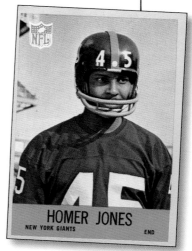

Homer Jones, shown on a 1967 Philadelphia card, caught 224 career passes.

Homer Jones, architect of the post-touchdown spike, catches a pass against the Cardinals in a 1967 game in St. Louis. Jones was a Pro Bowl receiver for the Giants.

Rivalry Born of Respect

Neither is the biggest rival of the other. The Redskins have the Cowboys; the Giants have the Eagles. Still, the Giants-Redskins series has produced several memorable games and plays over the years, along with a healthy amount of respect between two great franchises. Their rivalry dates to 1932, when the Skins were known as the Boston Braves.

"Even when they had bad teams," said Redskins linebacker Neil Olkewicz in 1986, "we respected the Giants. . . . The Giants are more like us, blue-collar guys who worked their way up to what they are."

Through the 2008 season, the Giants led the all-time series 87–61–4. Early in their existence, the Giants served as the Redskins' measuring stick for success. Washington battered New York on the final day of the 1937 season to win the East, and the following year the Giants turned the tables en route to an NFL title game win against the Packers.

At times during the 1970s, '80s, and '90s, it was the Giants trying to chase down the Redskins in the NFC East standings. A few of the series' most memorable moments include:

December 3, 1939: With another Eastern title on the line, the Redskins lined up for a winning field goal with 45 seconds to go. It was a chip-shot from 15 yards, and Bo Russell's boot looked good to his teammates. But referee Bill Halloran signaled "no good," leaving the Giants to celebrate a 9–7 victory.

October 28, 1962: Giants quarterback Y. A. Tittle had a record-setting passing day against the Redskins. His 505 passing yards shattered the previous franchise mark, and his seven touchdown tosses tied a record in a 49–34 win.

This program is from December 12, 1965, when New York beat the Redskins 27–10. Earl Morrall threw two TD tosses that day.

November 27, 1966: The Redskins routed the Giants 72–41 in a game that set NFL records for points scored by one team and points scored by both teams in a regular-season contest. Washington scored on offense, defense, and special teams and cranked up the heat on the rivalry by tacking on a field goal with seven seconds remaining in the game.

November 18, 1985: Many watching on TV opted to turn their heads or turn off their sets as the network replayed Lawrence Taylor's hit on Redskins quarterback Joe Theismann. Theismann's right leg had been caught in a precarious position, and the quarterback's tibia and fibula snapped—famously and grotesquely. Washington won, but a great career was ended.

Giants quarterback Tom Kennedy is forced into throwing an incomplete pass by Washington's Chris Hanburger. It was a rare example of defense in a 1966 game that the Redskins won 72–41, breaking NFL scoring records.

Getting Their Kicks

It's said that if you can make it in New York, you can make it anywhere. For an NFL placekicker, who can go from hero to goat with just one ill-timed miss, making it *anywhere* can be achievement enough.

That's why Pete Gogolak, the NFL's first soccer-style kicker, knows he can look back on his 11-year pro career and smile.

"I survived in New York, which is not easy," said the Budapest native, whose family survived the Hungarian Revolution in 1956 by fleeing with 14-year-old Pete and younger brother Charlie (who went on to kick for the Redskins and Patriots) to Austria, covering the final 16 miles on foot. "You know how it is—you have a couple of bad games, and you're gone. I just had a pretty good survival record."

Gogolak did much better than survive. He broke in with the Buffalo Bills in 1964, when his 102 points were one-quarter of the AFL team's total.

Until he arrived, pro football kickers approached the ball straight-on, making contact with the toe. Gogolak mastered the soccer style, approaching from the side and striking with his instep—a form that's used almost exclusively today. With it, he joined the Giants in 1966 and became one of the better kickers in the NFL.

When Gogolak retired after the 1974 season, he was the team's career scoring leader with 646 points. He also held franchise records for extra points attempted and made, field goals attempted and made, and extra points in a game (eight).

Pete Gogolak was the first soccer-style kicker in the NFL, revolutionizing the way field goals and extra points were struck. He became the Giants' all-time scoring leader at the time of his retirement.

Gogolak's final season was Dave Jennings's first, and the latter became to Giants punting what the former was to placekicking. Sure, fans don't care to see punters, since it means their team's offense has stalled. But Jennings's right leg was a valuable weapon for the club for more than a decade.

The New York native, who did not play high school football, led the NFL in total punts and punt yardage for the first time in 1979. The following year, he again led the league in punt yardage while also averaging a league-best 44.8 yards per kick.

In 11 seasons with the Giants, Jennings made the Pro Bowl four times and twice led the NFL in punts downed inside the 20-yard line. He spent the final three years of his career with the Jets and has since worked as a commentator for both of his former teams.

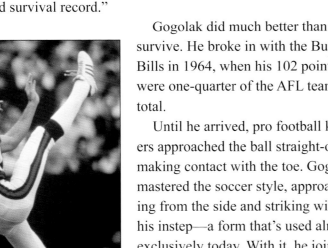

The right leg of Dave Jennings was a valuable weapon for the Giants for more than a decade. Jennings punted his way to the Pro Bowl four times.

Fran the Man

Sure, the Giants lost more games than they won with Fran Tarkenton calling the signals. The Hall of Fame quarterback posted a 33–36 mark as New York's starter from 1967 to 1971.

During those five years, though, watching a losing football team was well worth the price of admission, even if the price for obtaining Tarkenton's services from Minnesota was a steep one: two first-round and two second-round draft picks over a three-year stretch.

The Giants' front office felt it had to do something to boost interest and their team's chances. New York had won just one game in 1966, with three different QBs attempting 100 passes. In Tarkenton, the Giants landed a young weapon who made things happen with his arm and his legs.

"Scramblin' Fran" had made the Pro Bowl twice in his first five seasons with Minnesota. New York fans had never seen anything like him—a Houdini of a quarterback who could escape sure sacks to throw long touchdown passes on the run, or dodge defenders for huge ground gains.

"The first down is more important to him than possible injury," noted Dr. Don Lannin, Tarkenton's one-time physician with the Vikings. "He chews out pass receivers all the time for making their cut a half-yard short of a first down."

Tarkenton's presence made an immediate impact on his new team. The Giants improved to 7–7 in each of his first two years taking snaps and posted four successive second-place divisional finishes. Their 9–5 record in 1970 was the team's best mark since its '63 NFL runner-up campaign.

Tarkenton topped 3,000 passing yards in '67 and made the Pro Bowl in each of his first four years with the Giants. If New York fans appreciated the extra effort and the hits he was willing to take in the name of moving the chains, the former University of Georgia star was quick to return the adoration.

"New York fans are more demonstrative than any fans I ever played for," he said. "If you do anything worthwhile, they shake the stadium with noise and their appreciation."

Giants fans could appreciate Tarkenton for only one more season after a 9–5 1970 campaign. New York slipped to 4–10 in 1971. Following that season, Tarkenton returned to his original team in the second blockbuster trade of his career (the Giants acquired several players and two high draft picks). He led Minnesota to three Super Bowls, won the 1975 MVP Award, and became the Vikings' career leader in passing yards and touchdown passes.

Shown on a 1969 Topps card, Tarkenton eclipsed many of John Unitas's career passing records.

Though he played most of his Hall of Fame career with Minnesota, quarterback Fran Tarkenton spent five seasons keeping Giants fans on the edge of their seats with his mobility in the pocket.

New York's First 1,000-Yard Rusher

Firsts, by definition, happen but once. So you savor them. You remember them. And by them you compare those who follow.

As the franchise's first 1,000-yard rusher, Ron Johnson will forever hold a place in New York Giants history. In the early 1970s, he set the standard that the likes of Joe Morris, Ottis Anderson, Rodney Hampton, and Tiki Barber ran hard to uphold.

When Johnson was named chairman of the National Football Foundation & College Football Hall of Fame in 2006, NFF president Steven J. Hatchell noted, "Ron's on-field accomplishments, coupled with his success in business and the community, send a powerful message about the direction of our organization."

Likewise, Johnson's success with the Giants—though it came during a largely forgettable era in team history—had a powerful impact on the direction of the club. It was no coincidence that his two 1,000-yard seasons, 1970 and '72, powered the Giants to their only two winning campaigns between 1964 and 1980.

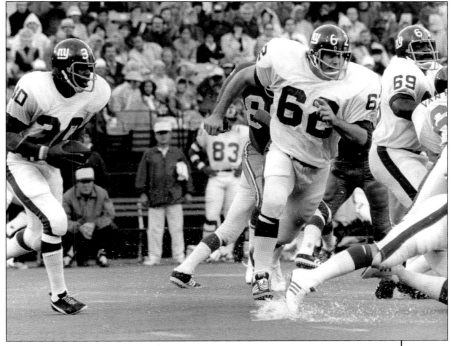

Ron Johnson (30) was the first 1,000-yard rusher in Giants history. In fact, his two 1,000-yard seasons helped New York to its only two winning seasons from 1964 to '80.

"Comeback-to-Back" Wins

Of Ron Johnson's 100-yard rushing games, no two were more memorable than those that helped the Giants to thrilling, back-to-back comeback wins at Yankee Stadium in 1970.

Dallas led 20–9 on November 8, but Johnson ran for a third-quarter touchdown and capped a Fran Tarkenton-led drive late in the game with another TD romp. The Giants went on to pull off a 23–20 win with three minutes remaining. Johnson finished with 136 yards on 23 carries.

One week later, Johnson and the Giants truly defied logic. Trailing the Redskins 33–14, they rallied for 21 fourth-quarter points on two Johnson runs and a 57-yard pass from Tarkenton to Tucker Frederickson for a 35–33 triumph. Johnson's nine-yard dash around end with one minute to go gave him 106 rushing yards and provided the winning points.

At Michigan, the Detroit native set an NCAA record (since broken) by rushing for 347 yards in a 1968 game against Wisconsin. In 1970, he became the Giants' first 1,000-yard rusher, eclipsing the mark in the last game of a 9–5 season. He finished with 1,027 rushing yards.

Two years later, in 1972, Johnson was even better, topping 1,000 yards in the 12th game of an 8–6 slate and finishing with 1,182. He led the NFL in rushing attempts and made the Pro Bowl in both 1970 and 1972.

Injuries began taking their toll, and Johnson retired after six seasons. A successful businessman, he earned his MBA from Fairleigh Dickinson University in 1980. His brother, Alex, was a big league baseball player who led the AL in batting in 1970.

GIANTS GALLERY

This signed photo of Ron Johnson resonates with Giants fans. Johnson was acquired in a trade with the Browns for flanker Homer Jones in 1970.

This lovable fellow is a highly collectible example of the classic bobblehead doll from the '60s.

Sports Illustrated

QUARTERBACK ON THE RUN
BY FRAN TARKENTON
OF THE NEW YORK GIANTS

"Scramblin' Fran" Tarkenton appears to be constantly in motion on this 1967 cover of *Sports Illustrated*.

JIM KATCAVAGE
NEW YORK GIANTS   END

JOE MORRISON
NEW YORK GIANTS   FLANKER

Jim Katcavage and Joe Morrison were key members of the Giants in 1967, when these Philadelphia cards were released.

Giants Upset Cowboys, 23-20, as Johnson Scores Twice in 2d-Half Comeback

Back Runs for 136 Yards; Triumph Is Fifth Straight

By LEONARD KOPPETT

Reproducing one of the classic competitions of antiquity—the race between the tortoise and the hare—the New York Giants scored their most notable triumph of recent years by beating the Dallas Cowboys, 23-20, at Yankee Stadium yesterday.

Bob Hayes, an Olympic champion sprinter, symbolized the hare by catching two touchdown passes, covering 38 and 30 yards, which helped Dallas to a 17-6 lead in the second quarter.

But the Giants, with Ron Johnson, plugged away in shorter strides throughout the second half and finally scored the winning touchdown with only 3 minutes 3 seconds to play.

Then the Giants' defensive unit, which let Dallas into only 145 yards aside from the two passes to Hayes, capped a magnificent performance by containing the Cowboys in a final exciting sequence in which a tying field goal or winning touchdown seemed possible until the last few seconds.

STATISTICS OF THE GAME

	Giants	Cwbys.
First downs	19	15
Rushing yardage	198	102
Passing yardage	136	161
Return yardage	22	0
Passes	15-25	10-22
Interceptions by	1	0
Punts	4-44	7-44
Fumbles lost	1	1
Yards penalized	30	81

29-Yard Attempt Misses

And when it was all over, the margin of victory in New York's fifth straight success stood as the record 54-yard field goal Pete Gogolak had kicked on the final play of the first half. He had others, of 40 and 42 yards, but missed a 29-yard try early in the fourth quarter, when the Giants were trailing by 4 points.

The significance of the victory was reflected in the standing and crowd reaction. Now embarked on their longest winning streak since 1962, the Giants have tied Dallas with a land

Gogolak's 40-yarder, but late in the first half Dallas reeled off two first downs to the Giant 38, and Hayes simply outran Ken Parker for Craig Morton's pass and a touchdown.

Gogolak cut the margin to 10-6 early in the second quarter, but two sequences later, after a punt into the end zone, Morton hung one out for Hayes, who made a running juggling catch on the Giant 30 after the ball had just cleared Willie Williams's fingertips. Hayes just kept going while Williams lay prone behind him.

As half-time neared, Gogolak missed a 55-yard field goal try, but the Giants got the ball back and made a first down on the Dallas 47 with 16 seconds left. After three incomplete passes, Gogo booted it, breaking by a yard a Giant record set by Don Chandler in 1962.

On the 71-yard march in the third quarter, Johnson carried on seven of the 10 plays for 54 yards. On the next drive, begun by a successful onside kickoff, he carried five times for 30 yards, but the drive failed.

The one that succeeded started with a 14-yard pass to Clifton McNeil (who suffered a broken nose in the first quarter but kept playing). Johnson ran for 2, then caught a pass for a 22-yard gain to the 17. Tarkenton, trapped, ran to the 13, and on third down hit Johnson...

2 Special Fans Watch Johnson

By AL HARVIN

Whether or not Ron Johnson, the Giants' star running back, had his biggest afternoon of the season yesterday against the Dallas Cowboys was of small moment to Mr. and Mrs. Arthur Johnson of Detroit. They were more than satisfied with their son's performance.

"This is the first time I've seen Ron play in person this season, but we went to all the games in Cleveland," said his father, who owns a trucking firm. "I'm very proud of all three sons."

Arthur Jr., the eldest, works in his dad's business. Alex, the next son in the family that includes two daughters, plays for the California Angels and won the batting crown this season. Ron is the baby.

"Now, you sound just like my mother," interrupted Ron, who has been a major factor in the big Giants' turnaround and five-game winning streak. "I'm the youngest but I'm not the baby."

Big Day 'Against Eagles

Since coming to the Giants this year in a trade with Cleveland, Johnson was switched from fullback to halfback and has matured into a bona fide star. His impressive showing...

confident in my ability and I knew things would work out."

Johnson appreciates his parents. "I was lucky. I didn't have to drop out of school or anything like that to go to work, even though my father only got as far as the fourth grade."

Next season there will be...

another Johnson rooting in the stands.

"I'm getting married during the Christmas holidays to Karen Lyons, whom I met in college," said Ron.

Clifton McNeil had his nose broken by Mel Renfro's elbow in the first quarter, but he continued to play...

Pro Football: 63-Yard Field Goal

By MURRAY CHASS

Although Tom Dempsey was born with half a right foot and a stub for a right hand, he doesn't consider himself handicapped. "I've always been able to do anything anybody else did," he says.

In New Orleans' game against the Detroit Lions yesterday, Dempsey did something better than anyone in pro football ever had done.

Using that half foot, he kicked a 63-yard field goal, 7 yards farther than the previous longest field goal in pro history, Bert Rechichar's 56-yarder for Baltimore in 1953.

And since it would have been a shame to waste such a prodigious feat on just any old 3 points, the 6-foot-1-inch, 264-pound Dempsey kicked it on the last play of the game and gave the Saints a 19-17 upset victory.

Special Shoe Helps

"I knew I could kick the ball that far, but whether or not I could kick it straight that far kept running through my mind," said Dempsey, who wears a special kicking shoe approved by the league.

The 23-year-old Saint, who booted the ball from the New Orleans 37-yard line—that's 3 yards farther back from the kickoff spot—said he couldn't see the ball clear the crossbar, which it did by inches.

four of five field goal attempts yesterday, was five for 15 going into the game.

It was a Johnson pass, though, that helped Kansas City break open a close contest. Bobby Bell, the Chiefs' agile linebacker, intercepted the pass in the fourth quarter and raced 45 yards for a touchdown.

Interconference

CARDINALS 31, PATRIOTS 0

St. Louis took over sole possession of first place in the National Conference's Eastern Division by posting its second straight shutout.

While the Cardinal defense was frustrating Boston's Joe Kapp, MacArthur Lane was sparking the offense with a three-touchdown, 71-yard rushing performance. The Patriots, who played their first game under Coach John Mazur, have scored only 13 points in the last four contests.

EAGLES 24, DOLPHINS 17

Powered by Norm Snead's three touchdown passes—two to Harold Jackson—Philadelphia won its first game of the season and its first since Nov. 23, 1969. In the interim, the Eagles had lost 16 games, including seven this season and five in the exhibition season.

The St. Louis and Philadelphia victories gave the National Conference a 16-3 lead over the American in interconference games.

American Conference

RAIDERS 23, BROWNS 20

George Blanda, whose 48-yard field goal with three seconds left gave Oakland a tie with Kansas City last week,

touchdown for the second week in a row.

BENGALS 43, BILLS 14

Buffalo lost not only the game but also its prize running back, O. J. Simpson, who suffered a knee injury on a kickoff return on the last play of the first half.

It was another kickoff return, by Cincinnati's Lemar Parrish, that helped beat the Bills. Parrish scampered 95 yards for a touchdown on the return for one of his two long scoring plays. The rookie also scooped up the ball after Ken Riley had blocked Grant Guthrie's field goal attempt and scooted 83 yards.

CHARGERS 24, BRONCOS 21

John Hadl's second touchdown pass to Gary Garrison, his third of the game, clinched the victory for San Diego. Garrison made a racing, fingertip grab of the pass with 5:22 to play.

National Conference

49ERS 37, BEARS 16

John Brodie wiped out a 16-10 deficit by throwing three touchdown passes in the second half, two to Gene Washington. Brodie completed 21 passes...

Nat'l Football League

YESTERDAY'S GAMES

New York Giants 23, Dallas 20.
St. Louis 31, Boston 0.
Cincinnati 43, Buffalo 14.
Oakland 23, Cleveland 20.
Kansas City 16, Houston 7.
New Orleans 19, Detroit 17.
San Diego 24, Denver 21.
Philadelphia 24, Miami 17.
Pittsburgh 21, Washington 10.
Minnesota 19, Chicago 14.
San Francisco 37, Chicago 16.

STANDING OF THE CLUBS

NATIONAL DIVISION

EASTERN DIVISION

	W	L	T	Pct.	Pts.	OP
St. Louis				.857	203	69
N.Y. Giants				.625	185	171
Dallas				.625	164	126
Washington				.375	156	145
Philadelphia				.250	109	201

CENTRAL DIVISION

Minnesota				.875	207	55
Detroit				.750	199	124
Green Bay				.250	127	164
Chicago				.250	104	173

WESTERN DIVISION

San Francisco				.750	212	135
Los Angeles				.625	209	164
Atlanta				.429	125	155
New Orleans				.250	104	175

AMERICAN CONFERENCE

Baltimore				.875	203	65
Miami				.625	190	116
Buffalo				.200	98	182
N.Y. Jets				.200	113	175

Captions (photos)

Smashing into Fran Tarkenton, Bob Lilly of Dallas Cowboys drops quarterback for a loss

In a more elusive moment, Tarkenton scrambles and leaves would-be tackler in the lurch

Dave Manders of Dallas and Jerry Shay of the Giants trading blows during a brief encounter in the second period.

This pin dates from the mid-1960s, when the Giants were just beginning their struggles under coach Allie Sherman.

Ron Johnson led the Giants to several exciting wins in 1970, including, as *The New York Times* reports, a come-from-behind victory on November 8 over the Cowboys.

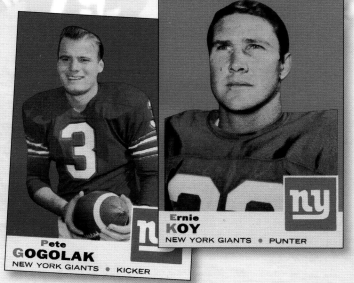

Pete
GOGOLAK
NEW YORK GIANTS • KICKER

Ernie
KOY
NEW YORK GIANTS • PUNTER

Pete Gogolak and Ernie Koy put the "foot" in football for the Giants in 1969, when Topps released these cards.

This rare matchbook schedule shows the lineup of games the dismal 1966 Giants would eventually traverse. The October 16 contest against Washington was their only win.

SUPERIOR MATCH CO., CHICAGO, U.S.A.

WNEW GIANTS SCHEDULE

PRE SEASON

AUG. 6	PITTSBURGH	2PM
AUG. 13	DETROIT	10PM
AUG. 21	ATLANTA	9PM
AUG. 27	GREEN BAY	2PM
SEPT. 3	PHILADELPHIA	2PM

REGULAR SEASON

SEPT. 11	PITTSBURGH	1:30PM
SEPT. 18	DALLAS	3:30PM
SEPT. 25	PHILADELPHIA	2PM
OCT. 2	CLEVELAND	1:30PM
OCT. 9	ST. LOUIS	1:30PM
OCT. 16	WASHINGTON	1:30PM
OCT. 23	PHILADELPHIA	1:30PM
NOV. 6	LOS ANGELES	4PM
NOV. 13	ST. LOUIS	1:30PM
NOV. 20	WASHINGTON	1:30PM
NOV. 27	CLEVELAND	1:30PM
DEC. 4	PITTSBURGH	1:30PM
DEC. 11	DALLAS	1:30PM
DEC. 18	...	...

WNEW 1130AM / 102.7FM

New York Giants

Monday Night Premiere Stumble

The bright lights of *Monday Night Football* did not shine favorably on the Giants on November 23, 1970. Where playoff hopes were concerned, it would have been appropriate for "Dandy" Don Meredith to sing from the broadcast booth, "Turn out the lights; the party's over."

The Giants had won six straight games entering their debut on *Monday Night Football*, ABC's weekly nationally televised game. It was the first year of the network's successful 35-year run of such telecasts, and on this chilly night the cameras rolled at Philadelphia's Franklin Field for a game between the surging Giants and the flightless Philadelphia Eagles, who had won just once in nine games.

New York prepared for a gambling, unconventional defense from the Eagles, but coach Alex Webster seemed confident Fran Tarkenton and his offense could solve it. All the quarterback would have to do is figure out a good play or two against that defense, Webster offered. "If you can sting it once or twice, chances are they'll come out of it and stay conventional."

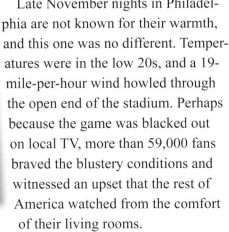

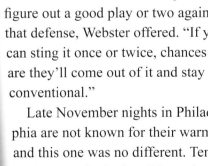

A new national happening in '70, Monday Night Football vexed the favored team, as *SI notes.*

Late November nights in Philadelphia are not known for their warmth, and this one was no different. Temperatures were in the low 20s, and a 19-mile-per-hour wind howled through the open end of the stadium. Perhaps because the game was blacked out on local TV, more than 59,000 fans braved the blustery conditions and witnessed an upset that the rest of America watched from the comfort of their living rooms.

The Giants offense did sting the Eagles a few times, as Webster had

The familiar face—and voice—of Howard Cosell was on hand for the Giants' first Monday Night Football *game against the Eagles in 1970, and for this one in Dallas the following season.*

hoped. Ron Johnson's second-quarter touchdown run helped New York to a 13–9 halftime lead, and a Tarkenton TD keeper in the third quarter gave the Giants a 20–16 edge.

New York's defense, though, broke down when it mattered most. The Eagles took a 23–20 lead—the final score—early in the fourth quarter, then held on to the ball for almost nine of the game's last 10 minutes as time ran out on the Giants.

Monday Night Football has not been kind to the Giants over the years. Through the 2008 season, their Monday night record was 18–31–1, including a 2008 upset loss at Cleveland. The Giants have never won more than two straight Monday night games, and once lost six in a row between 2001 and '03. At home, the Giants owned a 6–8 Monday night record through the 2008 season.

The Opposition Stops Here

How committed were the Giants to playing tough defense? So much so that they had one of their best receivers spending time at safety during the 1960s.

Joe "Old Dependable" Morrison retired in 1972 as the club's career leader with 395 receptions for 4,993 yards and 47 touchdowns. The fact that he doubled on defense occasionally and made a big impact on special teams demonstrated the value New York placed on shutting down opponents.

"He would do anything you asked him," Giants owner Wellington Mara once said.

The following is a look at some of the top defensive players who suited up for Mara's Giants during this era.

Troy Archer, Defensive Tackle (1976–78): Though he started for just two years, Archer recovered three fumbles in 1977 and returned one for a touchdown in '78.

Fred Dryer, Defensive End (1969–81): He played for the Giants only through 1971 before joining the Rams, but he led the team in sacks in each of his three seasons.

Jack Gregory, Defensive End (1967–79): During seven years with the Giants (1972–78), Gregory made 65 sacks (unofficially) and was voted to the Pro Bowl as a Giant in 1972.

Fred Dryer: Hunter of QBs and Crooks

Fitting, perhaps, that Fred Dryer became known to millions of Americans as star of the 1980s and early 1990s television series *Hunter*. Because the man who played Sgt. Rick Hunter was, for 13 seasons, a fine hunter of ball carriers for the Giants and Rams.

Dryer set an NFL record in 1973 by recording two safeties in one game, tackling two different Packers quarterbacks in the end zone on back-to-back possessions. *Hunter,* a police drama, aired for seven seasons on NBC. Dryer has also acted on the big screen (in *Death Before Dishonor*) and now owns his own production company.

Defense has defined the Giants throughout most of their history, and linebacker Brad Van Pelt holds a prominent place in that tradition as one of the club's best tacklers.

Brian Kelley, Linebacker (1973–83): A fixture in New York's linebacking corps for a decade, Kelley made 15 career interceptions. He enjoyed three seasons with three picks.

Carl "Spider" Lockhart, Defensive Back (1965–75): A takeaway machine, Lockhart amassed 41 interceptions and 16 fumble recoveries. He returned two picks for touchdowns in 1968, one of his two Pro Bowl seasons.

John Mendenhall, Defensive Tackle (1972–80): Before joining the Lions in his last pro season, the 255-pound Mendenhall played tackle, end, and even linebacker for the Giants.

Beasley Reece, Defensive Back (1976–84): Reece made 11 of his 18 career interceptions with the Giants (1977–83) before joining Tampa Bay and, eventually, entering the broadcast booth.

Brad Van Pelt, Linebacker (1973–86): During his 11 seasons with the Giants, Van Pelt made five consecutive Pro Bowls between 1976 and '80.

There's No Place Like Home

Brad Van Pelt played for just three NFL teams, but he might have been one of the most well-traveled players of his era. A number of his New York Giants teammates probably felt the same.

That's because Van Pelt and the Giants called four different stadiums home in less than five seasons, suiting up at Yankee Stadium until 1973, the Yale Bowl in 1973 and '74, Shea Stadium in '75, and Giants Stadium starting in 1976.

Legendary sports writer Red Smith once called the Van Pelt-era team the New York–New Haven–Long Island–New Jersey Giants, given their lack of a stable home.

It wasn't that the Mara family enjoyed living as NFL gypsies. After lengthy stays at the Polo Grounds (1925–55) and Yankee Stadium (1956–73), the Giants were forced to find a new "home" when the latter was scheduled for 1973 renovations. At first, the team was unable to strike a deal with either the Yale Bowl in New Haven, Connecticut, or Princeton University in New Jersey. In fact, when the 1973 NFL schedule was released, it did not indicate where Giants home games would be held.

Finally, commissioner Pete Rozelle modified the television blackout rule, which had been Yale's concern in negotiating a contract. It was determined that the Giants would move there after playing their first two games of the '73 slate at Yankee Stadium. After 1974, the club announced it would return to New York, sharing Shea Stadium with the New York Jets in '75, until Giants Stadium in East Rutherford, New Jersey, was completed the following season.

"When Pop [father Tim Mara] first got the franchise," Giants owner Wellington Mara noted in the midst of those tumultuous early 1970s, "we had practically no choice but to be tenants of the baseball Giants at the Polo Grounds. Then my brother Jack sensed some 30 years later that [baseball Giants owner] Horace Stoneham would move his ball club to San Francisco. That's when we shifted to Yankee Stadium, still tenants and still second fiddle to a baseball club.

"Over all those years as the tenants of the Giants and Yankees, I found myself likening it to a fellow living in the same house as his mother-in-law. The yearning kept growing to have a home of my own."

That yearning for a better home did not end with Mara's 2005 death. In 2010, the Giants and Jets are scheduled to move into a new stadium being built adjacent to the current Giants Stadium in the Meadowlands Sports Complex.

The Colts and Giants kick up dust at Shea Stadium in Flushing, New York, during a 1975 contest. Shea is just one of the venues the Giants and Jets have shared.

Where There's a Mill, There's a Way

Some called bars "gin mills" in the mid-20th century, and New York football fans came to know them well. Not that Giants fans drank more than their counterparts in opposing colors. It's just that New York's proximity to other states gave them more options when NFL blackout restrictions did not allow them to watch home games on television.

Before 1973, all NFL home games were blacked out locally (within a 75-mile radius). In '73, NFL commissioner Pete Rozelle altered the policy to lift blackouts when games sold out at least 72 hours prior to kickoff time.

When the Giants were blacked out, fans flocked to Connecticut and New Jersey to watch games at favorite watering holes, where

New York area fans went to great lengths to watch the Giants when a blackout rule kept the team off the local airwaves. Here, two fans are bundled up in director's chairs to cheer the Giants on a motel TV near the highway.

a beer might sell for less than a quarter. Motels in those states also did a brisk business on home football weekends, renting rooms to groups of Giants fans who might or might not actually spend the night.

"By age 10, I'd memorized all 40 Giant players' numbers, weights, heights, positions, and colleges," wrote Thomas R. Pryor in *The New York Times* of his 1960s fandom. "Dad saw most Giants home games. If he couldn't swindle a ticket, he'd drive to Connecticut with friends. They'd rent a motel room and watch the game on a station outside the blackout."

Pryor called the blackout "the most diabolical punishment ever devised to punish me."

Some New York fans would hoist antennae in an effort to intercept out-of-blackout TV signals, but with infrequent success. Fortunately, the popularity of Giants football has made the nonsellout days a series of road-trip tales from the past.

Bird Plucking

The Giants enjoyed just two winning seasons between 1964 and '80, but in '72 they established a franchise record for points in a single game. Philadelphia was an unfortunate foe on November 26, 1972, falling 62–10. The Giants' previous scoring record was a 56–0 rout of the same Eagles in Philadelphia's first NFL game, in 1933.

In the 1972 game, the Giants scored eight touchdowns and two field goals in 14 possessions. Ron Johnson ran for 123 yards, Pete Gogolak set a club record with eight extra points, and Bob Tucker caught eight passes for 100 yards. Giants quarterback Norm Snead threw three TD passes, while backup Randy Johnson threw two second-half scoring strikes. These two TD tosses sparked some debate about whether New York ran up the score.

Norm Snead

Official signals touchdown by Ron Johnson of the Giants, on the ground, during the first half of game here with the Philadelphia Eagles.

The New York Times/Patrick A. Burns

The New York Times discusses the Giants' 52-point crushing of the Eagles on November 26, 1972, noting that coach Alex Webster was embarrassed by the score.

OFFICIAL 1970 YEARBOOK · $1.25 · NEW YORK · GIANTS

Joe Morrison, featured on this Giants yearbook, was a starter as a fullback, halfback, and flanker in his career. He was a Giant from 1958 to 1972.

NORMAN SNEAD — NEW YORK GIANTS

Norm Snead, shown on this pin, took the reins of the Giants quarterback job in 1972 and led the NFL with a 60.2 completion percentage rate, as the Giants went 8-6.

CARL LOCKHART — NEW YORK GIANTS — DEF. BACK

Carl "Spider" Lockhart led the NFL in fumble recoveries in 1967, the year this Philadelphia card was issued. He was a Giant from 1965 through '75.

NEW YORK GIANTS

In 1975, the Giants replaced their familiar "NY" logo with a more stylized version. The logo didn't last long, but this pennant lives on.

1975 SPORTS FOCUS FOOTBALL ISSUE
New York Giants

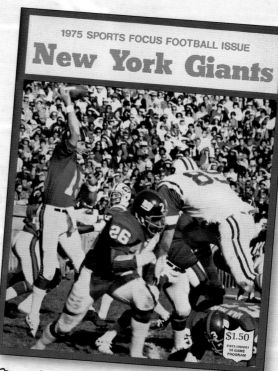

$1.50
EXCLUSIVE!
14 GAME
PROGRAM

This patch from the early 1970s helped fans show their allegiance, even though the Giants were not very good.

Quarterback Craig Morton (15) and running back Joe Dawkins (26) are featured on the 1975 Giants yearbook. The photo is from a 1974 game against the Jets.

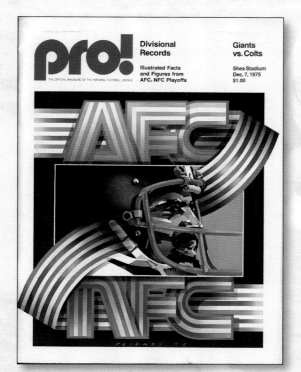

pro!

The Official Magazine of the National Football League

Divisional Records

Illustrated Facts and Figures from AFC, NFC Playoffs

Giants vs. Colts

Shea Stadium Dec. 7, 1975 $1.00

AFC
AFC
NFC

This program was available when the Giants hosted the Colts on December 7, 1975, at Shea Stadium. The Giants shared Shea with the Jets that season.

These gumball helmets sport the 1975 stylized "NY" logo. The short-lived logo helps make these items much more collectible.

Less Than Perfect

It was his "No-Name Defense" that made Bill Arnsparger a household name as a defensive football coach. That defense helped Don Shula's 1972 Dolphins secure the only perfect season in NFL history—a 14–0 campaign followed by a Super Bowl championship.

Unfortunately for the hardworking and low-key Arnsparger, he could not bring linebacker Nick Buoniconti or any of his other "No-Names" to New York when Arnsparger accepted the Giants head coaching job in 1974, after Miami's second straight Super Bowl victory.

Another Dolphin Import

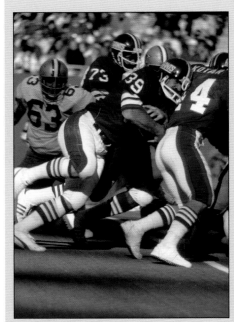

Larry Csonka

Bill Arnsparger was not the only Dolphin whose 1970s arrival in New York did not go swimmingly. Larry Csonka, who gave Miami's offense Hall of Fame power during two Super Bowl championships and was the first running back voted Super Bowl MVP, signed with the Giants in 1976 after the World Football League folded.

Csonka was a heralded addition. He enjoyed moderate success but never matched his Miami magic. In three seasons in New York, Csonka never topped 600 rushing yards in a season and was an outspoken opponent of the artificial turf at Giants Stadium.

Csonka made a comeback with the Dolphins in 1979, rushing for 837 yards on 220 carries—numbers the Giants would have loved.

Buoniconti would have been a star stopper anywhere, but even reserves on Arnsparger's Dolphins defense might have been prime-time players for his Giants. Arnsparger inherited a 2–11–1 team and went 2–12 in 1974, although the Giants did buy into their new coach's hard-hitting defensive philosophy and allowed 63 fewer points than the previous year.

For a while, Arnsparger looked to have the club heading in the right direction. He went 5–9 in 1975, with four losses coming by eight points or fewer. However, he began the '76 season with

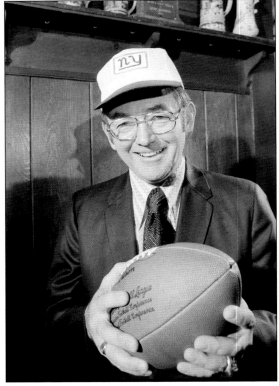

Bill Arnsparger was the defensive coach for six different teams that made the Super Bowl, including the 1968 Colts and the 1995 Chargers.

seven consecutive losses, at which point he was replaced by John McVay. By the time Arnsparger was ousted, only eight players remained from his '73 club.

Andy Robustelli, director of operations, said it was difficult informing Arnsparger of the Giants' decision. "It's tough here," the former Giants star said, "because football is a curious situation: People are always thinking they're going to win. And you're telling him, in effect, 'You lost.' Yet the guy didn't really lose. We lost."

Arnsparger finished with a 7–28 record. He rejoined the Dolphins as a defensive coach and later joined the college ranks as head coach at LSU and athletic director at Florida.

"Tuckering" Out the Opposition

The Giants struggled mightily in the 1960s and '70s, but they did lead the NFL in at least one offensive category—impact players named Tucker. Behind a line anchored by the durable Doug Van Horn, Bob Tucker became one of the best pass-catching tight ends of the era, while Tucker Frederickson battled injuries as an exciting young running back during trying times.

Following is a look at those three offensive standouts.

Tucker Frederickson, Running Back (Giants and career 1965–71): The Giants' first No. 1 overall draft choice since Kyle Rote in 1951, Frederickson arrived in 1965 having raced to SEC Player of the Year honors at Auburn. The 6'2", 220-pounder ran with a unique blend of power and speed.

If his arrival in New York was ominous—he had his new Corvette stolen on his first night in the city—his on-field debut went much better. Frederickson made the Pro Bowl as a rookie, running for 659 yards and five touchdowns and catching 24 passes.

However, an injury to his left knee sidelined Frederickson in 1966. He injured his right knee the following year, when he ran for 311 yards, and could never regain the burst and power that made him a top offensive weapon.

Tucker Frederickson made the Pro Bowl as a rookie in 1965, when the fullback rushed for 659 yards and five touchdowns. He is shown on this 1969 Topps card.

Bob Tucker, Tight End (Giants 1970–77; career 1970–80): Signed as a free agent from Pennsylvania's Bloomsburg University, Tucker surprised everyone by catching 40 passes as a rookie in 1970. The next season, he became the first tight end to lead the National Conference in receptions. His 59 grabs were just two behind Oakland's Fred Biletnikoff for the NFL lead.

The 6'3", 230-pounder caught at least 50 passes for three straight seasons from 1971 to '73 as one of the team's best weapons. By the time he was traded to Minnesota early in the '77 season, he had totaled 327 receptions for 4,376 yards—numbers that still rank high on the franchise's career charts.

Doug Van Horn, Guard-Tackle (Giants 1968–79; career 1966–79): An All-American at Ohio State, Van Horn was drafted by the AFL's Kansas City Chiefs and the NFL's Detroit Lions in 1966. He recovered a pair of fumbles as a rookie in Detroit before starting a 12-year run with the Giants in 1968.

From 1969 to '79, the 6'3", 245-pound Van Horn missed just three of a possible 158 games while blocking for Giants runners, protecting quarterbacks, and playing any line position that needed filling. He remains among the franchise's top 20 in career games played.

Tight end Bob Tucker caught 50 or more passes for the Giants in three straight seasons. Here, his grab helps New York to a 34–14 win against Houston in 1973.

Seeing Stars

A gentlemanly, deeply religious, fedora-wearing Texan fueled one of the NFL's fiercest rivalries. Well, Tom Landry didn't accomplish this by saying or doing anything hostile. He simply accepted the job as the first head coach of the newly formed Dallas Cowboys, and then he proceeded to turn them into Giant beaters.

New York fans struggled with this, because Landry was one of their own. He played for the Giants for six seasons, making the Pro Bowl in 1954, and coached their defense during their late 1950s glory days. One year after Vince Lombardi left the Giants as offensive coach to guide the Packers, Landry accepted the Cowboys post for their 1960 NFL expansion team debut. Giants followers knew they had lost another great one.

It did not take long for their fears to be realized. Landry's Cowboys played the Giants to a 31-all tie in their first meeting. The following year, the teams split two games. And in 1964, Dallas began a six-game winning streak in the series.

As the Cowboys emerged as "America's Team"—one of the NFL's most dominant clubs in the 1970s—the Giants fell on lean times. Starting in 1974, Roger Staubach quarterbacked Dallas to a string of 11 consecutive victories over New York.

The Cowboys had the Giants' number during the Roger Staubach (No. 12) era, but New York began to have better success against Dallas on its way to winning three Super Bowls.

Landry was not the only head coach to walk both sidelines in this series' history. Bill Parcells, who led the Giants to two Super Bowl titles, returned to Giants Stadium as the head coach of the Cowboys in 2003, adding more spark to a rivalry that does not lack for it.

"Every time we play them it's a college rivalry-type game," Giants receiver Amani Toomer said before that 2003 meeting. "We always have trouble with the Cowboys, and they always have trouble with us."

Through 2008, the Cowboys lead the all-time series 55–36–2.

Doomsday Deal

Shaky trades left the Giants shorthanded in the NFL Draft in the years preceding their 1970s downfall. The club did not have first-round picks in four drafts between 1967 and '75. What the Giants did in 1974 to land Dallas quarterback Craig Morton ranks among the worst of their bad deals through the years.

New York sent a first-round 1975 pick and a second-rounder in '76 for the veteran backup.

Craig Morton (No. 15)

Morton played three years for the Giants, throwing 49 interceptions against just 29 TD passes. Meanwhile, Dallas used the '75 first-round pick (second overall) to draft defensive tackle Randy White, who missed one game over 14 seasons, made nine Pro Bowls, and was enshrined in the Pro Football Hall of Fame.

Kotar Battled Toughest Foe

There was little not to like about Doug Kotar. With his shaggy beard and aw-shucks demeanor, he looked far more like a tailgating fan than an NFL running back. Teammates, coaches, and fans called him "Moe," though no one could ever explain why. And he toiled with all he had for every one of the 3,380 rushing yards he gained for the Giants from 1974 to '81.

Kotar was the pride of Muse, Pennsylvania—"population about a thousand, including the dogs," he was fond of saying—and was the fourth-leading career rusher in Giants history when news from a doctor rattled him like no linebacker ever could. In 1982, Kotar was diagnosed with a malignant, inoperable brain tumor. Sixteen months later, he died, at age 32.

"His courage in fighting the disease that took his life was in every way consistent with the toughness that made him the player and the person he was," said Giants general manager George Young of the undrafted and unheralded running back out of Kentucky.

Kotar "would dive, claw, scratch, do anything to get the extra yard," said future Hall of Famer Larry Csonka, who shared carries with Kotar for three seasons.

Kotar was the ultimate overachiever, and New York fans appreciated his work ethic. After joining the Giants in a 1974 trade from Pittsburgh, he led the team in rushing with 731 yards in 1976 and with 625 in '78. During the former campaign, he added a career-high 36 receptions and totaled 1,050 yards from scrimmage.

Kotar was the second Giants player in the 1980s to be diagnosed with a form of cancer. In 1980, linebacker Dan Lloyd was treated for a malignant lymphoma. He recovered and went on to coach high school football in California.

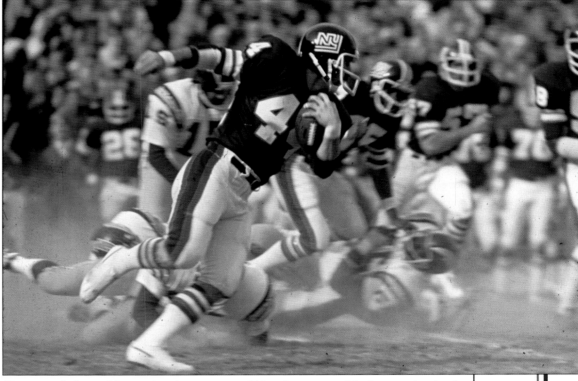

Known and cheered for getting the most out of his talent, overachieving running back Doug Kotar was diagnosed with brain cancer in 1982 and died 18 months later.

When former running back John Tuggle died of a rare blood vessel cancer in 1986 and tackle Karl Nelson was diagnosed with Hodgkin's disease in 1987, a two-year study was undertaken to determine whether there might be health risks stemming from radio towers or landfills surrounding the Meadowlands Sports Complex, as some suspected.

In releasing the results of that study in 1989, Dr. Frederick B. Cohen, director of oncology at Newark Beth Israel Hospital, said the players' cancers had begun before they joined the Giants and that, in effect, their illnesses were coincidental. Airborne levels of 14 different chemicals were tested around the facility, and all fell within "safe" levels.

New State, New Stadium...Same Giants

The New York Football Giants spent most of their existence feeling like second-class citizens in baseball stadiums. For their first 50 years, they played "second fiddle" to the baseball Giants at the Polo Grounds and to the Yankees at Yankee Stadium.

It was an existence that gave owner Wellington Mara all the strength he needed to counter the considerable opposition to his team's move to its own stadium in the "swamps of Jersey" in the mid-1970s. That opposition came from all angles.

New York fans were not pleased with the prospect of a bridge or tunnel trip to New Jersey to watch their favorite football team, though Mara pointed out that East Rutherford was 6.9 miles from Times Square, compared to Yankee Stadium's 6.6-mile distance from the same location. New Jersey taxpayers protested the cost of the Meadowlands Sports Complex, which would house Giants Stadium. The New York newspapers pointed out that "meadowland" was simply a euphemism for "swamp," and some began referring to the team as the New Jersey Giants.

"It's a thorny thing," said Yankees president Mike Burke in 1971 while insisting that the baseball team would stay in the Bronx. "When Pepsi-Cola goes to the suburbs, no one notices, but the psychological impact of the Yankees and Giants leaving the city would be disastrous."

Upon its completion in 1976, Giants Stadium in East Rutherford, New Jersey, stood as a state-of-the-art, football-only facility that would begin drawing fans from several nearby states.

Owner Wellington Mara wanted fans in New York to know that his Giants were not abandoning their roots by moving to New Jersey, but simply giving their longtime followers a better home.

One man's "disaster," in this case, was another's opportunity. Mara and the Giants had a hard time seeing primary tenancy in a state-of-the-art, 76,000-seat stadium with luxury suites and two instant replay boards as anything but a giant leap forward for a franchise that historically had to work its games around the schedules of Major League Baseball teams.

The idea was first pitched to Mara, ironically, by former AFL rival Sonny Werblin. A few years after Werblin lost his job with the New York Jets, he surfaced with a group that would become the New Jersey Sports and Exposition Authority, which pitched the idea of a multipurpose, $200 million sports complex housing a pro football stadium as its centerpiece.

"There was a time when Wellington Mara and I were competitors across one river," Werblin said upon the official announcement of the Giants' move, "but now we are partners on the same side of another."

"New York is not losing a team," added Mara, "but gaining a sports complex."

In hindsight, Mara's ability to secure a sweet deal for his club by pitting the New York and New Jersey contingents against one another was revolutionary. Other owners had moved pro teams to other states under similar circumstances, but Mara managed to do so while keeping the franchise in its general location, thus retaining a loyal fan base and generally keeping those fans' favor.

If only Mara could have worked the same magic with the product on the field. After playing in temporary homes at Shea Stadium and the Yale Bowl, the Giants were scheduled to open the 1976 season with four straight road games due to concerns that their new stadium would not be finished on time. They lost all four.

That slide continued in their Giants Stadium opener against Dallas on October 10, 1976. A packed house of 76,042 showed up to watch the first game at the $68 million stadium, cheering the Giants as they took the field. However, many booed before the end of a 24–14 setback. The Giants lost nine straight games before beating Washington 12–9 for their first win at Giants Stadium. Finally in a home of their own, they finished the year

Teamster in the End Zone?

You might have heard the story that late Teamsters president Jimmy Hoffa is buried under Giants Stadium. The mysterious circumstances surrounding his 1975 disappearance before his planned meeting with Mafia leaders led to the urban legend that has been told and re-told.

During a 2004 episode of the Discovery Channel show *Mythbusters,* hosts Jamie Hyneman and Adam Savage gained access to the stadium and used radar to investigate both end zones, the 10-yard line, midfield, and seating section 107—the most commonly rumored locations for the body.

Jimmy Hoffa

Like the Giants offense of the era in which Hoffa disappeared, the Mythbusters crew came up empty.

GIANTS GALLERY

Even though in the 1970s the Giants were in a down period, this 1976 Topps card still speaks to the longtime tradition of tough defense.

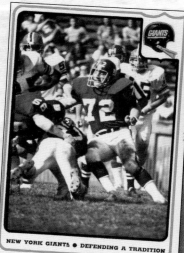

NEW YORK GIANTS • DEFENDING A TRADITION

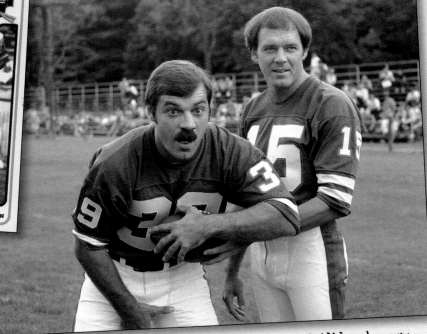

Craig Morton (No. 15) poses with new addition Larry Csonka (No. 39) before the 1976 season.

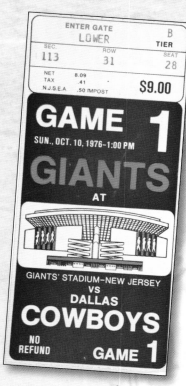

ENTER GATE B
LOWER TIER
SEC. 113   ROW 31   SEAT 28
NET 8.09
TAX .41
N.J.S.E.A. .50 IMPOST $9.00

GAME 1
SUN., OCT. 10, 1976-1:00 PM
GIANTS
AT
GIANTS' STADIUM-NEW JERSEY
VS
DALLAS
COWBOYS
NO REFUND   GAME 1

The inaugural game at Giants Stadium was against the Dallas Cowboys. The ticket price, including tax? $9.00.

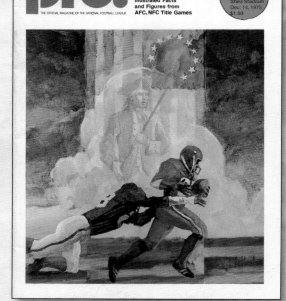

pro!
THE OFFICIAL MAGAZINE OF THE NATIONAL FOOTBALL LEAGUE

Championship Records
Illustrated Facts and Figures from AFC, NFC Title Games

Giants vs. Saints
Shea Stadium
Dec. 14, 1975
$1.00

This program is from the last game the Giants played at Shea Stadium, hosting the Saints, on December 14, 1975.

OPENING DAY
GIANTS STADIUM
OCTOBER 10th, 1976

This is a special pennant from the "Opening Day" of Giants Stadium, a state-of-the-art facility for its time.

As *The New York Times* notes, the $68 million Giants Stadium was called "The Pride of New Jersey" in 1976.

Giants Stadium in the Meadowlands of East Rutherford, N.J., as 76,042 fans watched yesterday as the Giants were beaten, 24-14, by the Cowboys, their fifth straight loss of the season. Stadium took about five years to build at a cost of $68 million. Building at upper left is race track clubhouse.

The New York Times/Robert Walker

$68 MILLION STADIUM FOR FOOTBALL GIANTS IS OPENED IN JERSEY

76,042 Fans Watch Cowboys Win by 24-14—Few Traffic Problems at New Meadowlands Plant

By NEIL AMDUR
Special to The New York Times

EAST RUTHERFORD, N.J., Oct. 10 — The opening of the $68 million Giants Stadium went more smoothly for the 76,042 spectators today than it did for their frustrated pro football team.

A 24-14 victory by the unbeaten

U.S. Dilemma: World Energy Need Encourages Spread of Atomic Arms

The following article was written by David Burnham

WASHINGTON, Oct. — ... tion of nuclear rea... for the production ... resulting spread of ... be used for making ... placing increasing p... States to devise ne... energy and internat...

The pressure stem... that the spread of re... increasing the availa... which can be used to ... This was stressed b... nuclear experts inte... weeks in the executive... industry and academic...

Major Statement...

APPOINTMENT OF HUA STILL UNCONFIRMED

Sergeants Balking At City Police Pact

BY PRANAY GUPTE

Delegates of the Sergeants Benevolent Association, apparently uncertain about a proposed new work chart under which New York City would require police sergeants to work an additional 10 days a year, refused yesterday to ratify a tentative settlement that their leaders had reached with the Beame administration last Friday.

The delegates directed the president of the 2,700-member union, Harold Melnick, to obtain more information from city officials on the proposed duty chart. Mr. Melnick, who had reportedly expected ratification yesterday, then got in touch with the city's chief negotiator, First Deputy Mayor John E. Zuccotti, who agreed to meet with him today.

The delegates' directive to Mr. Melnick came during a meeting yesterday morning in the Terrace-on-the-Park Restaurant in Flushing Meadow Park in Queens. But even as the 800 or so delegates considered the tentative contract, about 200 off-duty police officers picketed outside.

Continued on Page 23, Column 1

Rise in Dropouts In New York City Shocks Regents

By DAVID VIDAL

Although there is a dispute over just who is a dropout, the number of students who are leaving New York City high schools without earning a diploma is steadily rising, adding another worry to a school system that is already stumbling from the impact of repeated financial blows.

The dropout problem is being accompanied by persistently high absenteeism and truancy and a sharp climb in the number of pupil suspensions in the ... And even though the ... Regents has called the ... "intolerable," noting ... that "in New York ... percent of the public ... graduate," the situatio... worsen as the financi... education deepens.

"It is really sho... Theodore M. Black, sho... lor. "In New York City...

BEAME IS PREPARING DRASTIC CUTBACKS IN CITY'S SPENDING

$500 MILLION TARGET LISTED

High-Level Officials in Process of Selecting Services Slated for Further Reductions

By STEVEN R. WEISMAN

Amid fears that its worst budget crises are yet to come, the Beame administration is refining a harsh new program of drastic cuts and other steps to produce nearly $500 million in savings—beyond those achieved already—for the year beginning next July 1.

In the last week, high-level New York City officials have begun the process of selecting those services for further cutbacks—the details of which they said were too premature to discuss. But both city and state fiscal aides agreed that the new cuts might constitute the most trying phase of the effort to get city spending in line with income as required by Federal and state law.

Interviews with various budget experts disclose a common theme on the subject of the current status and prognosis for city finances—a theme that uncertainty surrounds virtually every projection on how the impending reductions and other measures will take shape in the months ahead.

This 1975 bobblehead sports the "Double-NY" logo on his helmet... just in time for the Giants to change their logo after the move to Giants Stadium.

Definitely a collectors' edition, this program is from the opening game at Giants Stadium, October 10, 1976.

pro!

GIANTS EDITION
Dallas vs. New York Giants
Oct. 10, 1976 · Giants Stadium · $1.00

THE OFFICIAL MAGAZINE OF THE NATIONAL FOOTBALL LEAGUE

GIANTS STADIUM

THE GIANTS, A CONTINUING TRADITION

RON JOHNSON
NEW YORK GIANTS

Ron Johnson, shown on this pin, had some injury woes by the end of his time with the Giants that limited his effectiveness, but he was with the team through the 1975 season.

The Fumble

Eagles fans remember it as "The Miracle at the Meadow-lands." Giants fans prefer calling it "The Fumble," though they'd rather block it out entirely. And however you refer to it, the finish of the November 19, 1978, game at Giants Stadium was the signature moment—rock bottom, if you will—of the most frustrating era in Giants football history.

All New York quarterback Joe Pisarcik had to do was take one more snap and fall on the ball to secure a win for his team. The Giants led the Eagles 17–12 with a half-minute to go, facing third-and-two in their own territory. CBS was rolling the credits at the end of its telecast. John Mara, team owner Wellington Mara's son, had been filling in as a "spotter" and was about to leave the press box for the locker room when, looking down toward the field, he could not believe his eyes.

Instead of falling on the ball to run out the clock, Pisarcik backed up from center and turned to hand the ball to Larry Csonka. The exchange was never made, the ball fell to the turf, and Eagles defensive back Herman Edwards scooped it up. Edwards was mobbed by his teammates after returning the fumble 26 yards for the winning score.

"I met Herman Edwards many years later and I introduced myself to him," John Mara said after becoming team president. "I said, 'I've never met you before, but I've hated you for many years.' We were in a terrible streak of lousy football teams and losing seasons. And to think that maybe you're starting to turn the corner a little bit and all of a sudden, to have that happen on a completely inexcusable play was really terrible."

Offensive coordinator Bob Gibson was fired the next morning, never to work in football again. He had scolded Pisarcik the previous week for changing plays at the line of scrimmage. Some of Pisarcik's teammates said they tried to convince the quarterback to ignore the call for a handoff and fall on the football, but that Pisarcik was afraid to do it.

"Three quarterback fall downs and we would have been out of there," Pisarcik noted. "The play should not have been called. But it wasn't just [Gibson's] fault. Everybody deserves a little bit of fault."

A win would have leveled the Giants' record at 6–6. Instead, they nosedived to a 6–10 finish, as some fans hired a plane to fly over Giants Stadium with a banner reading, "15 YEARS OF LOUSY FOOTBALL. WE'VE HAD ENOUGH."

One of the most infamous plays in Giants history saw Eagles cornerback Herman Edwards scoop up a botched handoff between Joe Pisarcik and Larry Csonka and run for the winning score in a 1978 game at Giants Stadium.

Eagles fans call Herman Edwards's 1978 fumble recovery and touchdown "The Miracle at the Meadowlands." Giants fans call it "The Fumble," frequently with an unprintable adjective or two thrown in for good measure.

Harry Carson: Rising to the Top

Harry Carson sat in the Giants' offices after a 28–7 loss to the Rams in 1980. The previous week, they had lost 35–3 to the Eagles. For the first time in his young career, fans had called him a "bum," a turn of events that—for a while—had the defensive star pondering quitting.

It was a fleeting thought. Carson had stopped in to tell coach Ray Perkins he was committed to the team and to winning. And when a member of the front office handed Carson his weekly share of his $125,000 annual salary, he refused it, believing he had not earned it with his performance.

If there was one player who could fully comprehend the depths from which the Giants climbed to reach the top in the 1980s, it was the soft-spoken and hard-hitting Carson. That's because Carson, perhaps more than anyone, led the long, arduous journey.

"He was a tremendous player and an integral part of one of the NFL's best two or three defenses for several years," said Bill Parcells upon learning of Carson's Hall of Fame election in 2006.

It became clear early in his career that Carson was an impact player. He was a defensive end at South Carolina State who was drafted in the fourth round and converted to middle linebacker. Carson won a starting job midway through his 1976 rookie year and rattled opponents for 13 seasons—all with the Giants.

Hall of Fame linebacker Harry Carson began his career in the Giants' lean years, but his play was integral in helping New York climb to the top of the National Football League.

Anywhere BUT New York

It wasn't just players who thrived elsewhere but struggled in New York during this era, though there were a few of those. Coach John McVay was promoted from the assistant ranks to replace Bill Arnsparger midway through 1976 and stumbled to a 14–23 record in two and a half years.

McVay's contract was not renewed after the '78 season, and he never coached again. However, he went on to great success. He was hired as vice president and director of football operations for the 49ers, whom he helped to five Super Bowl championships, and was voted NFL Executive of the Year in 1989.

Carson led the Giants in tackles in five of those seasons and made nine Pro Bowls. He served as team captain for 10 years, taking the club from its late-1970s misery to its 1986 Super Bowl title. Those who played with Carson compared him to the greatest middle linebackers of all time, including Dick Butkus and Mike Singletary.

"I'm a football player," Carson shrugged. "I enjoy playing the game."

This is a rare Dave Jennings card from 1978. In addition to being a longtime punter of the Jets and Giants, Jennings was also a longtime commentator for both teams.

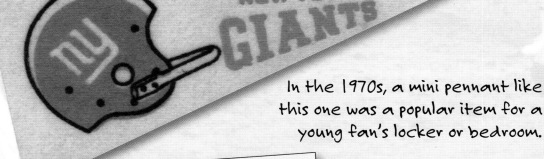

In the 1970s, a mini pennant like this one was a popular item for a young fan's locker or bedroom.

The New York Times registered disbelief that the Eagles could have won with 20 seconds left in "The Fumble" game.

Eagles' Herm Edwards grabbing fumble by Giants' Joe Pisarcik, on way to winning score with 20 seconds left in game.

SportsMonday

The New York Times

MONDAY, NOVEMBER 20, 1978   C1   L

Copyright © 1978 The New York Times

Jets Bow; Todd Reinjured; Giants Lose Unbelievably

20 Seconds Left As Eagles Win

By MICHAEL KATZ

Special to The New York Times

EAST RUTHERFORD, N.J., Nov. 19 — One of the simplest plays in football, a handoff to the fullback, was messed up by the Giants today and, with 20 seconds remaining, Herm Edwards of Philadelphia ran the ensuing fumble 26 yards for a touchdown to give the Eagles an unbelievable 19-17 victory.

Unbelievable, because the Giants had a 17-12 victory with 31 seconds remaining when Joe Pisarcik, against his better judgment and that of most of his teammates in the preceding huddle, took the center snap from Jim Clack and started to hand off to Larry Csonka.

The Eagles had no timeouts remaining.

The clock was running.

All the Giants had to do was fall on the ball, and the victory was theirs.

A 'Horrifying Ending'

"I never had control," said Pisarcik after Andy Robustelli fetched the quarterback from the sanctity of the trainer's room.

The ball bounced off Pisarcik's hand, bounced once on the artifical turf of Giants Stadium and Edwards, who had been at fault on one of Pisarcik's two first-quarter touchdown passes, picked it off in midair and ran untouched to the end zone.

"That's the most horrifying ending to a ball game I've ever seen," said a shaken Coach John McVay, whose job is now in real danger.

"It was the coaches' play, not the players."

The Giants call it a "pro 65 up," the

Continued on Page C4

Dave Anderson tells of Todd's fateful call, P. 4

Patriots Gain 19-17 Victory

By AL HARVIN

The 1978 comeback of Richard Todd as the New York Jets' No. 1 quarterback is over. It ended three-fourths of the way through the Jets' 19-17 loss to the New England Patriots yesterday at Shea Stadium.

Todd, back on the job only a week after having missed seven games with a broken left collarbone, cracked the same collarbone on a quarterback draw play that gained 7 yards at the end of the third quarter. He will be out for the remainder of the season.

The game was tied, 10-10, when Todd was reinjured. Matt Robinson, who substituted so ably for Todd when he was injured before, threw a spectacular 56-yard scoring pass to Wesley Walker in the last quarter, giving the Jets a 1-point lead, 17-16. Joe Klecko had blocked a Patriots' extra-point try earlier in the final period.

Penalty Costly to Jets

What lost the game for the Jets were two things: Pat Leahy's miss on a 33-yard field-goal attempt with 35 seconds left, and a costly penalty that allowed New England to continue a 71-yard drive and regain the head 19-17, on a 24-yard field goal by David Posey.

"I don't know what happened, I just missed it," said a disconsolate Leahy, who fell to the ground in frustration after his kick had hooked wide of the left upright. Steve Grogan, the New England quarterback, then fell down three times with the ball to consume the remaining time.

The Jets would not have needed the late field goal if New England had been halted a bit earlier. It was the key per-

Continued on Page C4

Mounting Drug Use Afflicts World Sports

By NEIL AMDUR

member, who has served as a team physician for United States Olympic squads as well as on the International Olympic Committee's medical

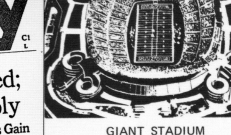

GIANT STADIUM

1   First National State

First National State Bancorporation
Executive Offices: 550 Broad Street, Newark, New Jersey 07102

The First National State Bank released this schedule for the 1978 season, which featured "Giant Stadium." The Giants went 6-10 that year.

Bobby Hammond

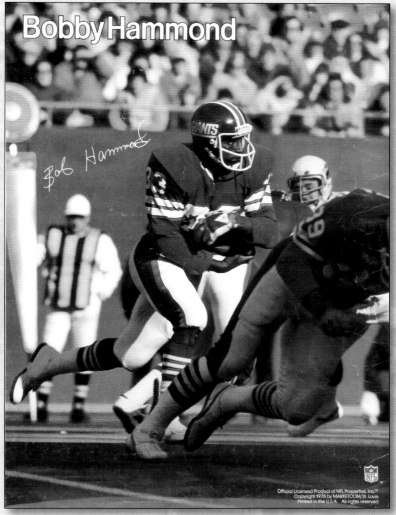

1979 GIANTS MEDIA GUIDE

Harry Carson is featured on the 1979 Giants media guide. He became a respected voice and face of the franchise.

This helmet was signed by Harry Carson, who arrived in 1976 and became a sterling example of the tough linebacker favored by the franchise.

This poster of Bobby Hammond was perfect for a fan's wall. Hammond made his mark in 1977 as a dangerous return man as well as a halfback.

NEW YORK GIANTS

DOUG VAN HORN

GIANTS

This is a 1970s-era Giants pennant. The Giants averaged only five wins a season in the decade, but it didn't take long in the next decade for the franchise to rebound.

Doug Van Horn, shown on this 1978 Topps card, was a stalwart on the Giants line from 1969 through 1979.

CHAPTER FIVE

Return to Glory

1979–1996

"I always said the Giants would make the Super Bowl. I just didn't know if I'd still be around."

GIANTS OWNER WELLINGTON MARA BEFORE NEW YORK'S VICTORY OVER DENVER IN SUPER BOWL XXI

Above: *By winning Super Bowl XXI, the 1986 Giants (shown on this pin) were finally the team to break the franchise championship drought, which had lasted 30 years.*
Right: *Quarterback Jeff Hostetler was one of several Giants who helped the franchise return to the top by winning their first two Super Bowls during this era.*

"Compromise" Pick Leaves Signature

Families feud. The family-run New York Giants were no exception. In 1979, they were a team in near-total turmoil. Coach John McVay had been fired. Operations director Andy Robustelli had quit. And the front office was operating dysfunctionally at best. Two of its top members, 50-percent owner Wellington Mara and his nephew, Tim, were not on speaking terms while attempting to hire a general manager.

The situation was so bad, NFL commissioner Pete Rozelle intervened. He gave the Maras a list of names from which to choose their new GM, knowing that Wellington and Tim would not reach an accord on their own. One name was agreeable to both men.

George Young had worked for several years as coach Don Shula's aide in Baltimore and was directing pro scouting for the Miami Dolphins when the call came from New York in 1979. He took over a Giants team that had not made the playoffs in 15 years. Under his direction, the feuding ceased interfering with the running of the football team. And the winning began.

Young's first draft choice in 1979 was quarterback Phil Simms, who became a Super Bowl MVP. He drafted Lawrence Taylor, one of the greatest linebackers ever to play the game. He hired Bill Parcells as defensive coordinator and later promoted him to head coach. Parcells built on a foundation laid by Ray Perkins—the coach who ended the Giants' 18-year playoff slumber in 1981—and guided the team to two Super Bowl championships.

Young, who played defensive tackle at Bucknell and began his

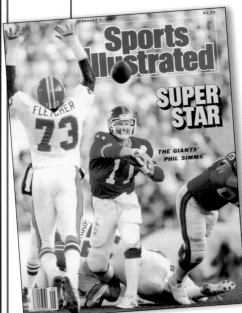

George Young's first draft pick, Phil Simms, was unpopular at first, but SI later called Simms a "Super Star."

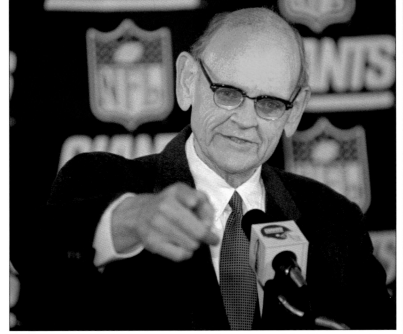

George Young spent 19 years as general manager of the Giants, turning the franchise from a cellar dweller into a two-time Super Bowl champion.

career as a teacher, was honored as NFL Executive of the Year five times.

"Without his support and help," Parcells said, "it would have been impossible for anyone to succeed, and I will always be grateful to George for that."

Parcells retired after his second Super Bowl season and was replaced by Ray Handley in 1991. It was a decision that began a phase in which some wondered whether the game had passed Young by. He stayed with the club through the 1997 season, and then took a post as the NFL's senior vice president for football operations. Young died at age 71 in 2001.

"George's legacy is greater than two Super Bowls," Wellington Mara said. "I think you have to measure it more in terms of the organization he built and the people he brought in to build it."

Return to Prominence

Some Giants veterans talked about staging an organized walkout if the club paid first-round draft choice Lawrence Taylor $750,000 in 1981. Coming off a 4–12 season, it was not the way to begin a march back to NFL significance.

Fortunately for Giants fans, the club did sign Taylor, and no such walkout happened. Instead, New York won four of its last five games in 1981 behind backup QB Scott Brunner and benefited from a final-weekend Jets win over Green Bay to make the playoffs for the first time in 18 years. It also marked the first time both New York teams made the NFL postseason in the same year.

The rookie Taylor made an immediate impact, joining Harry Carson, Brad Van Pelt, and Brian Kelley in the "Crunch Bunch," one of the sturdiest linebacking corps in the NFL. George Martin was also a defensive spark. He returned two fumble recoveries for touchdowns on his way to six career scores, an NFL record at the time for a defensive lineman. Only two NFL teams were stingier than the 1981 Giants, who yielded just 16.1 points per game.

Offensively, New York did not set the league on fire. Their 18.4-point offensive average was 22nd among 28 NFL teams. Without an elite runner, Brunner and starter Phil Simms did what

Kicker Joe Danelo is carried off the field by Giants coach Ray Perkins and teammates Ed McGlasson (left) and Harry Carson in 1981 after beating the Cowboys 13–10 on a field goal in overtime.

Running to a Playoff Win

An unconventional route paved the way to the Giants' first playoff win since the 1958 NFL championship game. Only three teams in the NFL were more futile than the Giants running the football in 1981, yet Rob Carpenter lugged it 33 times for 161 yards in a ball-hogging 27–21 triumph at Philadelphia in the NFC wild-card game.

Starting for the injured Phil Simms, Scott Brunner threw three touchdown passes. Mark Haynes recovered a fumbled kickoff in the end zone as the Giants raced to a 27–7 halftime lead before 71,611 fans at Veterans Stadium.

The Giants' magic ran out the following week in a 38–24 loss to Joe Montana and the eventual Super Bowl champion 49ers in San Francisco.

they could, with receiver Johnny Perkins hauling in 51 passes for 858 yards and six touchdowns in the best season of his seven-year career.

"I thought we would win nine games this year," said coach Ray Perkins after a 13–10 overtime thriller against the Cowboys in the finale capped a 9–7 slate. "And if we had a few breaks, 11 or 12.... Things got shaky toward the end of the first half of the season, but we hung in there."

Simms, That's Who

The New York media and Giants fans wondered, aloud, the same thing in 1979. "Phil who?"

The Giants' first-round draft choice that spring and the first draftee of GM George Young's tenure, Phil Simms had never in his life played in front of more than 25,000 fans. He had quarterbacked tiny Morehead State to four losing seasons. Giants fans, knowing that big names like Kellen Winslow and Charles Alexander were available with the No. 7 pick, were not impressed.

"Once in a while you get a chance to get a guy with a great arm and great potential and you'd darned sight better take it," Young said at the time, explaining the selection as a "value" choice. "Names, that's just feeding pablum to the fans."

What Giants fans wound up feasting on—thanks to Young's eye for talent and Simms's leadership—was victories, records, and a pair of Super Bowl championships.

Simms won the first five starts of his rookie season, finishing the year 6–4 as a starter. Injuries contributed to inconsistent play over

Giants quarterback Phil Simms shouts from the sideline during the first quarter of Super Bowl XXI in Pasadena, California, as the Broncos jumped out to a 10–7 advantage.

the next few seasons, but by 1984—when he threw for more than 4,000 yards and 22 touchdowns—it became clear the Giants had one of the NFL's best calling the signals.

Simms made his first of two Pro Bowls in 1985. The following season, he was an All-Pro quarterback and led the Giants to their first Super Bowl, earning MVP honors with a 22-for-25 performance in their win over the Broncos.

"I told Phil," Giants coach Bill Parcells said during the stretch run of that 1986 championship season, "'I think you're a great quarterback, and you got that way by being daring and fearless, so let's go.'"

With the blessing of his defensive-minded coach, Simms took chances and became a terrific clutch performer. His knack for leading two-minute drives and making pinpoint throws in tight situations set him apart from passers who may have had an edge in mobility or arm strength.

Simms led the Giants to an 11–3 start in 1990 before breaking his foot, and he watched as Jeff Hostetler completed another

Super Bowl MVP Phil Simms celebrates a touchdown pass to Mark Bavaro—one of three scoring strikes delivered by Simms—during Super Bowl XXI.

Super Bowl championship season. Simms eventually won the job back from Hostetler and led the team to an 11–5 mark in 1993, his second Pro Bowl season. However, a torn labrum and his 1994 release helped shape Simms's decision to retire.

"It took 15 years of hard work to earn your respect," Simms told Giants fans at a 1995 ceremony in which the team retired his No. 11 jersey. "And it was well worth the effort."

"No One," read a sign from a Giants Stadium fan that day, "Can Fill #11."

Sports Illustrated, in 2001, called Simms the most underrated quarterback in NFL history. He still holds several franchise records, including career attempts, completions, yards, touchdown passes, and 300-yard games.

Smart on the field and now perceptive from a booth high above it, Simms has gone on to a career as one of the NFL's top television commentators. He worked for NBC with Dick Enberg and Paul Maguire for a few years before joining CBS Sports in 1998 and eventually climbing to its top team with Jim Nantz. Phil's son, Chris, followed him to the NFL quarterbacking ranks.

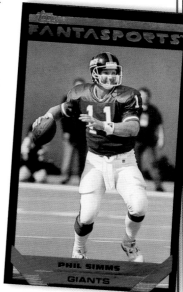

Phil Simms, shown on this 1993 Topps Fantasports card, was a leader among Giants.

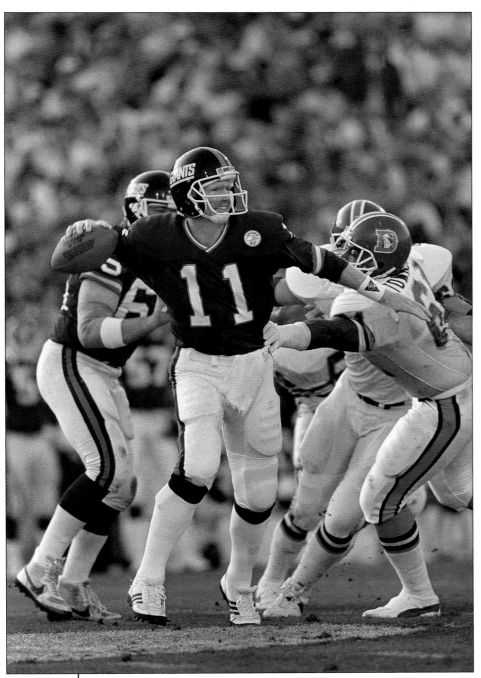

Phil Simms recorded the most accurate passing day in Super Bowl history, going 22 of 25 for 268 yards, three touchdowns, and no interceptions to lead the Giants to a 39–20 Super Bowl XXI win over Denver.

Simms's Record-Setting Game

Of the many Giants passing records that Phil Simms still holds, his arm-tiring effort against the Bengals on October 13, 1985, is not among his favorites. That's because the Giants lost 35–30 to Cincinnati.

Simms set three Giants single-game records that afternoon that have held up for more than two decades—62 attempts, 40 completions, and 513 passing yards. After the game, though, he was dejected about his two interceptions. Simms was also sacked seven times.

"I expect a little more from myself," he noted. "I don't expect to complete all my passes, but I don't expect to throw interceptions, either."

Landing the Big Tuna

The "Big Tuna" was almost yanked from the water after his first season as an NFL head coach. In 1983, Bill Parcells took over a Giants team that had enjoyed just one winning season in a decade, but one with enough young talent for its fans to expect a surge.

Instead, they got a 3–12–1 stinker. Before getting the head coaching job, Parcells was the former Giants and Patriots defensive coordinator. His biggest move in 1983 was benching quarterback Phil Simms for Scott Brunner. Parcells was rumored to be on his way out in favor of University of Miami coach Howard Schnellenberger.

But the Giants stood by Parcells—a hard-driving New Jersey native known for his love of the game and demand for excellence—and were rewarded with two Super Bowl championships.

As a youth, Parcells starred in football, baseball, and basketball, and he occasionally was tossed out of practices for his hot temper. Parcells could have played pro baseball or gone into law. But those were never really options.

"God put you on this earth to be a football coach," his high school coach, Vince Lombardi disciple Mickey Corcoran, once told Parcells.

Parcells made that clear with his success on the Giants sideline. He handed the offense to Simms in 1984, built one of the best defenses in the NFL, and ended years of franchise frustration. The Giants made the playoffs in 1984 and '85 and won their first Super Bowl in '86.

Parcells added a second Super Bowl title in 1990, then retired from football for the first of three (and counting) times to try the broadcast booth. In eight years at the Giants helm, he compiled a 77–49–1 record, including six winning seasons. He twice earned NFL Coach of the Year honors from at least one major media outlet (once as a Giants coach).

Brash and demanding coach Bill Parcells put his stamp on the Giants, winning five division titles and two Super Bowl championships in eight seasons at the helm.

Smashmouth Football

The term "smashmouth football" came into vogue in the 1980s. While the 49ers and other teams were winging the ball around in what came to be known as the West Coast offense, the Giants, Redskins, and others in the NFC East were knocking each other's helmets off.

"It's hammer city," Redskins coach Joe Gibbs once said of his team's physical battles with Bill Parcells's Giants.

With tough offensive linemen such as Bart Oates, Brad Benson, Chris Godfrey, Billy Ard, Karl Nelson, Jumbo Elliot, and William Roberts opening holes in a straight-ahead, low-risk offense, the Giants were built to thrive in such wars. It wasn't always pretty, but they did just that.

The Big and the Small of It

Little Joe Morris and big Ottis Anderson proved to be the perfect fit for the New York Giants' running game in the 1980s. One was a 5'7" dynamo who rushed for more yards at Syracuse University than Jim Brown, Larry Csonka, or Floyd Little. The other was an explosive 220-pounder who ran over and around defenders to become the first 1,000-yard rusher at the University of Miami. At the pro level, they each gave the Giants exactly what coach Bill Parcells craved—the ability to run the football, control the clock, and win championships.

Morris ducked and darted his way to a breakout season in 1985, his fourth year in the NFL. He paced the league with 21 touchdowns—all rushing—and enjoyed the first of his three 1,000-yard seasons in a Giants uniform.

With Morris suffering from a blood disorder in October 1986, Parcells went shopping for some backfield insurance and, in a trade with the Cardinals, acquired Anderson, who topped 1,000 yards five times with the Cards. It turned out Morris held up well, running for a career-high 1,516 yards and 14 scores. Morris and Anderson each ran for a touchdown in the 1986 Giants' 39–20 win against the Broncos in Super Bowl XXI.

Morris played two more seasons with the Giants. In 1988, he surpassed Alex Webster as the team's career rushing leader while breaking the 5,000-yard barrier.

"Before Joe emerged as a major threat we had a fullback-oriented rush," GM George Young said in '87. "We could rely on getting a one-yard, two-yard, or three-yard gain, but the bigger gains were not something we came by that often. Joe changed that."

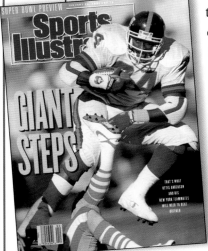

Veteran running back Ottis Anderson made the cover of Sports Illustrated *in 1991, but Giants fans remember him more as a Super Bowl hero than a cover boy.*

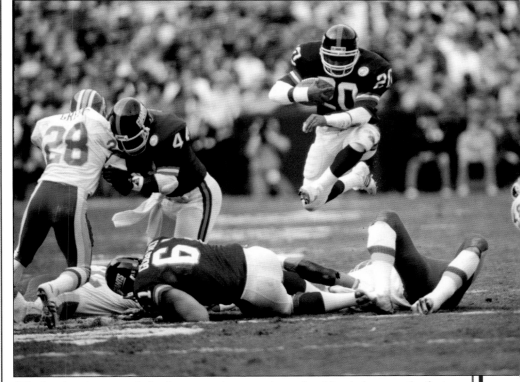

Whether leaping over defenders or racing past them, Joe Morris became the first player to rush for more than 5,000 career yards with the Giants.

Anderson became the starter upon Morris's departure in 1989 and added a sixth career 1,000-yard campaign to his résumé, earning NFL Comeback Player of the Year honors. The following year, he powered the Giants to a second championship with a Super Bowl XXV MVP performance, running for 102 yards and a score in a 20–19 win over Buffalo.

"Everyone else gave up on him," Parcells said of Anderson in 1991. "He's a tough, professional guy. He hasn't missed a practice since he's been here. He's played every role I've asked. I wish I had him his whole career."

Anderson retired following the 1992 season with more than 10,000 career rushing yards.

GIANTS GALLERY

As *The Giants Newsweekly* reports, losing Phil Simms to retirement was truly the end of an era.

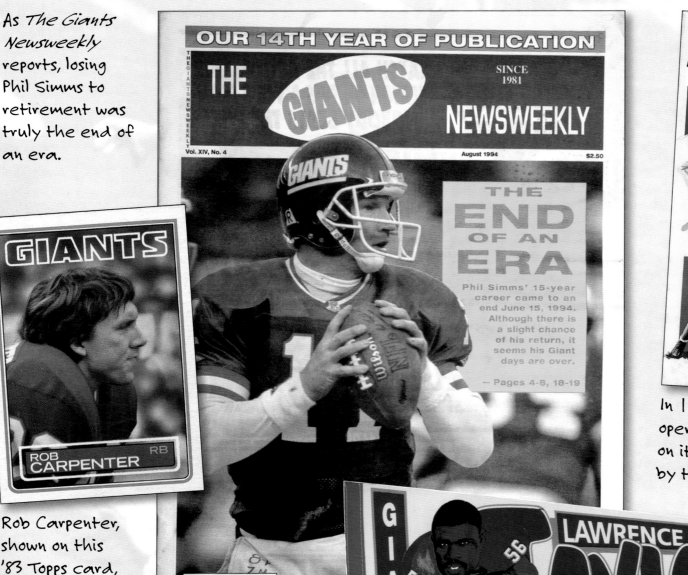

OUR 14TH YEAR OF PUBLICATION

SINCE 1981

THE **GIANTS** NEWSWEEKLY

Vol. XIV, No. 4   August 1994 $2.50

THE END OF AN ERA

Phil Simms' 15-year career came to an end June 15, 1994. Although there is a slight chance of his return, it seems his Giant days are over.

— Pages 4-8, 18-19

GIANTS

ROB CARPENTER   RB

GIANTS MEDIA GUIDE 1984

60th Season

Emlen Tunnell

Frank Gifford

Tim Mara

Mel Hein

Roosevelt Brown

Rob Carpenter, shown on this '83 Topps card, brought a tough, winning attitude to New York.

In 1984, its 60th year of operation, the team looked back on its rich history, as evidenced by this media guide cover.

GIANTS LAWRENCE TAYLOR 56

L. T., featured on this pennant from the '80s, was, and remains, a popular figure among Giants fans.

THE NEW YORK TIMES, MONDAY, DECEMBER 24, 1984

Haji-Sheikh's Foot Erases a Memory

By PETER ALFANO

Special to The New York Times

ANAHEIM, Calif., Dec. 23 — No one would have been very surprised if Ali Haji-Sheikh revealed that he changed his daily routine in preparation for his first playoff game, or trotted on the field at Anaheim Stadium for practice Saturday spreading incense and thinking positive thoughts about the faraway uprights. The nature and demands of being a place-kicker can make an eccentric of the most level-headed athlete.

But what makes Haji-Sheikh different in that he said he does not believe in lucky charms, incantation or even slumps, which he prefers to call "unfortunate luck." And, when questioned further, he says he doesn't really believe in luck either.

"Just hard work and preparation," he said. "I don't get mad and hardly raise my voice. I don't have idiosyncrasies. I don't even look at film of myself."

He does have a good memory, however, and the remembrances of his first game in this stadium last Sept. 30 were embarrassing. He said. That was when he missed one field-goal attempt, was wide on one conversion attempt and hit the goal post on another. That was the day the Giants lost to the Rams, 33-12.

Wanted Another Chance

"I've thought about that game a lot, and it eats at you," he said. "Every once in a while when I drive in my car, I think about it and get mad. I was just hoping I'd get another chance."

Today, he got that second chance and he kicked the three field goals that provided the winning points in the Giants' 16-13 victory against the Rams in the National Conference wild-card playoff game. His approach was business as usual, Haji-Sheikh said, although he admitted that he was nervous when he practiced here on Saturday.

"Then, I began laughing to myself about the first time," he said. "It was great to be here in the playoffs. And it's a great stadium to kick in. It's warm out here, there's plenty of sunshine and practically no wind."

In a season in which the Giants made the playoffs, their place-kicker struggled, converting 17 of 33 field-goal attempts but only 5 of 16 from 40 yards and farther. The Giants were

unaccustomed to his erratic performance after the rave reviews Haji-Sheikh received last year as a rookie, when he kicked 35 field goals in 42 attempts, and missed just one extra point, ironically against the Rams. Last year, when the Giants' offense was inept before a game, it would have sufficed to send out Haji-Sheikh and his holder.

Friends Can't Help

But the loneliness of the long-distance place-kicker is that no one can usually help him during those times when his kicks fall short, sail wide or hook as if they are about to come back like boomerangs. That is when the head coach places telephone calls to unemployed kickers tending bar and when teammates don't include the kicker in their social plans. That is when his holder can be the only source of sympathy.

"No kicker knows why it happens," Haji-Sheikh said. "You can lose a little confidence, but after the first Rams game I figured things couldn't get any worse. I talked to my wife a little about it, but otherwise all you can do it kick your way out of it. I didn't think much about the fact that I had never scored against them either."

He understood, he said, that there would be a period of adjustment when Jeff Rutledge, the Giants' reserve quarterback, became his holder after Scott Brunner was traded before the first game of the season. He ignored it when the fans began to call him "Ali Haji-Shank." Instead, he was boosted by the encouragement that he received from the coaching staff and his teammates. He was embraced when he could easily have been ostracized.

He responded by converting 12 of his last 13 attempts and then all three today, from 37, 39 and 38 yards. And at a time when Haji-Sheikh was almost matter-of-fact about his success, the biggest smile belonged to Rutledge.

"I figured that anytime you're in the playoffs, there is a better chance that the game will be decided by field goals," Haji-Sheikh said. "I was thinking that I couldn't afford to be three-of-five or two-of-four in a game like this.

"I didn't feel my rhythm was great today," he added. "It felt like an average day. I just did what I get paid to do. But you feel stupid when you don't do it."

The New York Times
Ali Haji-Sheikh kicking one of three field goals he made against R...

Giants' Rob Carpenter, far left, Phil Simms, Brad Benson and Chris Godfrey go after loose ball in the first quarter against the Rams. Giants recovered.
The New York Times/Paul Kennedy

Giants Halt Ram Rally for 16-13 Victory

Continued From Page 25

coverage on Mike Guman, who is ... blocking back. When Banks

On first down, Dickerson took a pitchout and ran 3 yards. On second down, Leonard Marshall, the Giants' defensive end, knifed between two Rams' linemen and threw Dwayne Crutchfield, the fullback and former ... loss. On third down,

Words of Encouragement

Special to The New York Times

ANAHEIM, Calif., Dec. 23 — Coach Bill Parcells of the Giants has ... Jim Burt, his nose tackle, "my kind of player," one whose ... much better. Today, Burt demon...

... Giants' 16-13 victory over the Rams, ... tackle, suffered bruised ribs. As ... the Giants sent in Conrad Goode, an ...

... ore Burt came running after him.
... your chance. Take advantage of it.' "
... ater," who was going into the biggest
... ve him confidence and make sure he

... ree plays before Nelson returned.
... said Goode. "It was thoughtful."

... help of the 10th penalty of the day ... against the Rams.
"Did Kemp fumble the ball?" said Taylor with a big smile. "I didn't know that. I thought it was a sack. He really fumbled? That's great."

So the Giants, instead of flying home after the game and cleaning out their lockers, are still alive. They plan to fly Monday morning to Fresno and train there until Friday, when they will move to Berkeley for the night. On Saturday, they play another game.

"The Giants are not going home for Christmas," Taylor announced. "We are sending someone else home."

PRO!

The Magazine of the National Football League

January 1983

Lawrence Taylor: Giants' Big Man

★ Eagles' Greatest Teams
★ Jets' Joe Klecko Unchanged by Superstardom
★ 20 Years With the Cardinals
★ Handball!: A Photo Essay
★ John Madden on Game Plans

The New York Times reports that the G-Men were on the right track, as evidenced by the 16-13 playoff win over the Rams in 1984.

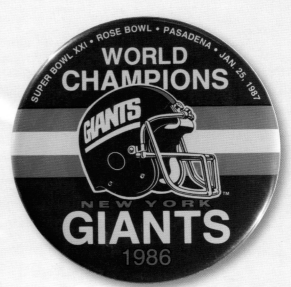

SUPER BOWL XXI • ROSE BOWL • PASADENA • JAN. 25, 1987

WORLD CHAMPIONS

GIANTS

NEW YORK

GIANTS

1986

The pin from 1986 shows that the Giants were focused on one goal: the Super Bowl.

Recognized as a force to be reckoned with just a few years into his career, Lawrence Taylor was featured in the NFL's magazine, *Pro!*

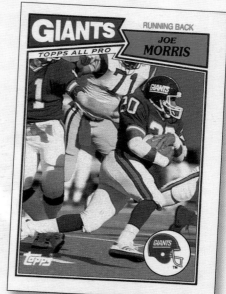

GIANTS   RUNNING BACK
TOPPS ALL PRO   JOE MORRIS

Shown on this rare 1987 Topps UK card, Joe Morris, all 5'7" of him, stood tall for the Giants at running back.

"L. T." Stands for "The Greatest"

The best outside linebacker in football history did not play the game until his junior year in high school, when the coach at Lafayette High in Williamsburg, Virginia, recruited him out of the hallway because he was big. Big as Lawrence Taylor was then, the imprint he left on the National Football League is much larger.

"In 30 or 40 years," said former Philadelphia running back Keith Byars, "I'm going to take out the tapes and show them to my grandkids, to show them I really played against Lawrence Taylor. The greatest."

"L. T." was an All-American at North Carolina and was drafted second overall—after running back George Rogers—by the Giants in 1981. At 6'3" and 240 pounds, Taylor was strong enough to shed blockers and bring down the toughest runners, fast enough to cover opposing receivers, and absolutely one of a kind when it came to harassing quarterbacks.

Combining his many physical and athletic gifts with unmatched intensity and a reckless disregard for his own well-being, Taylor threw himself into every snap, hurtling his body

His speed around the edge set Lawrence Taylor apart from any outside linebacker before him—or any since. There was virtually no keeping him out of the offensive backfield.

over, around, and through blockers to blow up plays before they started.

Taylor made 133 tackles and 9½ sacks as a rookie, winning the first of his three NFL Defensive Player of the Year Awards. He was named All-Pro in each of his first nine seasons. And when he recorded 20½ sacks while leading the Giants to a Super Bowl championship in 1986, he became the first defensive player since 1971 to be named A.P. NFL Most Valuable Player.

"Lawrence Taylor, defensively, has had as big an impact as any player I've ever seen," said former coach and TV commentator John Madden. "He changed the way defense is played, the way pass-rushing is played, the way linebackers play, and the way offenses block linebackers."

Rarely missing a game and coming up with countless key plays in clutch situations—"I want that last shot," he said, using a basketball metaphor—Taylor never let his own pain stand in the way of causing pain for others. In a memorable 1988 game against the Saints, he wore a harness to keep a torn muscle in place and recorded three sacks, seven tackles, and two forced fumbles.

"I was the king," he said. "And in the prime of my career, there was no one better. There was no one better."

Taylor's all-out style extended to his life off the field as well. He battled substance abuse, twice testing positive for drugs during his career. He was suspended for four games in 1988 but was in

fine form while leading the Giants to a second Super Bowl championship in 1990. He had said, unapologetically, that he lives life in the fast lane.

The fast lane—at least when it came to his performance on the field—led L. T. to the Pro Football Hall of Fame in 1999, five years after he was voted to the NFL's 75th Anniversary All-Time Team. At the time of his retirement after the '93 season, he ranked second in NFL history in career sacks, and he still stands among the all-time top 10.

Taylor credits golf with helping him overcome drugs, and he hits the little round ball much like he hit quarterbacks over the course of his 13 years with the Giants.

L. T. is one big hitter.

Lawrence Taylor is considered the greatest outside linebacker in pro football history. He set a new standard for pass rushers on his way to the Hall of Fame.

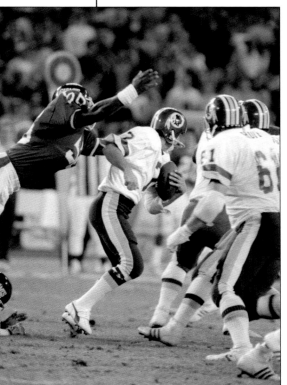

Lawrence Taylor's clean hit on Joe Theismann in a 1985 game caused a gruesome, career-ending fracture to the Redskins quarterback's leg.

Talkin' Taylor

Lawrence Taylor redefined the outside linebacker position during his 13-year career with the New York Giants. He also racked up numerous awards and achievements. Among them:

- Nine All-Pro selections
- Selected for 10 Pro Bowls
- NFL Most Valuable Player in 1986
- NFL Defensive Player of the Year in 1981, '82, and '86
- League-leading 20½ sacks in 1986
- Nine career interceptions, including two returned for touchdowns
- 132½ career sacks (not counting 9½ in 1981, before sacks became an official stat)
- Named to NFL 75th Anniversary Team, 1994
- Inducted into Pro Football Hall of Fame, 1999

Best 'Backers, Bar None

If Penn State University is known as "Linebacker U," the New York Giants were, for a long while, the National Football League equivalent—renowned for their ferocious hits and their ability to make game-changing plays along the second line of defense.

"Even in the 1950s, the Giants had impact players at the linebacker position," noted star 1970s and '80s inside linebacker Harry Carson. "It carried into the 1970s. Brad Van Pelt, then myself, and then into the 1980s with Lawrence Taylor. Then you had guys like Carl Banks and Pepper Johnson."

NFL analyst and former Raiders coach John Madden went as far as to say that the linebackers were the team's essence.

In the early 1980s, Taylor, Van Pelt, Carson, and Brian Kelley were known as the "Crunch Bunch," forming perhaps the most talented and cohesive groups of linebackers in the NFL. If no one thought it was possible to improve on a 'backing corps like that, the Giants proved them wrong with the addition of Banks, Johnson, and Gary Reasons.

Before Taylor came along and redefined the position, Van Pelt was the best outside linebacker in Giants history. In 1984, Van Pelt was replaced by Banks—another Pro Bowler—and the Giants did not miss a beat.

While Taylor and Banks were making life miserable for quarterbacks from their outside posts, Carson, Reasons, and Johnson smashed opposing ball-carriers from inside posts. For size, speed, talent, and depth, no team in the NFL could come close to matching the linebacking corps the Giants fielded for more than a decade. For duration of dominance, none has matched it since.

From 1976 to '90—a run of 15 consecutive seasons—the Giants had at least one linebacker in the Pro Bowl every winter.

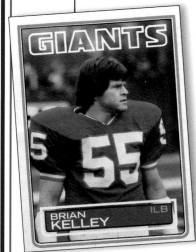

Inside linebacker Brian Kelley, shown on this 1983 Topps card, was a hard-hitting member of the "Crunch Bunch" linebacking corps.

One of the greats among an outstanding group of Giants linebackers was Carl Banks, who helped New York claim two Super Bowl championships.

Taylor, Banks, Carson, and Johnson combined for 21 Pro Bowl selections during their careers.

From 1981 to '91, those linebackers helped New York finish among the NFL's top seven in defense nine times, including three second-place rankings.

"I took it all for granted," said quarterback Phil Simms, who added that the strength of the Giants defense made the offensive players feel guilty every time they came off the field following a three-and-out series. "I look back [at the linebackers] and say, 'Wow, they were so good.'

"I do the same with the coaching staff. What a terrific staff we had under [Bill] Parcells. And we got hot with the draft. Every linebacker we picked was kicking butt."

The Legend of Rambo

Just two years into his pro football career, Mark Bavaro was called a "Legend In The Making" in a *Sports Illustrated* cover story.

"Oh, we've got one, even if he's only 24 years old," Giants quarterback Phil Simms told the magazine. "We've got our legend. Bavaaaro! Mark Bavaro. Great big kid. Real quiet. Some guys have never heard him talk. Loves to block, knock people down, plant 'em. First game [of 1985, Bavaro's rookie season] we rush for 192 yards, more than in any game the year before. Against

What a Drag

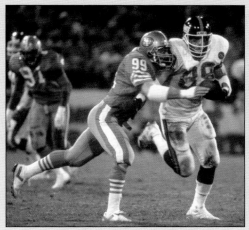

Bavaro's tackle-breaking catch and run against the 49ers in 1986 is considered one of the greatest plays in Monday Night Football *history.*

Even those rooting against the Giants became fans of Mark Bavaro on Monday night, December 1, 1986, after witnessing a play that epitomized the toughness of the tight end.

Against the 49ers, Bavaro caught a short Phil Simms pass across the middle and refused to be tackled. Seven different defenders—including All-Pro safety Ronnie Lott—got hands, arms, or helmets on him, and Bavaro dragged several of them some 20 yards. The play, considered one of the best in *Monday Night Football* history, sparked the Giants (trailing 17–0 at halftime) to a 21–17 win.

"I show people films of that play," said Phil McConkey, "and I have them count the people who had shots at Mark. One, two, three . . . seven total. On the sideline we just looked at each other in amazement."

Cincinnati, he breaks the club record with 12 catches for 176 yards. We're a veteran team, but we're a little bit in awe of this guy."

Some tight ends make their names as pass catchers. Others earn their paychecks doing the dirty work as punishing blockers. Bavaro, a fourth-round draft choice in 1985 after an All-America career at Notre Dame, was that rare tight end who did all that, and more.

His quiet, no-nonsense toughness and resemblance to Sylvester Stallone earned Bavaro the nickname "Rambo" during a 1985 season in which he made the NFL All-Rookie Team and set a Giants record for receptions in a game with those dozen against the Bengals.

The following year, the Massachusetts native topped 1,000 receiving yards on 66 catches, including several clutch grabs that helped the Giants win their first Super Bowl championship. It was his first of two All-Pro seasons.

In six seasons with the Giants—a span that included many games in which he played with cracked bones, sprained ankles, and bruises the size of plates—Bavaro caught 266 balls for 3,722 yards and 28 scores while opening countless holes for two Super Bowl-winning teams.

A legendary effort, some might say.

Mark Bavaro became one of the NFL's best pass-catching tight ends in no time flat, grabbing 66 balls for 1,001 yards in just his second season. It began a run of three straight years with 50-plus receptions.

1986: Simply Superb

It was a team of role players. Maurice Carthon. Phil McConkey. Mark Collins.

It was a team of stars. Lawrence Taylor. Phil Simms. Harry Carson. Joe Morris.

It was a team that adopted the personality of its hard-driving, no-excuses, get-out-of-our-bleeping-way head coach and muscled its way to glory, largely without ever looking glorious.

It was a team that accomplished a mission to win the franchise's first NFL championship in 30 years, and one that did so in impressive fashion.

"In my wildest dreams," said Simms, whose Super Bowl quarterbacking set a standard for precision that has yet to be broken, "I couldn't have hoped it would work out this way."

Even though the dominant Chicago Bears had "Super Bowl Shuffled" their way to a championship the previous year, many 1986 preseason forecasts picked the Giants to go all the way. Coming off a 10–6 season, they were balanced offensively, solid on special teams, made few mistakes, and fielded one of the hardest-hitting defenses in the NFL.

The ink on those preseason forecasts was barely dry, though, when New York dropped its opener 31–28 at Dallas after a Herschel Walker touchdown with 76 seconds remaining.

Walker was an import from the failed USFL, a league that contributed to the Giants' success as well. Fellow ex-USFLers Carthon, Pro Bowl punter Sean Landeta, and offensive linemen Bart Oates and Chris Godfrey were starters for the 1986 Super Bowl champs.

One game into the season, it was time to regroup, and the Giants did just that. They scratched out five straight wins, rally-

ing from behind in the fourth quarter to knock off the Raiders and Saints in back-to-back weeks.

Then, after a loss in Seattle, the Giants showed their mettle with a stretch of close wins that characterized their growing belief in themselves. They won six straight games by a touchdown or less, avenging the earlier loss to the Cowboys 17–14 in week nine. New York then capped a nine-game winning streak to end the regular season with a 24–14 victory at Washington and

George Martin, shown here on a 1983 Topps card, provided veteran leadership for the Giants in '86.

Jim Burt celebrates the Giants' 17–0 blanking of the Washington Redskins in the 1986 NFC championship game. It earned New York its first-ever Super Bowl berth.

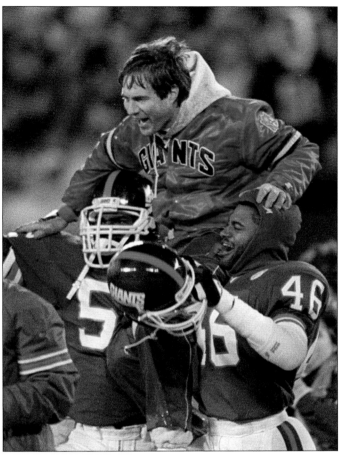

Before advancing to a championship head coaching career, Bill Belichick earned kudos—and a ride off the field after a 17–0 shutout of Washington in the 1986 NFC title game—for his work as a defensive coordinator.

confidence-building home romps over St. Louis and Green Bay.

At 14–2, the Giants tied the Bears for the best record in the NFL. If they got there by winning the close ones, their dominant play down the stretch had the Giants convinced they need not keep their fans biting their fingernails through the playoffs.

Nose tackle Jim Burt knocked 49ers quarterback Joe Montana out of the game in New York's first postseason tilt, causing an interception that Taylor returned for a touchdown in a 49–3 blowout. The next week, New York scored 17 first-half points and rode its dominant defense to a 17–0 shutout of the rival Redskins in the NFC championship game.

The Giants had not played a tight game in nearly two months entering Super Bowl XXI at the Rose Bowl in Pasadena, California, where the scene was far different from the last time the New Yorkers had won a championship some 30 years earlier.

The Super Bowl had become America's signature sporting event since the last time the Giants contended for a title. Seem-

ingly all eyes and ears were on every player, coach, cheerleader, statistician, and mascot involved. The previous year, the free-spirited Bears had cut a rap video, the "Super Bowl Shuffle," while filling newspapers with outrageous comments from players like Jim McMahon and William "The Refrigerator" Perry.

Under the glare of the New York media all season, the Giants took a vastly different approach—one that suited head coach Bill Parcells perfectly. They were calm, confident, and conservative. In fact, some wondered whether Parcells might be too conservative for his team's own good entering the biggest game of his life.

The Giants were favored by 9½ points against the Denver Broncos, who had gone 11–5 in the regular season and rallied past the Cleveland Browns for an upset win in a thrilling AFC title game. It seemed like a wide spread for a team that would have been perfectly comfortable slugging out a defensive battle in the single digits.

"Bill is conservative," noted Cowboys coach Tom Landry in assessing the Giants' chances and reflecting on their 17–0 NFC title game victory over the Redskins. "In the wind, with a 17-point lead, he sat on it for nearly three quarters.... Teams come back; then it becomes hard to get your team back up."

Such concerns dissipated not long

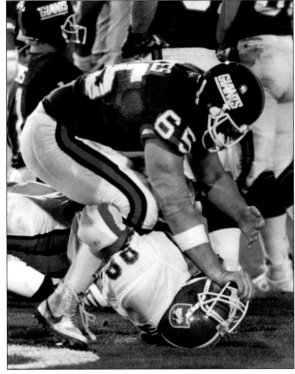

The 1986 Giants were known for their toughness. Here, Bart Oates works over Denver's Ricky Hunley during New York's 39–20 victory against the Broncos in Super Bowl XXI.

after Neil Diamond put the finishing touches on the National Anthem in front of 101,063 fans and an American television audience of some 130 million more. There would be no chance for the Giants to play conservatively, as John Elway and the Broncos jumped to first-half leads of 3–0 and 10–7. George Martin sacked Elway in the end zone late in the second quarter for a safety that cut the lead to 10–9 at halftime, and in the second half the Giants pulled out all the stops.

First, Parcells called for a fake punt on fourth-and-one, with backup quarterback Jeff Rutledge running for a first down that set up a 13-yard scor-

The Super Bowl XXI program displays the prize that the Giants were able to land, the Vince Lombardi Trophy.

ing pass from Simms to tight end Mark Bavaro as the Giants took the lead for good. Two possessions later, Simms hit McConkey on a flea-flicker that gained 44 yards to the Denver 1. Morris, who in 1986 had set a franchise single-season rushing record, ran in for the TD and a 26–10 advantage that put the game out of reach.

"I thought the flea-flicker just ended the game," said Simms, whose 22-for-25 passing performance set a Super Bowl accuracy record and earned him game MVP accolades. "I thought that was the difference—a great call."

Parcells put the credit right back on the arm of his quarterback, who threw three touchdown passes, racked up 268 yards through the air, and also rushed three times for 25 yards. Simms's completion percentage was not only the best in Super Bowl history but the best in NFL championship game annals.

"He quarterbacked as good a game as has ever been played," Parcells said.

"Right from the first day of practice I felt that I was going to have a good game," Simms said after the Giants outscored the Broncos 30–10 in the second half of a 39–20 win. "I felt good about throwing the ball. Conditions were just perfect for passing. The weather was great.

"I was used to throwing in the cold, but now I could grip the ball any way I wanted to. I could make it do anything I wanted."

Simms, as had become his custom, drove to the game with linemen

Giants defenders Lawrence Taylor (56), Erik Howard (74), and Leonard Marshall (70) join the Super Bowl XXI referees in putting their hands together after sacking Denver quarterback John Elway in the end zone for a safety.

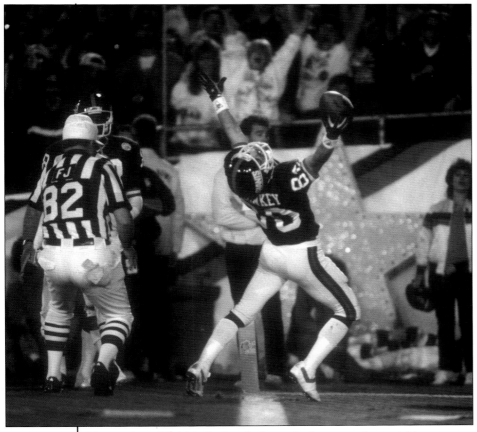

Unsung hero Phil McConkey looks to the heavens after catching a touchdown pass in Super Bowl XXI. The Giants reached the end zone three times via the air in their 39–20 handling of the Broncos.

Godfrey and Brad Benson. Benson, a Pro Bowler who was one-half of a bookend tackle tandem along with Karl Nelson, said he was nervous entering the game until Simms's confidence put his mind at ease. The rest was Giants football—balanced offense, solid special teams, few mistakes, and dominant defense.

"Now," offered Taylor, who that season became just the second defensive player voted A.P. NFL Most Valuable Player, "no matter what people say about our team, whether the Giants don't look good anymore or whatever, as long as I live I'll always have a Super Bowl ring. One time in my career, we are considered the best in the world."

Giants Pioneer "Gatorade Shower"

Gatorade was invented at the University of Florida as an athletic thirst quencher. Its most famous nondrinking use was invented by the New York Giants in 1985.

As the Giants prepared to halt a two-game skid against the Redskins, Bill Parcells taunted nose guard Jim Burt in practice all week about how Washington lineman Jeff Bostic was going to eat him alive. It was an effort to fire up Burt, but it came back to haunt Parcells after Burt and the Giants handed the Redskins a 17–3 setback at Giants Stadium.

As the clock ticked down, Burt grabbed a nearly full cooler of Gatorade, sneaked up behind his coach, and doused Parcells—a risky move. "I was the only one who had the guts to do it without knowing what his reaction would be," Burt said.

Soon, teammates' fears that Parcells might take offense to the gesture were laid to rest, and others—most notably linebacker Harry Carson—got into the act. The superstitious Parcells never objected to the showers as long as they signified victory. "It's fun," Parcells said. "It's not all life and death."

The following year, Parcells took his first Super Bowl championship Gatorade shower. Coaches have been getting drenched ever since.

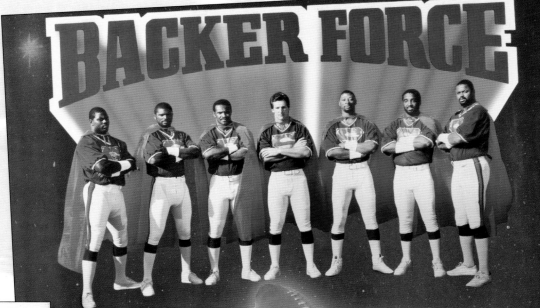

BACKER FORCE

WORLD CHAMPION
NEW YORK GIANTS
LINEBACKERS

T. JOHNSON, L. TAYLOR, H. CARSON, G. REASONS, C. BANKS, R. JONES, A. HEADEN

This poster celebrates the super linebacker corps, the heart and soul of the Super Bowl XXI-winning Giants.

This Super Bowl pin may have been purchased by one of the 101,063 in attendance at the Super Bowl.

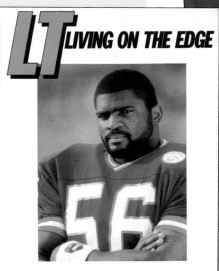

LT LIVING ON THE EDGE

LAWRENCE TAYLOR
and David Falkner

Like Sam Huff before him, L. T. was a crossover media star. He co-wrote this book at the height of his fame.

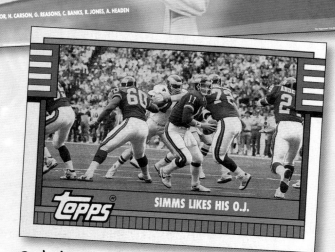

SIMMS LIKES HIS O.J.

O. J. Anderson brought some power-running juice to the Giant offense starting in 1986. Phil Simms appreciated it, according to this 1990 Topps card.

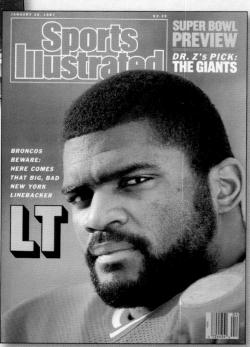

JANUARY 26, 1987 $2.25

Sports Illustrated

SUPER BOWL PREVIEW
DR. Z's PICK:
THE GIANTS

BRONCOS BEWARE: HERE COMES THAT BIG, BAD NEW YORK LINEBACKER

LT

Lawrence Taylor and the Giants were a popular pick, according to this issue of *Sports Illustrated*.

This pin pictures the 1986 Giants, who finally brought an NFL title back to New York.

The New York Times

"All the News That's Fit to Print"

Late Edition

New York: Today, at times a blizzard, with heavy snow ending this afternoon. High 14-22. Flurries tonight, tomorrow. Low, 21. High tomorrow, 23-28. Yesterday: High 24, low 8. Details, page C30.

NEW YORK, MONDAY, JANUARY 26, 1987

VOL.CXXXVI .. No. 47,031   Copyright © 1987 The New York Times

50 cents beyond 75 miles from New York City, except on Long Island.   30 CENTS

Giants Rout Broncos in the Super Bowl

Simms, Defense Excel As Team Takes First Title Since 1956

By FRANK LITSKY
Special to The New York Times

PASADENA, Calif., Jan. 25 — The Giants won the Super Bowl today, emphatically.

Yes, the Giants, who in the 1970's could hardly win anything. These Giants of 1987 were relentless on offense and especially defense. They emphasized the pass rather than the run, they mixed in two trick plays that led to touchdowns, and they trounced the Denver Broncos, 39-20.

This was Super Bowl XXI, the championship game of the National Football League. It attracted a screaming crowd of 101,063 in the Rose Bowl and millions of television viewers in the United States and 40 foreign nations.

Simms Most Valuable Player

The most super of the Giants was Phil Simms, the 30-year-old quarterback. For his eight years with the Giants, he has been maligned by the news media and the public, who said he was not good enough to win. Here, he was good enough and more.

Of the Giants' five touchdowns, Simms passed for three: 6 yards to Zeke Mowatt, 13 yards to Mark Bavaro and 6 yards to Phil McConkey, who caught a pass that bounced off Bavaro's hands. In addition, Simms set up one touchdown with a 44-yard pass to McConkey and one with a 22-yard run. His passing statistics were stunning: 22 completions in 25 attempts for 268 yards.

His completion rate of 88 percent was a Super Bowl record for passers with at least 15 completions in a game. In fact, it was the highest for any of the 213 postseason games in N.F.L. history.

"In my wildest dreams," said Simms, "I couldn't have hoped it would work out this way."

"That's as good as Phil has ever played," said Coach Bill Parcells of the Giants. "This dispelled for the last time any myth about Phil Simms. He was absolutely magnificent today."

Simms was a unanimous choice as the game's most valuable player. He and the other Giants were invited by President Reagan to reap the traditional reward of America's sports champions, a visit to the White House.

12th Consecutive Victory

Parcells reaped his traditional reward, too. This was the Giants' 12th consecutive victory, nine in the regular season and three in the playoffs. In the dying minutes of each previous victory in that streak, Harry Carson, the Giants' 33-year-old linebacker and defensive captain, doused Parcells with a bucket of icy Gatorade.

The dousing has become so much of a tradition that television cameras home

The New York Times/Vic DeLucia

Giants' Phil McConkey after catching touchdown pass in fourth quarter.

No More Waiting for No. 1; Giants' Fans Enjoy the Day

By JAMES BARRON

At the moment that Raul Allegre's toe touched the ball and the clock began ticking on Super Bowl XXI, Bruce Jagoda popped the cork on a bottle of champagne. "It's over now," said the 39-year-old financial analyst.

On Super Bowl Sunday — the one day when people who never worry about first downs, fumbles and interceptions worry about first downs, fumbles and interceptions — he and thousands of other fans were supremely confident that the Giants would do what they had never done

Before the homily at St. Gregory the Great Roman Catholic Church on the Upper West Side of Manhattan, the Rev. David A. Sork asked any Denver fans in the congregation to excuse his partisanship. He said he was rooting for the Giants.

Not certain that the Giants' past demonstrations of sheer power would carry the day, the secular community tried theology, too. At Manny's, a restaurant that is a kind of shrine to the

Continued on Page C4, Column 3

5-NATION PARLEY ON DOLLAR POLICY IS EXPECTED SOON

Meeting in Paris Feb. 7 of U.S. and Its Biggest Economic Allies Is Called Likely

By PETER T. KILBORN
Special to The New York Times

WASHINGTON, Jan. 25 — The United States and its biggest economic allies are negotiating arrangements for a meeting to discuss the dollar and the ways their economic policies affect it, European and Japanese officials said today.

They said a promising date for the meeting, probably in Paris, was Feb. 7, when Treasury Secretary James A. Baker 3d is scheduled to be on his way back to Washington from a visit to Saudi Arabia.

"Very soon there'll be a G-5 meeting," said a European diplomat, referring to what has become known as the Group of Five. "It's clearly in the air," added the diplomat, who like others here declined to be identified.

Uncertainty on Details

He and others said the timing and location were uncertain because the countries — the United States, Japan, West Germany, Britain and France — had not yet agreed on arrangements. They cautioned, however, that any one country could prevent a meeting.

Japan's Government-owned television station, NHK, reported today that the Group of Five would meet in Paris, probably on Feb. 7, but the Tokyo Government did not confirm it. The French Finance Ministry refused to comment.

The Treasury declined to comment.

Sees 'Excess' Market Volatility

Mr. Baker, appearing on NBC-TV's "Meet the Press" program today, said the dollar's decline had been helpful, but he added that he was helpful about "excess" volatility in the stock market. He said the Government should study such volatility. The Securities and Exchange Commission already has a study under way.

On Friday, the Dow Jones industrial average closed 44.15 points lower after gyrating wildly in an unusually tumultuous day. The stock market, according to Wall Street analysts, is likely to need at least a few days before recovering from Friday's session. [Page D1.]

An Administration aide said on Saturday that Mr. Baker and the chairman of the President's Council of Eco-

Continued on Page D10, Column 3

The New York Times

Dante B. Fascell, the chairman of House Foreign Affairs Committee

Anger Is Voiced Over Americans Still in Lebanon

By NEIL A. LEWIS
Special to The New York Times

WASHINGTON, Jan. 25 — The kidnapping of three American teachers in Beirut led today to expressions of resentment against Americans who have remained in Lebanon despite unequivocal warnings from the State Department that they cannot be protected.

"Americans who stay there are putting their whole country's policy at risk," said Representative Dante B. Fascell, a Florida Democrat and the chairman of the House Foreign Affairs Committee, reflecting the comments of many on Capitol Hill.

"They may stay there at what they think is their own risk, but it doesn't change the problem for the American Government," he added.

A Threat to Kill Hostages

A Lebanese radio station said today that two anonymous callers had claimed responsibility for the kidnappings Saturday in the name of an underground Moslem group. One reportedly threatened to kill hostages if the United States helped Iraq. [Page A10.]

Meanwhile, Administration officials asserted there would be no concessions made to the captors to obtain the release of the teachers.

Representative Robert G. Torricelli, a New Jersey Democrat and a member of the Foreign Affairs Committee, said it was "irresponsible" of Americans to remain in Lebanon in the face of all the

Continued on Page A10, Column 1

KOHL KEEPS POWER BY NARROWER EDGE IN WEST GERMANY

VOTE RESULT IS SURPRISE

Chancellor's Party Suffers Big Losses, While Its Partners Do Well — Greens Gain

By JAMES M. MARKHAM
Special to The New York Times

BONN, Jan. 25 — Chancellor Helmut Kohl's center-right coalition won a parliamentary majority today that will permit it to govern West Germany for another four years.

But Mr. Kohl's own party had its worst showing since 1949.

The coalition of the Chancellor's Christian Democrats and the small Free Democratic Party won 53.4 percent of the popular vote, which will translate into 266 of the 496 seats in the lower house of Parliament, down from 278 seats in the last Parliament.

Yet Mr. Kohl's Christian Democrats did considerably less well than opinion polls had predicted, winning only 44.3 percent of the popular vote, compared with 48.8 percent in the 1983 election. The poor performance, the party's worst since the founding of the West German state in 1949, appeared likely to weaken Mr. Kohl's personal authority within a fractious coalition.

Greens and Free Democrats Gain

The big winners were West Germany's two small parties — the centrist Free Democrats, junior partners in the coalition, and the anti-NATO Greens. The Free Democrats increased their share of the vote to 9.1 percent, from 7 percent in 1983, while the Greens jumped to 8.3 percent, from 5.6 percent.

The left-of-center Social Democrats did marginally better than most opinion polls had predicted and almost equaled their 1983 showing, drawing 37 percent, compared with 38.2 percent. The result four years ago had been the party's worst since 1961.

Although the performance was well short of the Social Democrats' goal of a majority in Parliament, Johannes Rau, the party's standard-bearer, did well in his home state of North Rhine-Westphalia. In the industrial state, with almost a third of West Germany's electorate of 45 million, the Social Democrats re-established themselves as the biggest party.

Many Split Ballots

Led by Foreign Minister Hans-Dietrich Genscher, the Free Democrats made deep inroads into the Christian Democratic camp by appealing to voters to split their ballots and give their "second votes" to the junior coali-

The New York Times notes that winning Super Bowl XXI was the Giants' first title since 1956.

Jim Burt carries his son around the field in celebration after the G-Men beat the Broncos in Super Bowl XXI.

Officially Licensed NFL Product

Super Bowl XXI

NEW YORK GIANTS

1986 NFC CHAMPS

January 25, 1987
Rose Bowl · Pasadena

This Super Bowl XXI pennant is a souvenir from the 39-20 whipping the Giants laid on the Broncos.

Wide Right Is All Right

National Football League dynasties are rare. Since the 1970s Steelers, no team had successfully defended a Super Bowl championship at the time the 1986 Giants earned the crown. Even getting to the Super Bowl, particularly for an NFC team, was a gargantuan feat during a period (1984 to 1996) in which 13 straight championships were won by teams from the Giants' conference. The Bears, 49ers, Redskins, and Cowboys often stood in the way.

Any New York fans expecting the "Big Blue" to dominate year after year were disappointed in a hurry. In the strike-ravaged 1987 season, the Giants—regulars and "scabs"—stumbled to a 6–9 record in defense of their first Super Bowl title. The running game that powered the '86 team fell apart in '87, as the Giants were one of five NFL teams to average less than 100 yards per game on the ground. New York finished last in the NFC East.

"We have a lot of talent in this room," offensive guard Billy Ard said before the 1987 finale, "but just because you were good last year doesn't mean you're good this year, obviously. You don't stay the same. You get better or you get worse."

A backup to Ottis Anderson in 1990, his rookie season, Rodney Hampton (No. 27) possessed power, vision, and ability—skills that were easy to see. Though he started only two games, Hampton gained 455 yards on 109 carries that season.

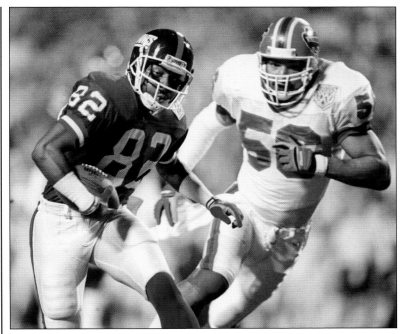

Receiver Mark Ingram caught five passes for 74 yards in Super Bowl XXV, helping the Giants hold on for a 20–19 victory over Buffalo and their second championship in five years.

By 1988, the Giants were getting better again. They still struggled to move the ball, but their defense returned to the NFL's top 10 and the result was a 10–6 record—one game shy of a wild-card playoff berth.

In '89, New York's defense replaced four starters and regained its edge, finishing first in the NFC and second in the NFL, while a rejuvenated Ottis Anderson rushed for 1,023 yards and 14 scores. The Giants returned to the top of the NFC East with a 12–4 record, earning a No. 2 seed in the playoffs.

An upset, overtime loss to the wild-card Rams left the Giants and their fans disheartened, but that game did not diminish the feeling that the franchise was once again on the cusp of something big.

"I'm excited about the future of this team with these young guys," linebacker Carl Banks offered after the 19–13 setback. "There's no team in this league we can't beat, so we build on what we accomplished this year and go on."

The Giants' optimism was well founded. And they wasted little time showing the rest of the league they were out to dominate in 1990, winning 10 consecutive games to start the season—the longest winning streak since they closed the '86 regular season with 12 straight (regular season and postseason) wins.

"The thing about this team is that we've played so consistent," Oates noted after the surge reached 10. "We're not playing to highs and lows. You don't see us with the cyclical swings. No one's scored a lot of points on us. And we've only scored as many as 30 points once or twice."

The Giants came crashing back to earth in their 11th game, a 31–13 loss in Philadelphia, and dropped a highly anticipated battle with two-time defending Super Bowl champ San Francisco the following week. The latter was a 7–3 defensive war between the NFC's two best teams.

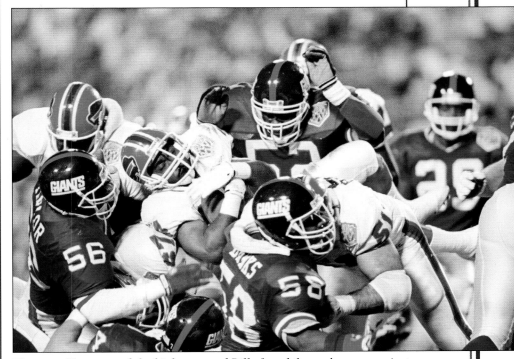

Thurman Thomas and the high-powered Bills found themselves up against a swarming Giants defense in Super Bowl XXV, and the Bills were unable to generate their usual offense.

The Giants were trailing Minnesota at halftime one week later at Giants Stadium and seemingly on the verge of a third straight loss, but Lawrence "L. T." Taylor delivered a brief halftime speech that seemed to hit its mark. "I'm going to start playing the way we're supposed to play," the All-Pro linebacker told his teammates. "If anybody wants to come along, fine."

New York rallied for a 23–15 victory over the Vikings, clinching a second straight division title. The Giants lost just once more down the stretch—a 17–13 home loss to the AFC-leading Bills in what turned out to be a Super Bowl preview—and a costly contest. Quarterback Phil Simms was sidelined for the remainder of the season with a broken foot.

Over the last two weeks of the regular season and into the playoffs, it would be 29-year-old Jeff Hostetler charged with avenging two of the Giants' three regular-season losses. Those games turned into a pair of classics.

A 31–3 rout of the Bears in the opening round set up the first one: a trip to the NFC championship game in San Francisco, where the defenses picked up where they left off in their regular-season tilt. Against a 49ers juggernaut led by Joe Montana, Jerry Rice, and Roger Craig, the Giants allowed just one touchdown—a 61-yard hookup between Montana and John Taylor that gave San Francisco a 13–6 third-quarter lead. Montana was knocked out of the game on Leonard Marshall's fourth-quarter sack.

While the Giants failed to reach the end zone, they did move the ball on the ground, and a key 30-yard gain by linebacker Gary Reasons on a fake punt set up Matt Bahr's fourth field goal of the day, cutting the lead to 13–12. Then, after L. T. recovered a Craig fumble with 2:36 to go, Hostetler again led the Giants into field-goal range, and Bahr hit his fifth three-pointer—the game-winner from 42 yards out as time expired. Giants 15, 49ers 13.

"We had them all the way," smiled Giants coach Bill Parcells after a landmark victory over the two-time defending champions.

It was a quip that held its humor after Super Bowl XXV, too—a rematch between the Giants and Bills that also came down to a kick.

Buffalo quarterback Jim Kelly, who like Simms had been injured in the regular-season battle between the Bills and Giants, was back under center for the big game in Tampa, Florida. While Kelly ran a no-huddle offense for a team that racked up points, the Giants tried to keep them off the field using a ball-control offense and power running by Ottis Anderson.

"We came out with three tight ends," said Mark Bavaro, one of those Giants tight ends, "fat slobs picking you up and moving you and letting you tackle O. J., if you could. And they couldn't. We just physically beat the Buffalo Bills."

Anderson carried 21 times for 102 yards and a touchdown, helping the Giants own the ball for more than two-thirds of the game and earning the Pete Rozelle Trophy as Super Bowl MVP. Despite having the ball for less than eight minutes in the second half, however, the Bills appeared poised to win when Scott Norwood lined up for a 47-yard field goal in the game's final seconds.

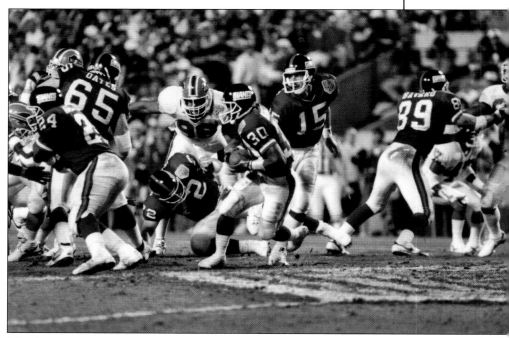

The diminutive Dave Meggett made an enormous play for the Giants on the opening drive of the second half in Super Bowl XXV, turning a short pass into a big gain on third-and-eight.

It was ready, aim, misfire for Scott Norwood and the Bills in the closing seconds of Super Bowl XXV in Tampa. Norwood missed a potential game-winning field goal wide right.

The lead had changed hands three times in the second half of an exciting game—once on Anderson's touchdown run, later on a 31-yard run by Buffalo's Thurman Thomas, and finally on a short Bahr field goal that put the Giants on top 20–19. As Norwood, normally reliable and a veteran of big games, lined up for the potential game winner, there was nothing most of the Giants could do but watch, hope, and pray.

The snap and hold were clean. The kick sailed wide right.

For the second time in five years, the New York Giants were Super Bowl champions.

"I realized a long time ago," said Parcells after being carried off the field by his players, "that God was playing in some of these games. He was on our side today. If we played tomorrow, they would probably win 20–19."

Hostetler: Yes, He Can

As the New York Giants celebrated their Super Bowl XXV victory over Buffalo, linebacker Pepper Johnson led a group of players over to the locker of 29-year-old quarterback Jeff Hostetler. They laughed and chanted:

You can't do it.

You can't do it.

They say you're just a backup.

You can't do it.

Indeed, Hostetler *was* a backup. He took over when starter Phil Simms was injured in Game 14 of the regular season. Hostetler started the final two games and all three playoff contests, including the Super Bowl win. His record in those five starts: 5–0.

Hostetler, it turns out, could get the job done. He threw three playoff touchdown passes without an interception. He used his superior mobility to keep plays alive. And he weathered a Super Bowl onslaught by Bruce Smith and the Bills defense with poise.

"I felt more confidence than any game I've ever played in," Hostetler said. "I was really excited to be in a Super Bowl, playing. I didn't have any nerves. I felt good. I just felt good."

Jeff Hostetler (No. 15)

GIANTS GALLERY

SportsMonday

The New York Times Copyright © 1991 The New York Times

MONDAY, JANUARY 28, 1991 L+C1

Giants Win

Bills' Kick Fails With :04 to Play In 20-19 Thriller

By FRANK LITSKY
Special to The New York Times

TAMPA, Fla., Jan. 27 — Last Sunday, the Giants got to Super Bowl XXV with a field goal on the final play of the game. Today, they won the Super Bowl when the Buffalo Bills missed a 47-yard field-goal attempt with four seconds left.

When the kick by Scott Norwood sailed wide to the right, the Giants were assured of a 20-19 victory and their second Super Bowl triumph in five seasons.

It was an exciting ending to the closest Super Bowl ever. It was a game of old-fashioned, in-your-face running by the Giants, who rushed for 172 yards. It was a game of finesse running by the Bills, who rushed for 166 yards. It was a game of big plays and deep thinking.

Giants Use Unusual Defenses

The Giants knew they could not completely stop the Bills' dangerous no-huddle offense. Their defensive plan was to stop the big plays, and they at least minimized them with novel defensive variations. They started the game in a 2-3-6 (two defensive linemen, three linebackers and six defensive backs) and switched early to a 2-4-5.

More so than ever, their offensive plan was to control the ball, to eat up yards and, at the same time, keep the ball from the Bills. That worked so well that the Giants had the ball for 40 minutes 33 seconds to the Bills' 19 minutes 27 seconds. Never had ever held the ball so long in a Super Bowl.

"We knew we could put points on the board and control the clock," said Ottis Anderson, one of the Giants' heroes.

That ball control depended on the passing and scrambling of Jeff Hostetler, a backup quarterback until five weeks ago, and the running of Anderson, at age 34 the oldest starting running back in the National Football League. Both made the big plays when they had to.

Anderson Named M.V.P.

Anderson rushed 21 times for 102 yards. That included runs of 24 and 18 yards with quickness you would have done a young buck proud. It also included a 1-yard run for the Giants' second touchdown.

Anderson won the first Pete Rozelle Award as the Super Bowl's most valuable player. He received seven and a half votes to four and a half...

Continued on Page C7

Coach Bill Parcells being carried from the field after the Giants' Super Bowl victory last night in Tampa, Fla. Giants' Ottis Anderson, the game's M.V.P., leaving the field after the 20-19 victory over the Bills. Scott Norwood, the Bills' kicker, leaving the field after his field-goal attempt went wide with four seconds left in the game.

Vic DeLucia/The New York Times

Anderson Is Most Venerable and Most Valuable

By MALCOLM MORAN
Special to The New York Times

TAMPA, Fla., Jan. 27 — Bart Oates stood at a podium, wearing a white T-shirt that somehow already read, "Giants 20, Bills 19."

His right arm cradled a long silver trophy with a metallic football at the top. In the bright lights, one could see fingerprints all over the Vince Lombardi Trophy, and most of them had to belong to the center of the New York Giants.

As Oates stood with the trophy, he talked about Ottis Anderson, the man he had been blocking for throughout the evening.

"It's the player that determines when he's going to retire," Oates said. "What he has left, and how he's going to perform. He's a tremendous role model for anyone out there that has somebody telling them they can't get the job done, that they're washed up."

"He was supposed to be washed up when he first came here, before the first Super Bowl," Oates said. "Another five or six years, and I think he'll be ready to retire."

"In '86, I was a backup to Joe Morris," Anderson said, remembering that championship season. "From then until 1985, I was a nominee for 'Where is he now?'"

The 34-year-old Anderson had just been voted the most valuable player. He gained 102 yards on 21 carries tonight.

In the second half, his 63 yards, on 14 carries, were a major reason why the Giants were able to establish the long, time-consuming drives that were a central part of their plans and their hopes.

The Giants' offense changed the direction of the game with a drive at the end of the second quarter, and another at the beginning of the third, that restricted Buffalo to one offensive play — Jim Kelly's drop to one knee at the end of the half — for a period of 13 minutes 28 seconds.

In the first drive, which began at the 30 with 3:49 to go in the first half, Hostetler completed 5 of 8 passes for 53...

Security slows the crowd's entry, C...

Hostetler's home rooting section, ...

Anderson on Parcells's plan, ...

Bill Parcells is shown in his last hurrah as Giants coach after Super Bowl XXV by *The New York Times.*

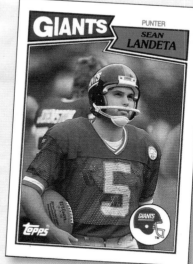

GIANTS PUNTER SEAN LANDETA

Sean Landeta is pictured on this 1987 Topps Mini card.

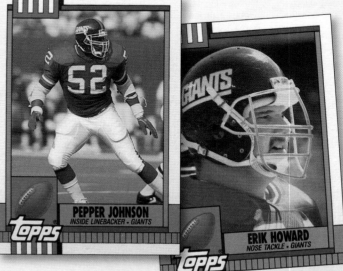

PEPPER JOHNSON
INSIDE LINEBACKER · GIANTS

ERIK HOWARD
NOSE TACKLE · GIANTS

These 1990 Topps cards feature Pepper Johnson and nose tackle Erik Howard, both of whom made the Pro Bowl that year.

Phil Simms, shown on this rare 1980s pennant, grew into the job as Giants quarterback. He retired with a franchise-record 199 touchdown passes.

Ron Kilbride (left) and Vincent Savino felt shaved by their love of the Super Bowl-bound Giants.

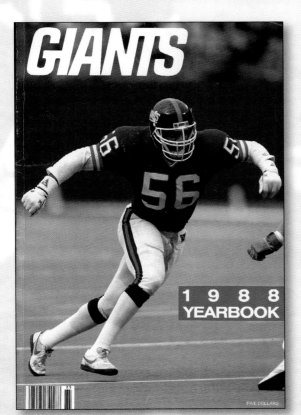

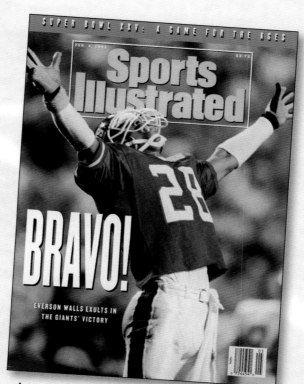

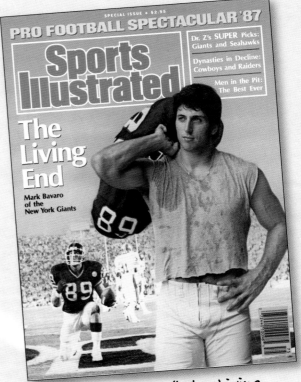

Though the Giants acquired great talent during the '80s, L. T. was still the big name, as evidenced by this 1988 yearbook cover.

This *Sports Illustrated* echoed what those who watched Super Bowl XXV thought: Bravo!

Mark Bavaro was "The Living End" to all Giants fans, as *Sports Illustrated* pronounced on this 1987 cover.

(Bad) Decisions, Decisions

The first time the Giants tried to repeat as Super Bowl champs, an NFL strike got in their way. The second time, New York simply struck out.

Defending a championship is never easy, and the Giants' task became mountainous when coach Bill Parcells announced his retirement four months after taking his 1990 team to the summit. "Mountainous" became "impossible" thanks to some ill-fated decisions by the club.

Defensive coordinator Bill Belichick was already being called a coaching genius long before Parcells decided to step down. His attacking schemes had maximized the talents of a Law-

One of Ray Handley's first big coaching decisions was benching Phil Simms (pictured) in favor of Jeff Hostetler to open 1991. Handley went 8–8 and 6–10 in his two seasons at the helm.

rence Taylor-led linebacking corps and caused fits for both run- and pass-oriented foes. Belichick, however, was allowed to take Cleveland's head coaching job after the Super Bowl win.

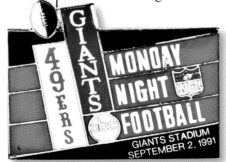

This pin was only given out to Giants fans attending the Monday night game on September 2, 1991.

So instead of getting a man who went on to win four AFC championships and three Super Bowl titles with the Patriots, the Giants named Ray Handley to replace Parcells. Handley had coached the offensive backfield and was considering quitting football in favor of law school before Parcells promoted him to offensive coordinator after the Super Bowl.

General Manager George Young brushed off a question about whether he felt the "real big fish," Belichick, had gotten away, saying Handley got the job because he was a good coach, not because he was an "heir apparent."

Handley's performance over the next two seasons left Giants fans unconvinced. His first major decision—whom to start at quarterback—backfired as loudly as Young's did. Handley went with Jeff Hostetler, the backup who had completed the 1990 Super Bowl run, over Phil Simms, who was returning from

an injury. Hostetler struggled, taking a 6–5 record into a game at Tampa Bay in which he suffered a back injury. Simms finished that win but went 1–3 in December, as the defending Super Bowl champs missed the playoffs at 8–8.

Giants Stadium signs proclaimed "From Super Bowl to Toilet Bowl" and "Thanks, Ray." Simms was back at the controls in 1992, but his team was no longer a contender, having watched the top players from two Super Bowl teams move on or become less effective.

After going 6–10 in that '92 season, Handley was fired. He was paid the $450,000 he was scheduled to earn in the final year of his three-year contract. Two years after considering leaving football, he did, never to coach in the NFL again.

"Some guys are meant to be head coaches," Giants linebacker Pepper Johnson said. "I don't know if Ray was."

Dan's the Man to Turn Giants Around

Having made a mistake in hiring Ray Handley, the Giants were not about to duplicate it when they went shopping for his replacement in 1993. Though they initially eyed Dave Wannstedt and Tom Coughlin, they landed a proven winner in Dan Reeves, architect of three AFC titles with the Denver Broncos.

Reeves was a protégé of former Giants assistant and Hall of Fame Cowboys coach Tom Landry in Dallas. Reeves also believed that New York had enough talent to return to contender status without a long rebuilding process. He was right, and his leadership helped it happen.

With 38-year-old Phil Simms playing like a quarterback in his prime and Rodney Hampton rushing for 1,000-plus yards for the third straight season, the 1993 Giants took their first three games impressively. Then, after a near win at Buffalo, they whipped division rivals Washington and Philadelphia on back-to-back Sundays. Two losses followed, but the Giants reeled off six straight wins in November and December toward an 11–5 record—the

Coach Dan Reeves discusses a play with quarterback Tommy Maddox during a 1996 preseason game. By then, winning records in Reeves's first two seasons with the Giants had been largely forgotten.

Bitter Cold a Blessing

It was bitterly cold on January 9, 1994, in New Jersey. A perfect day for football, the Giants would insist. New York won its first playoff game since the Super Bowl three years earlier, scoring 14 third-quarter points for a 17–10 NFC wild-card win over Minnesota.

Rodney Hampton rushed 33 times for 161 yards, tying club playoff records for carries and yardage. His 51-yard scoring scamper tied the game and his two-yard burst provided the winning margin. Meanwhile, the Giants defense stifled the Vikings all day. Keith Hamilton recorded two of New York's three sacks, and the Giants held Minnesota to 79 rushing yards.

The weather was warmer in San Francisco the following week, but all the Giants felt was the sting of a 44–3 loss that ended New York's "comeback" season.

best ever for a first-year Giants coach—and a wild-card berth in the playoffs.

Coming off a 6–10 season, it was enough to earn Reeves NFL Coach of the Year honors—not bad for a man who had been dismissed by the Broncos after 1992. Reeves, who won with a high-octane offense in Denver, did it with defense in New York. The Giants looked like the "Big Blue Wrecking Crew" of old at times, allowing a league-low 12.8 points per game.

"It's not me coming in here and all of a sudden they're successful because of me," said a vindicated Reeves after learning of his first Coach of the Year nod. "It's a combination of a lot of people working together to do a job."

Rodney Hampton: Quietly Productive

The first time he ever carried the football in an NFL game, Rodney Hampton broke the run for 89 yards and a touchdown against Buffalo. It was a preseason contest, so it didn't count toward his official statistics, but it served notice that the Giants had added a great weapon when they drafted the University of Georgia junior 24th overall in 1990.

Hampton backed up Ottis Anderson as a rookie, finishing second in rushing and third in receiving on a Super Bowl championship team. Thereafter, though it was anyone's guess as to which Giants quarterback might be starting, fans knew exactly what to expect out of the running back position—strong work by a difficult man to bring down.

Hampton powered for the tough yards between the tackles and could also break the long ones. Starting in his second season, he rushed for more than 1,000 yards in five straight years, topping out at 1,182 in 1995. He made the Pro Bowl in 1992 and '93 and retired in '97 as the franchise career leader with 1,824 carries, 6,897 yards, and 49 rushing touchdowns. Hampton played all of his eight NFL seasons with the Giants.

Hampton was a soft-spoken and unassuming man who was named Giants Alumni Man of the Year in 2008 for his many off-field contributions to camps and charities in New York, Georgia, and his hometown of Houston, Texas. "I have a lot of pride about my career," said Hampton. "I look back and I feel like I did pretty well. I get respect from the fans and I do a lot of things in the New York area. I've been blessed to have played in New York."

Right from his very first carry.

Unceremonious Ouster For Reeves

The Dan Reeves Era in New York started with fireworks and ended with no more than a flicker. After his NFL Coach of the Year campaign returned the team to the playoffs in 1993, the Giants slipped to 9–7 and out of the playoffs in '94. When the bottom dropped out with 5–11 and 6–10 seasons in '95 and '96—years in which Reeves and the front office bickered—Reeves was fired.

Dave Brown (No. 17), New York's quarterback in 1995 and '96, didn't blossom under Reeves.

"When it doesn't work out," Reeves said, "it's not one side that's wrong. It's both sides."

Reeves compiled a 31–33 record in four seasons with the Giants. A veteran of three Super Bowls as the coach of Denver, he returned to the Super Bowl in 1998 after a 14–2 season at the Atlanta Falcons helm.

Running back Rodney Hampton shattered Joe Morris's career Giants rushing record, amassing 6,897 yards on the ground from 1990 to '97.

Gentlemanly Giant: Jim Fassel

Legendary Fullerton College coach Hal Sherbeck vividly recalled the day he started quarterback Jim Fassel for the first time. The coach posted the lineup with the QB position blank and did not tell Fassel until after pregame warmups.

"Thank you, coach," a truly appreciative Fassel told him. "You won't be sorry."

Fassel threw for more than 300 yards and four touchdowns in the game, a 39–7 victory. It was not the last time the polite and humble son of hard-working parents made good on a promise.

Thirty years later, before the 1997 NFL season, Fassel was named head coach of the New York Giants. He led the team to the playoffs three times in seven years, including a 2000 campaign in which he famously predicted a playoff run after back-to-back losses dropped the Giants to 7–4. His players responded by charging all the way to the Super Bowl.

"He was always one who would never run from something," Sherbeck said.

Having served as offensive coordinator for Oakland, Denver, and Arizona, Fassel inherited a Giants team that had gone 11–21 over their previous two years. In his first season, he guided the club to a 10–5–1 mark and NFC East championship despite losing three of his first four games.

Fassel did not attain success by yelling, screaming, or berating his players. "Gentleman Jim," some called him. He chose to wear studious-looking glasses, parted his hair carefully, and demonstrated a propensity for substituting printable words for ones from the more typical, R-rated vocabularies of most coaches—at least when he was in front of public ears and microphones.

Though he didn't know Fassel before becoming a Giant, Michael Barrow said, "After I met him, I could see he was a good family man, a good leader, and that matters to a team. It has to be a family to win, and I could tell Jim was the man to bring that to us."

Fassel's Giants topped the NFC East again in 2000, going 12–4 in the regular season before falling to Baltimore in Super Bowl XXXV. Months later, terrorists attacked the United States, and Fassel went to the scene of Manhattan's Ground Zero to thank rescue workers.

The son of a fireman, Fassel decided then and there to set up a fund to help the families of firemen and policemen who lost their lives in the September 11 attacks. His generosity did not help him keep his job after a 4–12 season in 2003, but by then the Jim Fassel Foundation had raised $500,000. Some might call it making good on a promise.

The July 28 issue of The Giant Insider *got a good look at how Jim Fassel was going to run the Giants from the start.*

Jim Fassel was named NFL Coach of the Year in 1997, his first season at the Giants' helm. He guided the team through the 2003 campaign, on his way to amassing an overall record of 58–53–1.

As SI reported in 1993, John Elway and Dan Reeves feuded. After a few years of Dave Brown, Reeves might have missed Elway.

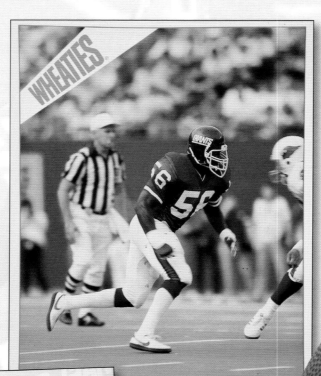

Lawrence Taylor
Linebacker   #56
New York Giants

Pictured on this rare 1987 poster from Wheaties, Lawrence Taylor had 12 sacks and three interceptions that year.

Dave Meggett, shown on this 1993 Topps Fantasports card, was an all-purpose runner and returner for the Giants.

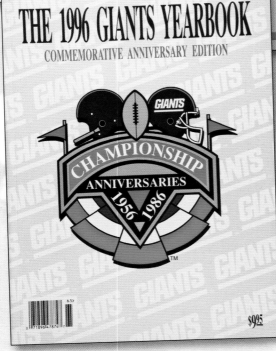

THE 1996 GIANTS YEARBOOK
COMMEMORATIVE ANNIVERSARY EDITION

GIANTS
CHAMPIONSHIP
ANNIVERSARIES
1956 ◆ 1986

$9.95

The 1996 Giants Yearbook celebrated the 10-year anniversary of the 1986 Super Bowl XXI champs and the 40-year anniversary of the 1956 title team.

Phil Simms is shown on this novelty football, produced after a 1991 season that saw him start only four games.

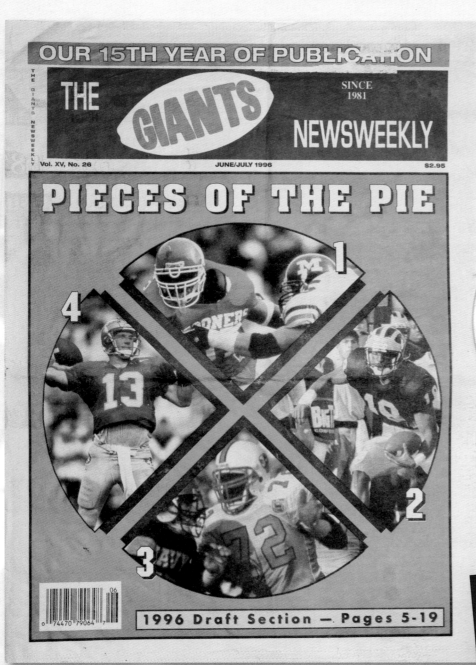

OUR 15TH YEAR OF PUBLICATION

THE GIANTS NEWSWEEKLY

SINCE 1981

Vol. XV, No. 26   JUNE/JULY 1996 $2.95

PIECES OF THE PIE

4

1

3

2

1996 Draft Section — Pages 5-19

In 1997, *Sports Illustrated* ran this striking portrait of a young Frank Gifford in full regalia.

This pin was given out to the lucky attendees who saw the Giants beat the 49ers 16-14.

PLAYOFF RIVALS COLLIDE

1981 1984 1985 1986

SF • GIANTS

10-6   12-5

JAN. 15 1994
Candlestick Park

1993   1990

A Gallery of Unforgettable Portraits

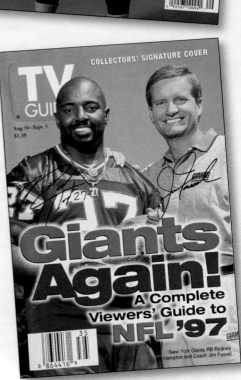

COLLECTORS' SIGNATURE COVER

TV GUIDE
Aug. 30–Sept. 5
$1.39

Giants Again!
A Complete Viewers' Guide to NFL '97

New York Giants RB Rodney Hampton and Coach Jim Fassel

The *Giants Newsweekly* reported on several of the Giants' draft prospects. The team ended up with Amani Toomer (right) and Roman Oben (bottom).

Michael Strahan became a starter in his second season, in 1994. He is shown here on a 2000 Topps card.

Running back Rodney Hampton and coach Jim Fassel were featured on this '97 issue of *TV Guide*.

CHAPTER SIX

Giants of Today

1997—Today

"It's the greatest victory in the history of this franchise, without question. I just want to say to all you Giants fans who have supported us for more than 30 years ... this is for you."

GIANTS CO-OWNER JOHN MARA AFTER SUPER BOWL XLII

Above: *The Super Bowl XLII champion New York Giants, who climbed back on top, signed this helmet.* Right: *If defense wins championships—and it does—the Giants have built their foundation on solid footing. Stopping opposing attacks remains the franchise's top priority.*

Revived Giants Suffer Playoff Shock

As surprising as the Giants' 1997 turnaround was, the way it ended was perhaps even more shocking. The Giants, 10–5–1 in Jim Fassel's first year as head coach, were the NFC East champs—a dramatic turnaround after a 6–10 1996 season.

Not that any Giants fan wants to recall the particulars, but the Minnesota Vikings scored 10 points in the last 90 seconds to stun the Giants in a first-round playoff game at Giants Stadium.

It was a loss that featured sideline bickering and a late collapse by a defense that had been one of the NFL's best that season.

Fassel could push no buttons to spare his team from the heartache of those final 90 seconds. Minnesota receiver Jake Reed somehow snuck behind a "prevent" defense for a 30-yard touchdown that cut a 22–13 Giants lead to 22–20. The Vikings then recovered an onside kick that somehow eluded the sure-handed Chris Calloway, setting up Eddie Murray's game-winning chip-shot field goal that left the Giants reeling as they trudged off the field in a bitter rain.

"We came apart at the wrong time," Giants defensive tackle Keith Hamilton said. "We unraveled. I've never seen anything like it."

Perhaps the most painful aspect of the Giants' sudden collapse was that it followed such a promising resurgence. Because the team was adjusting to a new coach after a dismal '96 season, few would have been alarmed had the Giants missed the playoffs altogether.

Instead, they did something no NFC East team before them had ever done. They went through the regular season unbeaten in divisional play, capping a 7–0–1 record against division rivals with a meaningless 20–7 win over the Cowboys on the final weekend.

Meaningless? In the standings, yes, but not in the minds of the players.

"If you think of all the great Super Bowl teams that have come out of the NFC East," said linebacker Corey Miller, "and you realize none of them got through the division undefeated, that makes us pretty special. In a season when people expected so little from us, to make history is truly satisfying."

Though Fassel's background was as an offensive coordinator, his first New York team won the "Giants' way." That is, with defense. Opponents averaged just 16.6 points per game against New York—third in the NFL. Six of those foes failed to top 10 points against a Giants team that was dominant against passing offenses, notching 54 sacks and intercepting a league-best 27 balls.

Tight end Aaron Pierce holds up the ball as an official signals a touchdown for the Giants, but it was Vikings safety Robert Griffith (No. 24) who celebrated after a wild-card upset at the Meadowlands.

Giants safeties Sam Garnes and Tito Wooten walk dejectedly from the field after watching a 10–5–1 regular season and NFC East title quickly become distant memories in a wild-card loss to the Vikings.

Accorsi: More Than a Manning Man

His coveting and acquisition of quarterback Eli Manning in the 2004 NFL Draft will remain Ernie Accorsi's signature achievement as general manager of the New York Giants. If the measure of a man's success is the legacy he leaves, Accorsi must be judged a winner.

He ran three of the NFL's storied franchises: the Giants, Colts, and Browns. After serving for four years as an assistant to Giants GM George Young, Accorsi took over in 1998 and led four playoff teams in nine seasons. His 2000 team reached Super Bowl XXXV, and Manning's addition led to a Super Bowl title one year after Accorsi stepped down in January 2007.

Accorsi was a member of the front office of the 1970 Super Bowl–winning Baltimore Colts. Also known as the drafter of such QBs as John Elway (Colts) and Bernie Kosar (Browns), Accorsi ran the Giants without concern for making headlines or winning front-office awards. He was a student of the game and its history, a fan of its greats, and a believer in common sense.

A keen eye for quarterbacks had Giants GM Ernie Accorsi (right) sold on luring Eli Manning to New York to give Tom Coughlin (left) a signal-caller around whom the coach could build an offense.

Not every move he made was lauded or panned out (see Ron Dayne), but each was made because Accorsi felt it would help the organization.

"He's one of the most outstanding and talented general managers in the business," said former Browns and Baltimore Ravens owner Art Modell. "I didn't realize how good he was until he left me."

Believing Manning was a championship-level talent, Accorsi traded first-rounder Philip Rivers and three picks to San Diego to land the QB in 2004. Giants fans cheered the move, but some of his colleagues in the front office believed their GM was pinning too much hope on one prospect. Thus far, the deal has paid substantial dividends for the Giants.

For his part, Accorsi never cared much about how his moves were regarded. His legacy was not of interest to him, he said in an e-mail to a *New York Times* reporter shortly before stepping down after the 2006 season, declining personal interviews so as not to distract his team from its postseason quest.

"I don't care what exit polls say. Whatever people think of the job I did will be determined on the field by the players that have played for me over a long period of time. How I feel about my work matters to me and, obviously, what people I respect think."

Accorsi was hired as an NFL consultant and GM advisory committee co-chair in 2008, building on a career in the league that has spanned four decades.

Strahan the Sack Man

The accomplishments speak volumes: two trips to the Super Bowl, the single-season NFL record for sacks, and a Super Bowl championship in the final game of his career. Life in the NFL was good to Michael Strahan, whose gap-toothed smile, candor, and wit have also played well in a budding TV career.

"I'm a lot younger than these guys," the former defensive end said of Terry Bradshaw, Jimmy Johnson, and Howie Long when it was announced in 2008 that Strahan would join the trio on Fox's NFL pregame show. "A lot better looking, too."

Strahan looked great to Giants fans in his No. 92 jersey, making life hell for opposing quarterbacks for 15 seasons. The youngest son of an Army major, he moved to Germany at age 9 and did not play football until his senior year of high school. His 6'5" size, power, and speed made him a natural at shedding blockers and pounding quarterbacks.

After Strahan had an All-America career at Texas Southern, the Giants drafted him in the second round in 1993. He won a starting job in his second season and made the Pro Bowl for the first of seven times in 1997, when he totaled 14 sacks. He broke Mark Gastineau's single-season NFL record with 22½ in 2001, earning the NFL Defensive Player of the Year Award. Strahan again led the league with 18½ in '03.

Strahan went out on top. He recorded nine sacks in his final season while leading the '07 Giants to a Super Bowl championship. When he announced his retirement that offseason, his 141½ career sacks ranked fifth in NFL history.

"Michael is not only one of the great Giants of all time," said former teammate Tiki Barber, "but also one of the great defensive players in NFL history."

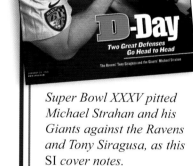

Super Bowl XXXV pitted Michael Strahan and his Giants against the Ravens and Tony Siragusa, as this SI cover notes.

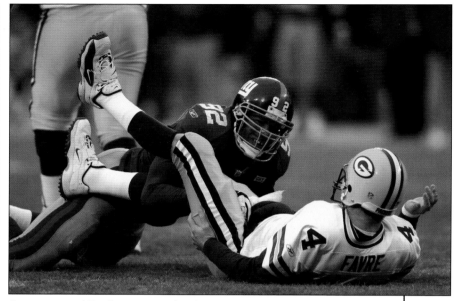

Some accused Packers quarterback Brett Favre of assisting Michael Strahan in his quest for the NFL single-season sack record. Helping hand or not, Strahan was a force along the defensive line.

A Gift from Brett

Needing one sack to break Mark Gastineau's single-season record of 22 in 2001, Michael Strahan chased Brett Favre around Giants Stadium all day in the season finale, laughing with the Packers quarterback each time he came close.

Then, with Green Bay comfortably ahead in the final minutes, the record fell in questionable fashion. Favre simply fell down with Strahan in the vicinity, giving the Giants defensive end 22½ sacks and the mark he was chasing.

Favre called it a "keep pass" that went awry. Others called it a gift. Some called it a joke, or even a mockery of the game.

Favre took heat for it in the media, and Strahan had the legitimacy of his record questioned. No asterisk appears in the books, however. And there's no denying the greatness of Strahan's record-setting season.

Sibling Rivalry

"**J**-E-T-S! Jets! Jets! Jets!" For Giants fans, those syllables can make the blood boil.

It's natural, of course, for the New York Giants and New York Jets to feud, just as baseball's Yankees and Mets and hockey's Rangers and Islanders do. Each wants to be top dog in its town.

The Giants-Jets rivalry, however, has an added fuel source. Because they share not only a city's name, but a home venue, their efforts to be No. 1 are not unlike two brothers competing for their parents' attention.

Largely, it's a rivalry that's contested off the field among fans of both teams, in subway stations and sports bars in the metropolitan area. That's because the teams have met just 11 times in the regular season, with the Giants holding a 7–4 series edge. Ironically, some of the most intense moments in this rivalry took place in an exhibition game.

"I never felt such tension in a locker room or on a bus going over to a stadium, other than maybe a Super Bowl or a big playoff game," Giants co-owner John Mara said of a 1969 preseason game between his NFL club and the defending Super Bowl champion Jets of the rival AFL—the first-ever confrontation between the teams. "It was incredible."

The Giants were fearful of losing some of their longtime fan base to Joe Namath and the AFL newcomers, while the Jets were eager to parlay their Super Bowl title into status as champions in the hearts of New Yorkers. Even though the game didn't count in the standings, 70,874 fans came out to the Yale Bowl in Connecticut to witness the Jets' hard-hitting, 37–14 victory.

It was not the last time the Jets and Giants shared antagonism in an exhibition setting. A 2005 training camp scrimmage between the teams in Albany, New York, produced fisticuffs, shoving matches, and two wild, sideline-clearing skirmishes.

There have also been meaningful regular-season battles between the Giants and Jets. In the 1988 season finale, for instance, a 27–21 Jets victory dropped the Giants to 10–6 and kept them out of the playoffs. And in 2007, the Giants rallied from a 24–14 deficit with 21 unanswered points for a 35–24 win that provided a boost toward their eventual Super Bowl championship.

The rivals have had to work together off the field. They shared a home at Shea Stadium, they currently share Giants Stadium at the Meadowlands, and—together—they are building a new stadium both will call home.

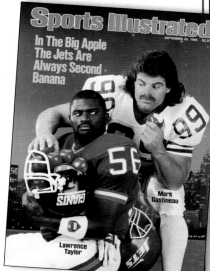

A 1986 Sports Illustrated *cover recognized the Giants' overwhelming popularity in the New York metropolitan area, pointing out that "the Jets are always second banana" in the Big Apple.*

Face paint or not, Giants and Jets fans do not see eye to eye. If the teams squared off against each other more frequently, the potential would exist for one of the most bitter rivalries in sports.

Tiki Takes Off

Don't let their suave looks, NFL success, and comfort in front of the television cameras fool you. The Barber twins, Tiki and Ronde, have been fighters since they entered the world prematurely in Roanoke, Virginia, in 1975. And Tiki's determined legs carried the New York Giants running attack for the better part of a decade.

"Tiki is definitely a foot-forward type of guy, an initiative type of person," Ronde said. "He's always kind of done things first and often a little better.

"If we were doing calculus or something that was difficult, he'd read it one time, have it figured out, and I would be like, 'OK, what did you do there? Help me out!' His commonsense meter runs pretty high, and he never panics with things."

Tiki, born seven minutes after Ronde, was never content to come second thereafter. He screamed so loudly and frequently in his early hours of life that his mother, Geraldine, named him Atiim Kiambu, or "Fiery-Tempered King."

"It was like he was yelling, 'Let me out of here. I don't want to be held down,'" Geraldine recalled. "Ronde was more like, 'OK, I'm going to take advantage of this moment to rest, and then I'm going to come out and kick your butt.' And that's still how they play football."

Tiki, following in the footsteps of Walter Payton, his boyhood hero, played running back, while Ronde starred as a cornerback. Both attended the University of Virginia, where Tiki set a career rushing record. Tiki became the first player in school history to rush for 1,000 yards in back-to-back seasons, tied the school long jump record, and took his studies seriously, earning a commerce degree with a concentration in management information systems.

Drafted in the second round in 1997, Tiki was expected to contribute for New York as a third-down back while players like

Tiki Barber used his charisma (and football ability) to become a popular figure among Giants fans.

Tiki Barber owns the top three single-season rushing totals in Giants history, thanks to his ability to chew up yardage both inside and outside the tackles.

Rodney Hampton, Tyrone Wheatley, Charles Way, and Gary Brown handled the bulk of the rushing duties. By 2000, though, Barber had become the team's top ground weapon, and his emergence as a 1,000-yard rusher that season coincided with the Giants' return to the Super Bowl.

"Some people succeed because they are destined to," Barber said during his rookie year, "but most succeed because they are determined to."

Barber's emergence was just the beginning. He powered past 1,200 rushing yards in five of his six remaining NFL seasons. He used a patient, cerebral approach in which he would wait for lanes to develop while also showing the power to gain tough yards and the speed to break long runs.

He shattered franchise records for career rushing yards (10,449), rushing touchdowns (55), and all-purpose yards (17,359). He also set numerous other Giants rushing marks, including most rushing yards in a game (234), most yards in a season (1,860 in 2005), most 100-yard games (38), and longest run from scrimmage (95 yards).

"If there is such a thing as a 21st-century football player, it is Barber," wrote Mike Freeman in *The New York Times*. "He is part great athlete, with a catlike burst of speed; part intellectual, who designed his own Web site and graduated from the University of Virginia; and part nice guy, who greets almost everyone with a smile. The NFL wishes it had a thousand players like Barber."

Though he left the Giants while still in 1,000-yard form and had some question his loyalty to the only team he played for in his career, Barber wanted to set the record straight while beginning his career as a television personality.

"I'm a Giant, through and through," he said, "and I always will be."

Barber recorded twice as many 100-yard rushing games (38) as any other back in Giants history on his way to a franchise-record 10,449 career yards on the ground.

Barber a Fit in New Role

It's not unusual for a football star to become a TV personality, but usually such fame comes in the broadcast booth. For Tiki Barber—author, intellectual, playwright, family man—a gig on NBC's *Today* show was never much of a stretch.

Barber began laying the groundwork for a television career while still playing for the Giants, shaking hands with the right connections and flashing his personable smile. A student of history and government, Barber has an affinity for politics that played well when he was a correspondent for Fox News Channel's morning show and hosted a Sirius Radio Show, *The National Sweep*.

He joined NBC in 2007, working both for *Today* and *Football Night in America*. If his TV career goes anything like his football one, the best is yet to come.

Tiki's bright smile, outgoing personality, and considerable smarts translate well to his new job on television. His TV work has not been limited to sports, though he did cover the Giants' Super Bowl XLII win in Arizona.

A Guarantee Satisfied

Though he never uttered the word "guarantee," Giants coach Jim Fassel's words following a 2000 loss to Detroit certainly qualified as such. "This team's going to the playoffs," he said, his club having dropped back-to-back games to stumble to 7–4. "I'm going to define where we're going. I'm not afraid to say one thing: We're going to the playoffs."

What Fassel told his players was even more direct. They had been awful on special teams in that 31–21 loss to the Lions, so the coach called a meeting for his coverage and return teams and said he was considering putting offensive and defensive starters in their places, moves that would result in job losses for some.

Whatever threats the coach made—subtle or otherwise—worked. The Giants were much improved on special teams and in virtually every other aspect of the game in winning their last five starts. Their 12–4 record won the NFC East.

"The first 11, 12 games are about setting yourself up," general manager Ernie Accorsi said. "Then you hit the homestretch, and Jim knew exactly when to push the button with this team."

Fassel gathered his captains after making his "guarantee" and told them he needed their support. He forbade his coaching staff from talking with the media and ordered his players not to talk about one another publicly. "He's all over the place making sure everything is done to his liking," said Lomas Brown, one of the captains. "His attitude has been that if he was going down, he wanted to know he was in control of everything."

This pin is a memento from Super Bowl XXXV. Jim Fassel seemingly willed the 2000 Giants to get to this game.

If Fassel's job was on the line following a 7–9 season in 1999, he secured it when the 2000 Giants reeled off those five straight wins and then powered their way to their third Super Bowl berth.

Ron Dixon returned the opening kickoff 97 yards for a touchdown in the first playoff game, and the Giants held Philadelphia to fewer than 200 yards in a 20–10 win. In the NFC championship the following week, Kerry Collins threw five touchdown passes, and New York's defense smothered Minnesota in a 41–0 laugher.

Everyone knew there would be no 40-point outburst in the Super Bowl against Ray Lewis and a Ravens defense some were call-

Ron Dixon races 97 yards on a kickoff return for the Giants' only touchdown in Super Bowl XXXV. Unfortunately for New York, Ravens return man Jermaine Lewis went 84 yards for a matching score on the ensuing kick.

Though the season ended with a one-sided Super Bowl loss, running back Greg Comella and the Giants could celebrate a 2000 season in which they went 12–4 and shut out Minnesota for the NFC title.

ing the best in NFL history. How dominant was the Baltimore D? Dominant enough to carry a team that went five straight games without an offensive touchdown all the way to Super Bowl XXXV in Tampa, Florida. Dominant enough that the Ravens, a wild-card team, were listed as slight favorites over the NFC's No. 1 seed.

The Giants had added the power running of rookie Ron Dayne to their offensive arsenal in 2000, but it was the emergence of Tiki Barber that gave the team its legs. Barber ran for 1,006 yards—his first 1,000-yard season—and Dayne added 770 for a team that also relied on its defense.

None of it mattered much once the Backstreet Boys put the finishing touches on the national anthem. Baltimore's defense overwhelmed New York from the start. The Ravens raced to a 17–0 lead, their second touchdown coming on an interception return by Duane Starks. The only points the Giants could muster came on Dixon's 97-yard kickoff return. Baltimore even had an answer for that, with Jermaine Lewis running back the ensuing kick 84 yards for a matching score.

The final was 34–7. The Ravens became the third team in history to shut out the opposing offense in a Super Bowl game.

A Giants win, in all likelihood, would have vaulted Fassel's guarantee into the stratosphere of Joe Namath's Super Bowl III guarantee. As it was, postgame chatter centered largely on whether the Ravens defense—the only group ever to yield fewer than 1,000 rushing yards and 180 points (165) over a 16-game season—could be called the best in NFL history.

"Other than the kickoff return, against our defense, it was a goose egg," Ravens defensive end Michael McCrary noted. "A goose egg in the Super Bowl speaks for itself."

"We talked all week and backed up what we said. We're the best defense ever to play the game straight out," defensive tackle Tony Siragusa added. "We *are* the best."

Fans in New York react to the television screen as they watch a Baltimore interception in the first half of Super Bowl XXXV in Tampa, Florida. The Giants fell 34–7.

GIANTS GALLERY

This pin was issued in 1999, when the Giants franchise marked 75 years.

This 1997 pennant cheers the Giants' NFC East title, though they were on their way to a devastating playoff loss.

COLLINS

NEW YORK GIANTS
OFFICIAL INFORMATION GUIDE

2000

$7.00

Sam Garnes and Jessie Armstead, shown on these 2000 Topps cards, keyed the Giants defense. Armstead was an All-Pro five times, including 2000, while Garnes started as a rookie that year.

Kerry Collins got his own bobblehead after becoming a New York fan favorite. He led the 2000 Giants to Super Bowl XXXV against the Ravens.

"Team" seems to be the theme of this 2000 Giants media guide. The Giants improved to 12-4 that year from a 7-9 record in 1999.

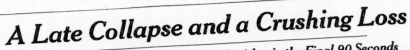

The New York Times
Sports Sunday

Sunday, December 28, 1997

L+   Section 8

A Late Collapse and a Crushing Loss

Giants' 9-Point Lead Over the Vikings Vanishes in the Final 90 Seconds

A Big-Play Afternoon

Fumbles, interceptions, defensive stops and an onside kick all made for an eventful first-round playoff game. Here is the rundown of big plays.

1ST QTR

2:30 Goal-Line Stop — After 2d turnover, they stop Giants at 4-yd. line to keep damage to field goal.

7:34 Takeaway I — Fumble is recovered at Viking 23-yd. line. Result: FG

6:35 Takeaway II — Fumble is recovered at Viking 46-yd. line. Result: FG

SCORE 0   6

2D QTR

3:11 Takeaway — Toomer fumbles away punt return at Giant 27. Result: FG

13:32 Reception — 37-yd. pass to Patten to Viking 2. Result: TD

6:33 Interception — Sehorn returns it 36 yds. to Viking 47. Result: FG

0:15, FG

SCORE 3   19

3D QTR

10:31 Turnover — Barber fumbles, recovered by Vikings at Giant 4. Result: TD

3:35 Disaster Averted — Recovers own fumble for 1st down. Result: FG (in 4th Qtr.)

3:49 Bad Punt — Maynard punts only 14 yds. to Viking 40.

SCORE 10   19

4TH QTR

1:38 Unlikely Flash — 30-yd TD pass to Reed is followed by successful onside kick. Vikings go 56 yds. on 7 plays for game-winning field goal.

12:43 Conversion — 18-yd. pass to Patten on 3d and 9 to keep drive alive. Result: FG

FINAL SCORE 23   22

Barton Silverman/The New York Times

The Vikings celebrated after recovering an onside kick that set up their game-winning field goal. "I should have had it," said the Giants' Chris Calloway, who could not corral the kickoff.

Sam Garnes and Tito Wooten took a slow, sad walk off the field after the Giants let a playoff victory slip away in the final 90 seconds yesterday. Wooten missed the final few plays with an injury.

By BILL PENNINGTON

EAST RUTHERFORD, N.J., Dec. 27 — With two minutes to play, through a driving rain and beneath darkening skies, the Giants still saw it all the way to Green Bay.

With a victory, that would be their second-round playoff destination, and victory was all the Giants could see in their future as they watched the game against the Minnesota Vikings unfolding before them.

And then the sky collapsed. The Giants saw that a season of magical turnarounds had limits. Their future held only a trip home.

In a dizzying succession of misplays, ill-timed bounces and penalties in the final 90 seconds, the Giants today lost a 9-point lead and a wild-card playoff game to the Vikings, 23-22, at Giants Stadium.

It was a stunning reversal of a game the Giants had controlled for most of the afternoon. The Vikings scored a touchdown with 1 minutes 30 seconds to play, recovered the ensuing onside kickoff, then used a pass interference penalty on Giants cornerback Phillippi Sparks to set up Eddie Murray's game-winning 24-yard field goal with 10 seconds left in the game.

Just like that the Giants, who had led by 16 points at halftime and who were looking forward to a second-round game with the defending Super Bowl champion Green Bay Packers, were out of the play... Giants suffered their most her... since the 1989 season, wher... ended with the Los Angeles R... son's overtime touchdown...

The outcome stagg... their locker room wor... opportunities and sr... second half. The G...

VIKINGS	23	
GIANTS	22	

NFL PLAYOFFS ROUND 1

MIXING IT UP IN THE MEADOWLANDS
Giants' defense ends up distracted by on-field feuding. Araton, Page 3.
Scrappy Vikings scuffle with Giants in a brawl at halftime. Page 2.

DOING A DANCE IN DENVER
Broncos 42, Jaguars 17 Page 4.

The 1997 playoff loss to the Vikings, in which the Giants allowed ten points in the final 90 seconds, was a "crushing loss," according to *The New York Times*.

These Giants and Ravens pins were souvenirs of Super Bowl XXXV; the Giants pin is not as valuable a collectible today.

This football was signed by the first five Giants backs to have gained 1,000 yards in a season: Ron Johnson, Joe Morris, Ottis Anderson, Rodney Hampton, and Tiki Barber.

Collins Calls Big Audible

Quarterback Kerry Collins has played for five NFL teams, but the biggest audible of his career was his swapping of partying for the game. Fortunately for the Giants, it was a decision the Penn State product made shortly after signing with New York in 1999.

Collins said in '99 that since he had been in the NFL, only four years at that point, "I had never not drank and not partied and really dedicated myself and life to the game." The former first-round pick of the Carolina Panthers said that he changed his hard-partying ways because he had talent, and "I think that a wasted talent is the biggest crime you can have. I made that decision, and I stuck with it."

Collins had been arrested for driving while impaired four months before joining the Giants. Through an NFL program, he checked himself into rehab in Kansas and straightened out his priorities.

"Once I met with Kerry," said Giants general manager Ernie Accorsi, "I immediately trusted him and liked him. And I knew he was serious."

Though some wrote Collins off before he ever took a snap in New York, his first full season with the Giants was the best of his career. He completed nearly 59 percent of his passes in 2000, throwing for 22 scores and leading the Giants to a 12–4 record and a Super Bowl appearance.

"Kerry Collins took the New York Giants to the Super Bowl," said Jim Fassel, coach of those 2000 Giants. "But that's not the success story here. The success story is Kerry Collins himself."

Collins threw 19 touchdown passes in each of the next two seasons, topping 4,000 passing yards for the first time in 2002. The best Giants quarterback between Phil Simms and Eli Manning, Collins threw 81 scoring strikes in five seasons with New York. That total is almost double his total for any other team. He threw 41 while directing Oakland's pass-heavy attack in 2004 and '05.

Collins signed with Tennessee in 2006, and in '08 he joined Brett Favre and Payton Manning as the only active quarterbacks to reach 35,000 career passing yards while helping the Titans

Kerry Collins completed more passes in a Giants uniform than any quarterback not named Phil Simms. Collins still holds several club passing marks.

claim the AFC South title. Collins has also served as a mentor to Titans quarterback Vince Young, having learned plenty of lessons—the hard way—in his own younger days.

"I can definitely be a good resource for him," Collins said. "I certainly had my struggles."

Targets for Praise, Criticism

One made four Pro Bowls and countless headlines as a brash and bold Giants pass catcher. The other has never been to a single Pro Bowl, though he stands as the most productive receiver in franchise history.

Jeremy Shockey and Amani Toomer couldn't be more different. But they have at least one thing in common: a place among the elite targets in New York Giants aerial history.

Toomer, a 13-year veteran, is the Giants' career leader in receptions, receiving yards, and touchdown grabs. Having played on the 2000 runner-up and the 2007 Super Bowl championship teams, this second-round 1996 pick out of Michigan is also tops in club history in virtually every playoff receiving category.

A consummate professional, Toomer has gone about his business as quietly as is possible for a record-setting athlete in New York. If he's been something of a locker room prankster along the way—and he has—his high jinks have never been the kind to land him in trouble or provide locker room bulletin-board material for the opposition.

"I just do my job and figure out where I kind of fit in," said Toomer, who produced five consecutive 1,000-yard receiving seasons between 1999 and 2003. "Why have I not gotten into trouble? I didn't think it was that hard to not get in trouble."

In 13 years, from 1996 to 2008, Amani Toomer became the Giants' career leader in receptions, receiving yards, and touchdown grabs.

Toomer's teammate for six seasons, Shockey arrived from the University of Miami in 2002 with a brash and bold personality, along with big-play ability that few tight ends can match. His 74 catches for 894 yards in his debut season earned him All-Pro status and some Rookie of the Year consideration.

Although he offended some coaches, teammates, fans, and opponents with his outspoken style, Shockey grabbed at least six touchdown passes in three straight seasons. A tight end with receiver skills, he was always open, and he would be the first to tell you about it—sometimes in unprintable terms.

Wrote Ralph Vacchiano in the *New York Daily News,* "It's hard to pinpoint the exact moment when Shockey turned from the second coming of Mark Bavaro into a carnival sideshow—you know, the kind that make you cringe and say 'I can't watch this,' just before you sneak a peek...."

"I was relieved," Shockey said after being traded to the Saints before the 2008 season. "I wasn't surprised.... If I had gone back to the Giants, no matter what, it would have been a circus."

Tight end Jeremy Shockey backed up his bravado with exceptional pass-catching skills. He caught at least one pass in each of the 83 games he played for the Giants from 2002 to 2007.

NFL to Giants: "Sorry"

Sorry, Giants.

It's safe to say New York fans still have not accepted the NFL's apology for botching a call that ended the Giants' one-game stay in the 2002 playoffs. Nor will they ever, in all likelihood.

New York botched a snap on a potential game-winning field goal on the final play of a 39–38 loss at San Francisco. Holder Matt Allen picked up the ball and threw a pass to guard Rich Seubert, who before the game had reported as an eligible receiver on all placekicks.

San Francisco's Chike Okeafor clearly interfered with Seubert on the play, but the only flags that flew charged the Giants with having an ineligible receiver downfield. That call, on a different Giants player, was correct. However, an interference call on the 49ers would have resulted in offsetting penalties and given New York one more chance at a winning 41-yard kick.

Mike Pereira, the NFL's director of officials, admitted the error and apologized to the Giants the following day. "It doesn't do us a damn bit of good," noted coach Jim Fassel.

The same could not be said for late-night talk show hosts, who should have thanked the NFL for the material. David Letterman aired the "Top Ten NFL Referee Explanations" for the blown call, including "Not actually a referee, I'm just a guy who works at Foot Locker" and "It's all part of God's plan, and God doesn't like the Giants."

If the aftermath of the game was "Sorry, Giants," their collapse from a 38–14 lead was simply a matter of them being sorry Giants. At the time, the 24-point meltdown—the result of a second half of senseless penalties, dropped passes, and poor tackling—was the second-largest blown lead in NFL playoff history, trailing only the Houston Oilers' infamous 32-point collapse against Buffalo ten years earlier. "It just got away from us," Fassel said. "It was tragic."

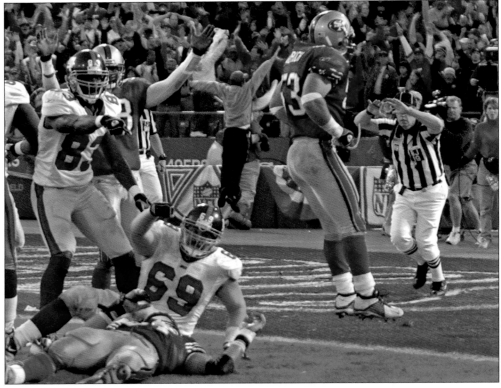

Giants players, including intended "receiver" Rich Seubert (69), point to San Francisco's Chike Okeafor after the final play of the 49ers' 39–38 win over New York. NFL officials later admitted that pass interference should have been called on Okeafor.

The controversial loss ended a season in which the Giants charged into the playoffs at 10–6 by winning their last four games. They rebounded from a dreary 7–9 campaign in 2001, thanks to the running of Tiki Barber (1,387 rushing yards), the arm of Kerry Collins (a career-best 61.5 percent completion rate and 4,073 passing yards), and a defense that was one of just three in the NFL to limit opponents to fewer than 300 points for the season.

While sorry play and stupid penalties made the 49ers game closer than it should have been, the fact is that New York would have preferred to have its fate decided according to the rules.

Giants Honor Wellington Mara

Some pro sports owners are considered meddlers. Others are in it for the investment rewards. Precious few have virtually universal respect from everyone involved in their organization and league, and fewer still maintain that respect for more than a half-century in their business. But there is one name that stands clear: Wellington Timothy Mara.

When Mara died at age 89 on October 25, 2005, the Giants—from top management to the maintenance workers—felt they'd lost their glue. The NFL lost an ambassador and an innovator. Pro sports lost an icon.

From the time he served as a 9-year-old ballboy for the team his father purchased to the day he died 80 years later, Mara gave everything he had to the Giants. Once you were a Giant, he believed, you were a Giant for life.

Mara rewarded his players and coaches, helped former players and their families when he learned of illnesses or setbacks, and frequently found scouting or advisory jobs for former Giants who needed work and could help the team. He was the kind of man who was perfectly comfortable being called "Well" or "Duke," but also the kind of man who'd earned such respect that even those who knew him well sometimes called him Mr. Mara.

"My wife said it best when we talked about Mr. Mara and the fact that he was very ill," said quarterback Phil Simms. "She said, 'There are so few icons left.' That's what Mr. Mara was.

"He was from an era where there were certain men who handled themselves differently than everybody else. I don't know if you can be that person anymore in this day and age. I don't know if society would let you be like him."

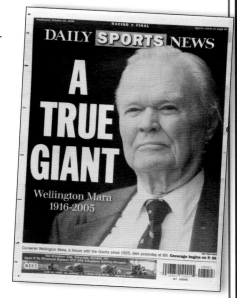

A football man first and foremost, Wellington Mara was truly an icon among Giants fans.

Though the Giants lost an owner, they were not about to lose a football game dedicated to him. After Kate Mara sang the national anthem to honor her late grandfather in the Giants' first game since his death, with 35 other grandchildren behind her, New York pounded the Washington Redskins 36–0 at Giants Stadium.

They did it in traditional Giants style, just as Mara would have wished. Tiki Barber rushed for a career-high 206 yards, and the defense threw a wall in front of everything Washington tried. New York's players wore "WTM" patches on their jerseys.

"I know that my grandfather would be very happy right now," said another of those grandchildren, an emotional 22-year-old Tim McDonnell. "It really was a perfect game."

Kate Mara, granddaughter of the late Wellington Mara, sings the national anthem before the Giants' 36–0 shutout of the Washington Redskins on October 30, 2005.

GIANTS GALLERY

This team photo was a promotional item at Giants Stadium in 2005, when the team went 11-5 and won the NFC East.

2005 NEW YORK GIANTS

ROW 5- CHARLES WAY-DIR. OF PLAYER DEVELOPMENT; TIM SLAMAN-ASST. EQUIPMENT MANAGER; 82-VISANTHE SHIANCOE-TE; 84-TIM CARTER-WR; 85-DAVID TYREE-WR; 86-JAMAAR TAYLOR-WR; 87-WILLIE PONDER-WR; 88-SEAN BERTON-TE; 90-RYAN KUEHL-LS; 91-JUSTIN TUCK-DE; STEVE KENNELLY-ASST. ATHLETIC TRAINER; BYRON HANSEN-ASST. ATHLETIC TRAINER.

ROW6- ED WAGNER, JR-EQUIPMENT/LOCKER ROOM MANAGER; JOE SKIBA-ASST. EQUIPMENT MANAGER; ED SKIBA-ASST. EQUIPMENT MANAGER; 92-MICHAEL STRAHAN-DE; 93-ERIC MOORE-DE; 94-WILLIAM JOSEPH-DT; 95-ADRIAN AWASOM-DE; 97-KENDERICK ALLEN-DT; 98-FRED ROBBINS-DT; 99-DAMANE DUCKETT-DT; ED TRIGGS- ASST. VIDEO DIRECTOR; CARMEN PIZZANO-ASST. VIDEO DIRECTOR; DAVE MALTESE-VIDEO DIRECTOR.

ROW 7- ANDY BARNETT-ASST. STRENGTH & CONDITIONING; JOHN DEFILIPPO-OFFENSIVE QUALITY CONTROL; DAVE DEGUGLIELMO-ASST. OFFENSIVE LINE; PAT FLAHERTY-OFFENSIVE LINE; KEVIN GILBRIDE-QUARTERBACKS; JERALD INGRAM-RUNNING BACKS; MICHAEL POPE-TIGHT ENDS; JOHN HUFNAGEL-OFFENSIVE COORDINATOR; TIM LEWIS-DEFENSIVE COORDINATOR; DAVID MERRITT-DEFENSIVE ASSISTANT; RON MILUS-SECONDARY; MIKE PRIEFER-ASST. SPECIAL TEAMS; BILL SHERIDAN-LINEBACKERS; MIKE SULLIVAN-WIDE RECEIVERS; MIKE SWEATMAN-SPECIAL TEAMS COORDINATOR; MIKE WAUFLE-DEFENSIVE LINE; JERRY PALMIERI-STRENGTH & CONDITIONING.

PHOTO BY JERRY PINKUS & EVAN PINKUS

Visit the Dunkin' Donuts Fan Poll on www.giants.com and ente... ...away trip (D...

2 lbs. of Coffee for $10.99 + appl. tax
At Participating Metro New York Area Stores. Offer Expires December 26, 2005. N... ...ecessary.

This pin celebrates the Giants playing the Houston Texans (an expansion franchise) in their first-ever game in 2002.

AFC — NFC HALL OF FAME GAME AUGUST 5, 2002

TV CABLEVISION EDITION GUIDE

SPECIAL PREVIEW

WIN A TRIP TO THE BIG GAME IN JANUARY! SEE INSIDE

AUG. 28-SEPT. 3 $1.79

Giants WR Amani Toomer

RISIN' GIANTS!

THE COMPLETE VIEWER'S GUIDE TO NFL '99

COLLECTOR'S SIGNATURE COVER

0 864415 2 35

Amani Toomer graces the cover of this *TV Guide* in 1999, when he moved into a starting role and had his first 1,000-yard receiving season.

NEW YORK GIANTS 2000 NFC CHAMPIONS

SUPER BOWL XXXV

This pennant commemorates the 2000 NFC title. The G-Men beat Minnesota 41-0 in the title game.

Vol. 6, No. 20
January 6, 2002

THE GIANT INSIDER

TGI adds
Ottis Anderson
to lineup

The
Will
to win

Candid
Conversation:
STs Coach
Van Appen

Rookie corner impressive

Get Giants news all y...

Will Allen
and his
outstanding
2001 rookie
season were
acclaimed
on this cover
of *The Giant
Insider.*

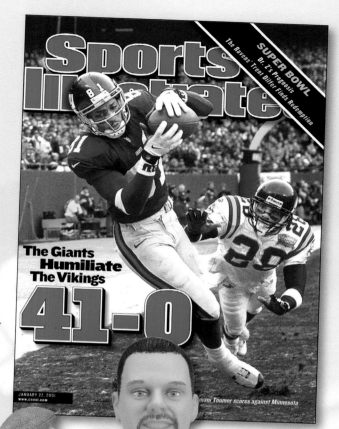

Sports Illustrated

SUPER BOWL
Dr. Z's Prognosis
The Ravens' Trent Dilfer Finds Redemption

The Giants
Humiliate
The Vikings
41-0

JANUARY 22, 2001
www.cnnsi.com

...mani Toomer scores against Minnesota

Sports Illustrated
found the Giants'
manhandling of the
Vikings cover-worthy
in 2001.

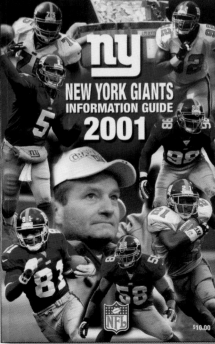

ny
NEW YORK GIANTS
INFORMATION GUIDE
2001

$10.00

The 2001
team media
guide observed
the 2000 NFC
champs.

For two seasons, the
Collins-to-Shockey
combination
excited New York
fans, and the two
players even shared
a bobblehead.

COLLINS

SHOCKEY

Bleeding Red, White, and Giants Blue

Eddie Friend has been in the middle of tailgating Giants fans for years. The manager of Manny's HD, a popular Giants-oriented restaurant and gathering spot one mile from the Meadowlands in Moonachie, New Jersey, Friend describes those fans matter-of-factly.

"Very dedicated," Friend said. "Also very vocal, when the team is winning. A little subdued when they're not—unlike Philadelphia fans, who are running their mouths all the time. And very knowledgeable. Giants fans are very knowledgeable, not just about their team, but about the whole league and sports in general. They're big sports fans. They know their stuff."

If you think Friend is biased about the Giants because he's a supporter, think again. He's a Cowboys fan.

Whether celebrating a Super Bowl, a victory, or merely a first down, Giants fans are known as some of the most passionate in the National Football League.

"That's made for some interesting Sundays," he chuckled.

Most Sundays, Friend revels in the popularity of the Giants, as it's made Manny's a place to be each fall. For $40 per person, patrons can park their cars at the restaurant, enjoy a pregame buffet, and ride a shuttle to and from Giants Stadium for the game. Between 50 and 100 people generally take advantage of the offer, he said, and scores of others stick around and watch the game on the high-definition televisions that dominate the decor. "It gets really loud," Friend said.

Bill Parcells had his own table at Manny's, where he could be seen plotting defensive schemes over solo lunches. Another former Giants coach, Jim Fassel, was also a regular. Signed photos of Harry Carson, Frank Sinatra, Roger Staubach, and George Carlin—to name a few—line the walls of a restaurant that's been a hangout for Giants fanatics for some 40 years.

Of course, Manny's is one of literally thousands of restaurants and watering holes in the New York metro area that qualify as hot

New York fans care about their sports, and those who follow the Giants have been called some of the most knowledgeable—and loudest—in the business.

In 2008, officials decided to open Meadowlands parking lots just five hours before kickoff, instead of seven, in an effort to crack down on rowdy behavior at games. Suffice it to say that loyal Giants fans take full advantage of whatever time they've allotted to game day—whether that time is spent in a parking lot, restaurant, sports bar, or living room.

Such loyalty dates way back, said Joe Healy, a fan who began attending Giants games in the mid-1950s—to when there was a vastly different dress code in the stands.

Attending a New York Giants game was a special event, Healy said. "You wore a jacket and tie. As the old guard started dying off, you see a difference in the fans."

Giants Stadium is a place where people from different walks of life come together. Fans from New Jersey and New York set their state-line rivalry

Several hours before a game, the Giants Stadium parking lots fill with fans who break out their barbecue grills and coolers for some of the NFL's best tailgating.

spots for Giants fans. The top spot on game days is the large parking lot at the Meadowlands, where some of the best tailgating in the NFL takes place.

Giants fans of all ages, shapes, and sizes fire up grills, throw footballs, drain their favorite beverages, and discuss their team's chances. It's a hearty bunch, braving temperatures that can be among the most bitter in the league.

aside for several hours on Sundays and unite for one common cause—a Giants victory.

"They're the New York Giants," Friend said, "but they're every bit as much New Jersey's team. You see people from Poughkeepsie, Long Island, Boston . . . you name it. They all come here and get loud. They're Giants fans. That's all that really matters."

Manning Becomes "The Man"

Pedigree was never a question surrounding Eli Manning. The son of Mississippi legend and longtime Saints quarterback Archie Manning and the younger brother of two-time NFL MVP Peyton Manning arrived in New York in 2004 with the bloodlines to be a star.

The question, primarily, was leadership. Could this soft-spoken young man from the Bayou—with his aw-shucks approach—handle the pressure of the big city, the tough New York media, and the task of reviving a Giants team that had stumbled to a 4–12 record the year before his arrival?

The answer: Yes.

It didn't happen right away. Eli—whose strong arm and poise turned Ole Miss from an SEC also-ran into a Cotton Bowl champion during his record-setting college career—struggled as a rookie. He replaced veteran Kurt Warner midway through 2004, won just one of his seven starts, and had fans wondering whether GM Ernie Accorsi had made a huge mistake in sending Philip Rivers and three other draft picks to San Diego for Manning's services.

Predictably, Manning stayed stoic amid the criticism. His teammates began to rally around him late in his rookie season, and he engineered a late touchdown drive to beat the rival Cowboys for his first victory, in the season finale. The quarterback entered 2005 as the starter, and he engineered a stunning turn-around that netted an NFC East title and 11–5 record.

He did it rather quietly, getting the ball in the right hands frequently enough to help the Giants finish third in the NFL in scoring. Manning didn't snag loads of individual accolades, but he didn't care.

Manning's leadership became evident to the sporting world in 2007, when he won the Super Bowl MVP Award, joining his brother Peyton, who won the honor in 2006. Eli led the Giants to a 10–6 record during a regular season, then directed the G-Men to three consecutive road victories for a trip to the Super Bowl.

Against the heavily favored and previously undefeated Patriots in Super Bowl XLII, he steered the Giants to two fourth-quarter touchdowns, throwing the game-winning scoring pass to Plaxico Burress in the final minute. Manning was 9-of-14 for 152 yards in the final frame.

The aw-shucks demeanor is still there, but so is proven leadership from a QB who threw 20 or more TD passes each season from 2005 to '08.

When the Giants swapped picks with the Chargers in 2004 to acquire top draft choice Eli Manning, no one was bold enough to predict he would produce a Super Bowl title in his fourth season.

From his position as the No. 1 overall pick in 2004, quarterback Eli Manning quickly climbed the charts among the most accomplished passers and field generals in New York Giants history.

Coughlin: Survivor, Champion

The New York Times, in 2008, referred to Tom Coughlin as "Santa Claus in a headset." It's further evidence of a stunning transformation for the New York Giants head coach, who early in his Giants tenure more resembled the lead character from *How The Grinch Stole Christmas!*

A disciple of the hard-driving Bill Parcells, Coughlin was hired by the Giants in 2004 to rescue a team that had won just four games the previous season. He had won two division titles in eight seasons with Jacksonville, but some considered his strict rules, grueling practices, and no-nonsense style to be better suited for the college game than the NFL.

His every tactic heated by the magnifying glass of the New York media, Coughlin weathered numerous barbs in his first three seasons—a roller-coaster ride that included 6–10 and 8–8 marks surrounding a 2005 division title campaign. Finally, in 2007, "Colonel Coughlin" made a few subtle changes and was embraced as a kinder and gentler boss. Winning a Super Bowl championship can endear you to people.

Even a "kinder, gentler" Tom Coughlin ranks among the most demanding and passionate head coaches in the NFL. It's a combination that has worked well for the Giants.

Behind the Grimace

Some folks in Jacksonville and, yes, even Boston were cheering for Tom Coughlin when his Giants beat the New England Patriots in Super Bowl XLII. That's because in the cities where his demanding approach has made an impact on the field, his heart has made a difference away from it, too.

Most notably, Coughlin founded the Jay Fund in 1996 while coaching the Jaguars. Named in honor of Jay McGillis, a former Boston College player who developed leukemia and died during Coughlin's tenure there, the foundation has not only raised money to fight cancer—it has become a passion for Coughlin.

"I know you see this wild, angry guy on television," says Helena Richards, a clinical social worker in Jacksonville. "I know him as a different guy. He'll do anything to help these families."

Without question, Coughlin toned down the "tough love" and put more trust in his players. It was not a change in philosophy as much as a change in the messenger. Rather than jump on Giants who were not performing at peak level, Coughlin created a "players leadership council" of veterans who would meet with the coach and hold their teammates accountable.

By playoff time, Coughlin had a 10–6 wild-card team believing it could win a Super Bowl. Three road wins and a stunning Super Bowl upset of New England later, his altered approach had produced that very result.

"These guys played with great heart," Coughlin said. "They're tough-minded. They never say die. They just keep coming."

A reflection, some might say, of their coach.

Unfathomable Tops Unbeaten

Just think of the Yankees-Red Sox or the Knicks-Celtics or the Rangers-Bruins. In the heated history of the New York-Boston sports rivalry over the last century, the 2007 NFL season belongs at or near the top of any New Yorker's list.

The 2007 New England Patriots were an immovable force and an indestructible object all rolled into one juggernaut of a football dynasty. Their quarterback, Tom Brady, could dissect any defense with pinpoint passing. Their coach, Bill Belichick, could draw up a defense to stop any high-powered attack. Their players, to a man, bought into a principle that team success trumps individual accomplishment, and the result was the first 16–0 regular season in history.

Their Super Bowl XLII opponent, surprisingly enough, was a New York Giants squad that had lost its first two games of the 2007 season before rallying to finish a relatively modest 10–6. The Giants were the No. 5 seed in the NFC playoffs, and they became the first team in conference history to advance to the Super Bowl by winning three straight postseason road games.

Of course, conventional wisdom held that whichever NFC team advanced—even those stronger than the Giants—would be little more than the final speed bump on the Patriots' road to a fourth Super Bowl championship in seven years. Still, it was an opportunity the underdog Giants craved, and one they seized impressively.

Kicker Lawrence Tynes watches the winning 47-yard field goal split the uprights at Lambeau Field as the Giants defeat the Packers 23–20 in overtime in the NFC title game.

Michael Strahan (right) and the Giants defense made life miserable for Tom Brady and the Patriots in Super Bowl XLII, ruining New England's bid for a perfect season.

New York finished 7–1 on the road and just 3–5 at Giants Stadium in 2007, an anomaly no one could adequately explain but one that had the Giants confident entering the playoffs with a "road warrior" mentality.

Defensive end Justin Tuck credited the success to "leadership. Whenever you can go into a hostile environment, fight all the adversity we did . . . I think it's that leadership. It starts with the coaches and goes right down to the veterans and it also goes down to the young guys and rookies, being able to understand the importance of what guys are telling them about playing on the road."

Coach Tom Coughlin gave his team a simple message before its NFC wild card game at Tampa Bay. "Let's keep playing," he instructed.

The Giants did just that. Their 24–14 wild card win against the Buccaneers snapped a four-game postseason losing streak that had begun in Super Bowl XXXV at Tampa's Raymond James Stadium. The week after the wild-card win, New York avenged its only road loss of the season with a 21–17 upset of the top-seeded Cowboys, when R. W. McQuarters intercepted Tony Romo's pass in the end zone with nine seconds remaining.

As a reward, New York earned a trip to the NFC Championship Game in Green Bay to play in what turned out to be the coldest game in Giants history. The temperature was –1 degree Fahrenheit at kickoff, the third-coldest in NFL history. Factor in a 12-mile-per-hour wind, and the wind chill was –23 degrees Fahrenheit.

Green Bay quarterback Brett Favre, usually unbeatable in such bone-chilling conditions, came up short against New York QB Eli Manning (21-for-40 for 251 yards) on this night. In fact, Favre's final pass in a Packers uniform was intercepted by Corey Webster in overtime, setting up Lawrence Tynes's 47-yard, game-winning field goal.

The Giants' improbable road trip had taken them to Glendale, Arizona, where they were nearly a two-touchdown underdog

The Patriots were chasing perfection, but it was Michael Strahan's Giants who left Arizona with a championship after one of the biggest upsets in Super Bowl history.

against a Patriots team that had shown no significant weaknesses in winning 18 consecutive games, including a 38–35 win at Giants Stadium in the regular-season finale.

Boston, it seemed, was destined to get the better of New York once again.

But a funny thing happened to the Patriots on their way to being coronated as the greatest team in pro football history. A Giants team galvanized by its road success, its carefree young quarterback, its opportunistic defense, and its hard-hitting, play-till-the-final-whistle approach pulled off one of the greatest upsets in Super Bowl history: Giants 17, Patriots 14.

The surprise champs, the Giants were only able to capture the title as a team.

"Nobody's Perfect," read several newspapers' headlines the following morning, as the general slant fell on the Patriots' failure to uphold their end of the bargain. In the Giants' camp, however, the focus was squarely on one of the most amazing triumphs in New York sports history.

"It's the greatest victory in the history of this franchise, without question," Giants co-owner John Mara exulted in a hoarse

One of the greatest, and most important, grabs in Super Bowl history saw New York's David Tyree secure the ball against his helmet and retain control for a critical first down during the Giants' winning drive in Super Bowl XLII.

voice after the game. "I just want to say to all you Giants fans who have supported us for more than 30 years at Giants Stadium, for all those years in Yankee Stadium, and some of you even back to the Polo Grounds, this is for you."

Manning, fulfilling the promise the franchise had placed in him three years earlier, completed 19 of 34 passes for 255 yards and two fourth-quarter touchdowns to earn Super Bowl MVP honors. He connected with Plaxico Burress on a 13-yard fade pattern with 35 seconds remaining to clinch David's win over Goliath.

"There's something about this team," Manning said. "The way we win games, and performed in the playoffs in the stretch. We had total confidence in ourselves. The players believed in each other."

Hang around in the Super Bowl, the Giants strategized, and anything could happen. They set the tone on the game's opening drive, milking almost ten minutes off the clock while marching 63 yards for a field goal and the early lead.

If keeping Brady and the Patriots' precise offense off the field was the Giants' top strategy, disrupting that offense with an aggressive defensive game plan was a close second. They sacked Brady five times and frustrated the Patriots time and again. Tuck's second sack forced a fumble late in the second quarter and kept New England from padding a 7–3 lead entering the break— a margin that held up through a scoreless third frame.

For throwing two fourth-quarter touchdown passes and engineering one of the most memorable two-minute drives in championship history, Eli Manning was named Super Bowl MVP.

The final quarter featured three lead changes—a first in Super Bowl history. Manning's five-yard touchdown pass capped an 80-yard drive and gave the Giants a 10–7 edge. However, Brady took advantage of Webster's slip and found Randy Moss for a touchdown that put New England on top with 2:42 on the clock.

"That's a position you want to be in," Manning said of his opportunity to direct an 83-yard drive in those final minutes. "You can't write a better script. There were so many big plays on that drive."

The biggest play was a 32-yard Manning-to-David Tyree toss on third down that Tyree caught one-handed against his helmet after the Patriots came oh-so-close to making a game-deciding sack. It gave the Giants the first down they needed to set up Manning's game-winning pass to Burress, which set off a Giants celebration as Patriots players held their heads in their hands, looked to the heavens, or simply stood silently, awed at their fate after a record-setting season.

"We played them five weeks ago and it was a three-point game," Brady said. "And they made enough changes and really eliminated what we did offensively."

"Every team is beatable," Coughlin said after his Giants improved to 11–1 in games away from Giants Stadium. "You never know. The right moment, the right time, every team is beatable."

Those who thought the 2007 season was the Patriots' moment, the Patriots' time—a time for Boston to revel in a glorious sports victory at the expense of a New York rival—had overlooked the Giants.

"Of course, they were surprised," defensive end Michael Strahan said. "We shocked the world. We shocked ourselves."

Giants receiver Plaxico Burress celebrates after hauling in the game-winning touchdown pass from Eli Manning in Super Bowl XLII.

"Catch 42" Sparks Giants

Giants coach Tom Coughlin called it one of the greatest plays in Super Bowl history. If Joe Montana-to-Dwight Clark in the 1981 NFC Championship Game was "The Catch," Giants fans can consider Eli Manning-to-David Tyree in Super Bowl XLII "Catch 42," as a poll in the *New York Daily News* dubbed it.

The catch, by itself, was worthy of such praise. Tyree outleaped Rodney Harrison and cradled the ball against the top of his helmet near midfield as Harrison and gravity were bringing him to the ground. You truly had to see it to believe it. Consider that the play covered 32 yards on a key third-and-five during the Giants' last-minute, Super Bowl–winning drive, and that Manning somehow scrambled out of a certain sack before delivering the throw, and, well....

"An amazing play," Coughlin noted, "in the middle of an amazing drive." One of the greatest in Super Bowl history, to be sure.

GIANTS GALLERY

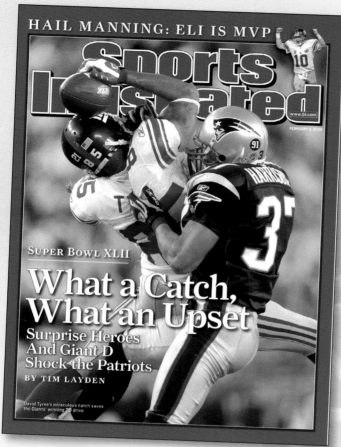

In 2008, Topps released these special cards after Super Bowl XLII: Jay Alford and his Giants teammates harassed Tom Brady throughout the Super Bowl. Plaxico Burress's 13-yard touchdown reception is the one that won the game, allowing Eli Manning and Tom Coughlin to hold up the big prize: the Lombardi Trophy.

Sports Illustrated was among the media outlets that thought David Tyree's grab was the play of the game.

This pin was given out to those attending the "Duel at the Meadowlands," featuring the Manning brothers, in 2006.

This novelty football honors the Giants' NFC title-game win over the Packers in −24 degrees Fahrenheit wind chill conditions at Lambeau Field on January 20, 2008.

This Amani Toomer bobble-head was issued to immortalize Super Bowl XLII.

Eli Manning, here in bobblehead form, is one of the most popular Giants.

The New York *Daily News* agrees that one play—"Catch 42"—came to symbolize the 2007 Giants' determination to win.

The Giants and the Dolphins played in the first game outside of North America at London's Wembley Stadium in 2007, when this pin was issued.

Big Success, Hard Fall

Eli Manning mustered a brief smile after one of the most heartbreaking setbacks of his young career, a 23–11 loss to Philadelphia in the 2008 divisional playoffs. The Giants quarterback knew that, despite the pain of becoming the first No. 1 seed to ever fall to a No. 6 in the NFC playoffs, there was much to celebrate in the way his team wore its 2007 Super Bowl crown.

"We were a good team," Manning said. "It was a fun year. We played really well this year, for most of the season."

The knowledge that the Giants went 12–4 in the regular season to earn the NFC's top seed did not ease the sting of their early playoff exit, which followed their unlikely run to the 2007 championship.

"We didn't have exit meetings last year," tight end Kevin Boss explained after the playoff loss. "We won the Super Bowl and rode off into the sunset. This year we have to do the painful stuff, like clean out the locker."

Before they tidied up for the offseason, the 2008 Giants proved that the previous year's championship was no fluke, winning the NFC East and looking—for most of the season—like a team that plans to contend for more titles in the years to come.

New York took 11 of its first 12 games in 2008, the best start for a defending Super Bowl champion since the New England Patriots followed their 2003 victory with a 12–1 start in '04. Included in the 2008 Giants' season-opening run was a torrid, seven-game winning streak in which they defeated all four conference championship game qualifiers—Philadelphia, Arizona,

Sports Illustrated *had some fun with David Tyree's helmet-aided Super Bowl reception in the 2008 training camp issue of the magazine. It was, indeed, a reception worthy of front-page play.*

Derrick Ward is chased by Carolina defenders as his overtime run sets up a Giants victory against the Panthers on December 21, 2008.

Pittsburgh, and Baltimore—along with San Francisco, Dallas, and Washington.

They did it in traditional Giants style, playing stout defense and running the football better than any team in the NFL.

Despite losing sack masters Michael Strahan to retirement and Osi Umenyiora to a season-ending knee injury in the preseason, the Giants finished fifth in the NFL in scoring defense. They ranked among the league's top 10 in both rushing and passing defense.

Offensively, Manning cut his previous year's interception total in half, throwing just 10 while completing more than 20 touchdown passes (21) for the fourth straight season. It was a topranked running attack, however, that powered the Giants.

Brandon Jacobs (1,089 yards, 15 TDs) and Derrick Ward (1,025) became just the fourth teammate tandem in NFL history to rush for more than 1,000 yards in the same season. With the powerful Jacobs carrying the load early, Ward sparking the offense in the third and fourth quarters, and Ahmad Bradshaw (355 yards) rounding out what became known as the "Earth, Wind, and Fire" backfield, New York was the only NFL team to top 2,500 rushing yards in 2008.

Derrick Ward's fancy footwork could not keep the Giants from falling to the Eagles in their 2008 playoff game. The loss brought a promising 2008 season to a premature end for the Giants, who were 12–4 in the regular season.

"It's difficult," Jacobs said, "when you have such a great team and you're around guys with great character who wanted to win and had such a great opportunity in front of us to go take advantage of going back to the Super Bowl."

Counting the playoff loss, the 2008 Giants dropped four of their last five games after their 11–1 start. Their season-ending slump, not coincidentally, followed the suspension of Plaxico Burress after the talented receiver accidentally shot himself in the thigh in December.

Brandon Jacobs, shown on this '08 Topps card, proved to be a franchise player that year with his second straight 1,000-yard rushing season.

With Burress (35 receptions) in the lineup, Manning threw 19 touchdown passes in the first 12 games. Without him, he threw for just two TDs in the last five games.

While players and coaches alike downplayed the effect of the "distraction" in the locker room, performing without one of their top offensive weapons clearly hurt the Giants down the stretch.

"'Plax' has a presence out there, and has an uncommon skill set, and you just don't replace that," Giants general manager Jerry Reese noted. While the team made some adjustments, the results just weren't there at that point of the season, he added.

Having made the playoffs four years in a row, the Giants wear the look of a team that expects to be there, and one built to succeed over the long haul.

Linebacker Danny Clark said that without a doubt the Giants will be back, mostly because of the resilient players who are on the team. A team leader, he added that as the Giants have shown in the past, there is a core of guys that can be successful.

GIANTS GALLERY

A collection of "realistic" bobbleheads like this can give fans a sense of pride...or a slightly queasy feeling.

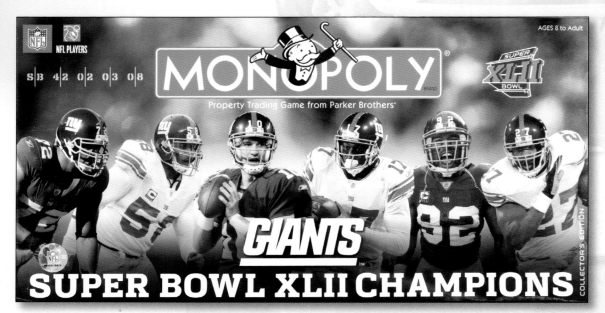

Sure to be a collector's item, this super Super Bowl XLII-edition Monopoly game lets you land on Eli Manning, a space that promises "Free Parking."

This novelty ball doesn't tell the whole story of the franchise. The Giants have a new stadium planned for 2010.

This Giants helmet was signed by Osi Umenyiora ("ny" side) and Brandon Jacobs ("FedEx" side). Umenyiora was a Pro Bowler in 2007, while Jacobs ran for 1,000 yards in both 2007 and '08.

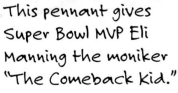

This pennant gives Super Bowl MVP Eli Manning the moniker "The Comeback Kid."

This wastepaper basket pictures Super Bowl XLII, in which the Giants trashed the Patriots.

The Giants and the city have always had a special relationship, as this 1990 pin (which includes the World Trade Center) reminds us.

Leaders and Legends
New York Giants, Year by Year

Year	Coach	Record	Result/Postseason	Year	Coach	Record	Result/Postseason
1925	Bob Fowell	8–4–0	4th	1953	Steve Owen	3–9–0	5th
1926	Joe Alexander	8–4–1	6th	1954	Jim Lee Howell	7–5–0	3rd
1927	Earl Potteiger	11–1–1	1st/NFL champions	1955	Jim Lee Howell	6–5–1	3rd
1928	Earl Potteiger	4–7–2	6th	1956	Jim Lee Howell	8–3–1	1st/NFL champions
1929	LeRoy Andrews	13–1–1	2nd	1957	Jim Lee Howell	7–5–0	2nd
1930	LeRoy Andrews/Benny Friedman	13–4–0	2nd	1958	Jim Lee Howell	9–3–0	1st/Eastern champions
1931	Steve Owen	7–6–1	5th	1959	Jim Lee Howell	10–2–0	1st/Eastern champions
1932	Steve Owen	4–6–2	5th	1960	Jim Lee Howell	6–4–2	3rd
1933	Steve Owen	11–3–0	1st/Eastern champions	1961	Allie Sherman	10–3–1	1st/Eastern champions
1934	Steve Owen	8–5–0	1st/NFL champions	1962	Allie Sherman	12–2–0	1st/Eastern champions
1935	Steve Owen	9–3–0	1st/Eastern champions	1963	Allie Sherman	11–3–0	1st/Eastern champions
1936	Steve Owen	5–6–1	3rd	1964	Allie Sherman	2–10–2	7th
1937	Steve Owen	6–3–2	2nd	1965	Allie Sherman	7–7–0	2nd
1938	Steve Owen	8–2–1	1st/NFL champions	1966	Allie Sherman	1–12–1	8th
1939	Steve Owen	9–1–1	1st/Eastern champions	1967	Allie Sherman	7–7–0	2nd
1940	Steve Owen	6–4–1	3rd	1968	Allie Sherman	7–7–0	2nd
1941	Steve Owen	8–3–0	1st/Eastern champions	1969	Alex Webster	6–8–0	2nd
1942	Steve Owen	5–5–1	3rd	1970	Alex Webster	9–5–0	2nd
1943	Steve Owen	6–3–1	2nd	1971	Alex Webster	4–10–0	5th
1944	Steve Owen	8–1–1	1st/Eastern champions	1972	Alex Webster	8–6–0	3rd
1945	Steve Owen	3–6–1	3rd	1973	Alex Webster	2–11–1	5th
1946	Steve Owen	7–3–1	1st/Eastern champions	1974	Bill Arnsparger	2–12–0	5th
1947	Steve Owen	2–8–2	5th	1975	Bill Arnsparger	5–9–0	4th
1948	Steve Owen	4–8–0	3rd	1976	Bill Arnsparger/John McVay	3–11–0	5th
1949	Steve Owen	6–6–0	3rd	1977	John McVay	5–9–0	5th
1950	Steve Owen	10–2–0	2nd	1978	John McVay	6–10–0	5th
1951	Steve Owen	9–2–1	2nd	1979	Ray Perkins	6–10–0	4th
1952	Steve Owen	7–5–0	2nd				

Year	Coach	Record	Result/Postseason
1980	Ray Perkins	4–12–0	5th
1981	Ray Perkins	9–7–0	3rd
1982	Ray Perkins	4–5–0	10th
1983	Bill Parcells	3–12–1	5th
1984	Bill Parcells	9–7–0	2nd
1985	Bill Parcells	10–6–0	2nd
1986	Bill Parcells	14–2–0	1st/Super Bowl champions
1987	Bill Parcells	6–9–0	5th
1988	Bill Parcells	10–6–0	2nd
1989	Bill Parcells	12–4–0	1st/NFC East champions
1990	Bill Parcells	13–3–0	1st/Super Bowl champions
1991	Ray Handley	8–8–0	4th
1992	Ray Handley	6–10–0	4th
1993	Dan Reeves	11–5–0	2nd
1994	Dan Reeves	9–7–0	2nd
1995	Dan Reeves	5–11–0	4th
1996	Dan Reeves	6–10–0	5th
1997	Jim Fassel	10–5–1	1st/NFC East champions
1998	Jim Fassel	8–8–0	3rd
1999	Jim Fassel	7–9–0	3rd
2000	Jim Fassel	12–4–0	1st/NFC champions
2001	Jim Fassel	7–9–0	3rd
2002	Jim Fassel	10–6–0	2nd
2003	Jim Fassel	4–12–0	4th
2004	Tom Coughlin	6–10–0	2nd
2005	Tom Coughlin	11–5–0	1st/NFC East champions
2006	Tom Coughlin	8–8–0	3rd
2007	Tom Coughlin	10–6–0	2nd/Super Bowl champions
2008	Tom Coughlin	12–4–0	1st/NFC East champions
Totals		**618–510–30**	

Playoff Results

Dec. 17, 1933: NFC Divisional–Chicago Bears 23, N.Y. Giants 21

Dec. 9, 1934: NFL Championship–N.Y. Giants 30, Chicago Bears 13

Dec. 15, 1935: NFL Championship–Detroit 26, N.Y. Giants 7

Dec. 11, 1938: NFL Championship–N.Y. Giants 23, Green Bay 17

Dec. 10, 1939: NFL Championship–Green Bay 27, N.Y. Giants 0

Dec. 21, 1941: NFL Championship–Chicago Bears 37, N.Y. Giants 9

Dec. 19, 1943: Eastern Division–Redskins 28, N.Y. Giants 0

Dec. 17, 1944: NFL Championship–Green Bay 14, N.Y. Giants 7

Dec. 15, 1946: NFL Championship–Chicago Bears 24, N.Y. Giants 14

Dec. 17, 1950: American Conference–Cleveland 8, N.Y. Giants 3

Dec. 30, 1956: NFL Championship–N.Y. Giants 47, Chicago Bears 7

Dec. 21, 1958: Eastern Conference–N.Y. Giants 10, Cleveland 0

Dec. 28, 1958: NFL Championship–Baltimore 23, N.Y. Giants 17 (OT)

Dec. 27, 1959: NFL Championship–Baltimore 31, N.Y. Giants 16

Dec. 31, 1961: NFL Championship–Green Bay 37, N.Y. Giants 0

Dec. 30, 1962: NFL Championship–Green Bay 16, N.Y. Giants 7

Dec. 29, 1963: NFL Championship–Chicago 14, N.Y. Giants 10

Dec. 27, 1981: NFC Wild Card–N.Y. Giants 27, Philadelphia 21

Jan. 3, 1982: NFC Divisional–San Francisco 38, N.Y. Giants 24

Dec. 23, 1984: NFC Wild Card–N.Y. Giants 16, L.A. Rams 13

Dec. 29, 1984: NFC Divisional–San Francisco 21, N.Y. Giants 10

Dec. 29, 1985: NFC Wild Card–N.Y. Giants 17, San Francisco 3

Jan. 5, 1986: NFC Divisional–Chicago 21, N.Y. Giants 0

Jan. 4, 1987: NFC Divisional–N.Y. Giants 49, San Francisco 3

Jan. 11, 1987: NFC Championship–N.Y. Giants 17, Washington 0

Jan. 25, 1987: Super Bowl XXI–N.Y. Giants 39, Denver 20

Jan. 7, 1990: NFC Divisional–L.A. Rams 19, N.Y. Giants 13 (OT)

Jan. 13, 1991: NFC Divisional–N.Y. Giants 31, Chicago 3

Jan. 20, 1991: NFC Championship–N.Y. Giants 15, San Francisco 13

Jan. 27, 1991: Super Bowl XXV–N.Y. Giants 20, Buffalo 19

Jan. 9, 1994: NFC Wild Card–N.Y. Giants 17, Minnesota 10

Jan. 15, 1994: NFC Divisional–San Francisco 44, N.Y. Giants 3

Dec. 27, 1997: NFC Wild Card–Minnesota 23, N.Y. Giants 22

Jan. 7, 2001: NFC Divisional–N.Y. Giants 20, Philadelphia 10

Jan. 14, 2001: NFC Championship–N.Y. Giants 41, Minnesota 0

Jan. 28, 2001: Super Bowl XXXV–Baltimore 34, N.Y. Giants 7

Jan. 5, 2003: NFC Wild Card–San Francisco 39, N.Y. Giants 38

Jan. 8, 2005: NFC Wild Card–Carolina 23, N.Y. Giants 0

Jan. 7, 2007: NFC Wild Card–Philadelphia 23, N.Y. Giants 20

Jan. 6, 2008: NFC Wild Card–N.Y. Giants 24, Tampa Bay 14

Jan. 13, 2008: NFC Divisional–N.Y. Giants 21, Dallas 17

Jan. 20, 2008: NFC Championship–N.Y. Giants 23, Green Bay 20 (OT)

Feb. 3, 2008: Super Bowl XLII–N.Y. Giants 17, New England 14

Jan. 11, 2009: NFC Divisional–Philadelphia 23, N.Y. Giants 11

Head Coaches
(Records do not include playoff games)

Coach	Seasons	Record
Bob Folwell	1925	8–4–0
Joe Alexander	1926	8–4–1
Earl Potteiger	1927–1928	15–8–3
LeRoy Andrews	1929–1930	24–5–1
Benny Friedman	1930	2–0–0
Steve Owen	1931–1953	153–100–17
Jim Lee Howell	1954–1960	53–27–4
Allie Sherman	1961–1968	57–51–4
Alex Webster	1969–1973	29–40–1
Bill Arnsparger	1974–1976	7–28–0
John McVay	1976–1978	14–23–0
Ray Perkins	1979–1982	23–34–0
Bill Parcells	1983–1990	77–49–1
Ray Handley	1991–1992	14–18–0
Dan Reeves	1993–1996	31–33–0
Jim Fassel	1997–2003	58–53–1
Tom Coughlin	2004–2008	47–33–0

Most Pro Bowl Appearances

Lawrence Taylor	10	(1981–1990)
Rosey Brown	9	(1955–1960, 1962, 1964–1965)
Harry Carson	9	(1978–1979, 1981–1987)
Emlen Tunnell	8	(1950–1957)
Frank Gifford	7	(1953–1956, 1958–1959, 1963)
Michael Strahan	7	(1997–1999, 2001–2003, 2005)

Most Consecutive Pro Bowl Appearances

Lawrence Taylor	10	(1981–1990)
Emlen Tunnell	8	(1950–1957)
Harry Carson	7	(1981–1987)
Rosey Brown	6	(1955–1960)
Jimmy Patton	5	(1958–1962)
Brad Van Pelt	5	(1976–1980)
Jesse Armstead	5	(1997–2001)

Retired Numbers

1	Ray Flaherty, E (1928–1929, 1931–1935)
4	Tuffy Leemans, RB (1936–1943)
7	Mel Hein, C (1931–1945)
11	Phil Simms, QB (1979–1993)
14	Y. A. Tittle, QB (1961–1964)
16	Frank Gifford, HB (1952–1960, 1962–1964)
32	Al Blozis, OT (1942–1944)
40	Joe Morrison, RB, WR (1959–1972)
42	Charlie Conerly, QB (1948–1961)
50	Ken Strong, HB (1933–1935, 1939, 1944–1947)
56	Lawrence Taylor, LB (1981–1993)

Giants in Pro Football Hall of Fame

Red Badgro, E, 1981

Roosevelt Brown, T, 1975

Harry Carson, LB, 2006

Benny Friedman, QB, 2005

Frank Gifford, HB, 1977

Mel Hein, C, 1963

Sam Huff, LB, 1982

Tuffy Leemans, HB, FB, 1978

Vince Lombardi, Coach, 1971

Tim Mara, Founder, 1963

Wellington Mara, Co-owner, 1997

Steve Owen, Coach, 1966

Andy Robustelli, DE, 1971

Ken Strong, HB, 1967

Lawrence Taylor, LB, 1999

Y. A. Tittle, QB, 1971

Emlen Tunnell, DB, 1967

Arnold Weinmeister, DT, 1984

Players in the Hall of Fame with Giants Experience

Larry Csonka, FB, 1987

Ray Flaherty, E, Coach, 1976

Joe Guyon, HB, 1966

Pete Henry, HB, 1963

Arnie Herber, QB, 1966

Cal Hubbard, T, 1963

Don Maynard, WR, 1987

Hugh McElhenny, HB, 1970

Fran Tarkenton, QB, 1986

Jim Thorpe, HB, 1963

Special Awards

Associated Press NFL MVP Award
1963 Y. A. Tittle Quarterback
1986 Lawrence Taylor Linebacker

Pro Football Writers Association NFL MVP Award
1986 Lawrence Taylor Linebacker

United Press International NFL MVP Award
1956 Frank Gifford Running back
1962 Y. A. Tittle Quarterback

Newspaper Enterprise Association NFL MVP Award
1956 Frank Gifford Running back
1959 Charlie Conerly Quarterback

1961 Y. A. Tittle Quarterback
1963 Y. A. Tittle Quarterback
1986 Phil Simms Quarterback

The Sporting News NFL MVP Award
1962 Y. A. Tittle Quarterback
1963 Y. A. Tittle Quarterback
1986 Lawrence Taylor Linebacker

Joe F. Carr Trophy NFL MVP Award
1938 Mel Hein Center

Maxwell Football Club Bert Bell Award NFL Player of the Year
1962 Andy Robustelli Defensive end
1986 Lawrence Taylor Linebacker

Super Bowl MVP Award
1987 Super Bowl XXI Phil Simms Quarterback
1991 Super Bowl XXV Ottis Anderson Running back
2008 Super Bowl XLII Eli Manning Quarterback

Associated Press NFL Defensive Rookie of the Year
1981 Lawrence Taylor Linebacker

Associated Press NFL Coach of the Year
1961 Allie Sherman
1962 Allie Sherman
1986 Bill Parcells
1993 Dan Reeves
1997 Jim Fassel

The Sporting News NFL Coach of the Year
1950 Steve Owen
1956 Jim Lee Howell
1986 Bill Parcells
1993 Dan Reeves
1997 Jim Fassel

Maxwell Club Earle "Greasy" Neale Award (NFL Coach of the Year)

1993	Dan Reeves

United Press International NFL/NFC Coach of the Year

1961	Allie Sherman
1962	Allie Sherman
1970	Alex Webster
1986	Bill Parcells
1993	Dan Reeves
1997	Jim Fassel

NFL-NFC Rookie of the Year

1974	John Hicks	Guard

NFL Defensive Rookie of the Year

1981	Lawrence Taylor	Linebacker

Newspaper Enterprise Association NFL Rookie of the Year

1981	Lawrence Taylor	Linebacker

All-Time Leaders: Passing Yards

	Name	Years	Att	Comp	Yards	Pct	TD	INT
1.	Phil Simms	1979–1993	4,647	2,576	33,462	55.4	199	157
2.	Charlie Conerly	1948–1961	2,833	1,418	19,488	50.0	173	167
3.	Kerry Collins	1999–2003	2,473	1,447	16,875	58.5	81	70
4.	Eli Manning	2004–2008	2,284	1,276	14,623	55.9	98	74
5.	Fran Tarkenton	1967–1971	1,898	1,051	13,905	55.4	103	72
6.	Y. A. Tittle	1961–1964	1,308	731	10,439	55.9	96	68
7.	Dave Brown	1992–1997	1,391	766	8,806	55.1	40	49
8.	Scott Brunner	1980–1983	986	482	6,121	48.9	28	48
9.	Craig Morton	1974–1976	884	461	5,734	52.1	29	49
10.	Norm Snead	1972–1974, 1976	713	416	4,644	58.4	27	45

All-Time Leaders: Rushing Yards

	Name	Years	Carries	Yards	Avg	LG	TD
1.	Tiki Barber	1997–2006	2,217	10,449	4.7	95	55
2.	Rodney Hampton	1990–1997	1,824	6,897	3.8	63	49
3.	Joe Morris	1982–1989	1,318	5,296	4.0	65	48
4.	Alex Webster	1955–1964	1,196	4,638	3.9	71	39
5.	Ron Johnson	1970–1975	1,066	3,836	3.6	68	33
6.	Frank Gifford	1952–1960, 1962–1964	840	3,609	4.3	79	34
7.	Doug Kotar	1974–1981	900	3,380	3.8	53	20
8.	Eddie Price	1950–1955	846	3,292	3.9	80	20
9.	Tuffy Leemans	1936–1943	919	3,132	3.4	75	17
10.	Brandon Jacobs	2005–2008	555	2,620	4.7	44	35

All-Time Leaders: Receptions

	Name	Years	Total	Yards	Avg	LG	TD
1.	Amani Toomer	1996–2008	668	9,497	14.2	82	54
2.	Tiki Barber	1997–2006	586	5,183	8.8	87	12
3.	Joe Morrison	1959–1972	395	4,993	12.6	70	47
4.	Jeremy Shockey	2002–2007	371	4,228	11.4	59	27
5.	Ike Hillard	1997–2004	368	4,630	12.6	59	27
6.	Frank Gifford	1952–1960, 1962–1964	367	5,434	14.8	77	43
7.	Chris Calloway	1992–1998	334	4,710	14.1	68	27
8.	Bob Tucker	1970–1977	327	4,376	13.4	63	22
9.	Kyle Rote	1951–1961	300	4,797	16.0	75	48
10.	Mark Bavaro	1985–1990	266	3,722	14.0	61	28

All-Time Leaders: Interceptions

	Name	Years	Total	Yards	Avg	TD
1.	Emlen Tunnell	1949–1958	74	1,240	16.8	4
2.	Jim Patton	1955–1966	52	712	13.7	2
3.	Spider Lockhart	1965–1975	41	475	11.6	3

	Name	Years	Total	Yards	Avg	TD
4.	Dick Lynch	1959–1966	35	568	16.2	4
4.	Willie Williams	1965, 1967–1973	35	462	13.2	0
6.	Tom Landry	1950–1955	31	360	11.6	3
7.	Terry Kinard	1983–1989	27	574	21.3	2
8.	Terry Jackson	1978–1983	24	282	11.8	2
9.	Phillippi Sparks	1992–1999	22	163	7.4	0
10.	Frank Reagan	1941, 1946–1948	20	376	18.8	0

Single-Season Leaders: Passing

Pass Attempts

	Name	Att	Season
1.	Kerry Collins	568	2001
2.	Eli Manning	557	2005
3.	Kerry Collins	545	2002
4.	Phil Simms	533	1984
5.	Kerry Collins	529	2000
5.	Eli Manning	529	2007
7.	Eli Manning	522	2006
8.	Kerry Collins	500	2003
9.	Phil Simms	495	1985
10.	Phil Simms	479	1988
10.	Eli Manning	479	2008

Pass Completions

	Name	Comp	Season
1.	Kerry Collins	335	2002
2.	Kerry Collins	327	2001
3.	Kerry Collins	311	2000
4.	Eli Manning	301	2006
5.	Eli Manning	297	2007
6.	Eli Manning	294	2005
7.	Eli Manning	289	2008
8.	Phil Simms	286	1984

	Name	Comp	Season
9.	Kerry Collins	284	2003
10.	Phil Simms	275	1985

Passing Yards

	Name	Yards	Season
1.	Kerry Collins	4,073	2002
2.	Phil Simms	4,044	1984
3.	Phil Simms	3,829	1985
4.	Kerry Collins	3,764	2001
5.	Eli Manning	3,762	2005
6.	Kerry Collins	3,610	2000
7.	Phil Simms	3,487	1986
8.	Phil Simms	3,359	1988
9.	Eli Manning	3,336	2007
10.	Eli Manning	3,244	2006

Touchdown Passes

	Name	TD	Season
1.	Y. A. Tittle	36	1963
2.	Y. A. Tittle	33	1962
3.	Fran Tarkenton	29	1967
4.	Eli Manning	24	2005
4.	Eli Manning	24	2006
6.	Fran Tarkenton	23	1969
6.	Eli Manning	23	2007
8.	Charley Conerly	22	1948
8.	Earl Morrall	22	1965
8.	Phil Simms	22	1984
8.	Phil Simms	22	1985
8.	Kerry Collins	22	2000

Passer Rating

	Name	Rating	Season
1.	Y. A. Tittle	104.8	1963
2.	Charley Conerly	102.7	1959

	Name	Rating	Season
3.	Phil Simms	92.7	1990
4.	Phil Simms	90.0	1987
5.	Y. A. Tittle	89.5	1962
6.	Phil Simms	88.3	1993
7.	Fran Tarkenton	87.2	1969
8.	Phil Simms	87.0	1991
9.	Kurt Warner	86.5	2004
10.	Eli Manning	86.4	2008

Single-Season Leaders: Rushing

Rushing Attempts

	Name	Carries	Season
1.	Tiki Barber	357	2005
2.	Joe Morris	341	1986
3.	Rodney Hampton	327	1994
3.	Tiki Barber	327	2006
5.	Ottis Anderson	325	1989
6.	Tiki Barber	322	2004
7.	Joe Morris	307	1988
8.	Rodney Hampton	306	1995
9.	Tiki Barber	304	2002
10.	Ron Johnson	298	1972

Rushing Yards

	Name	Yards	Season
1.	Tiki Barber	1,860	2005
2.	Tiki Barber	1,662	2006
3.	Tiki Barber	1,518	2004
4.	Joe Morris	1,516	1986
5.	Tiki Barber	1,387	2002
6.	Joe Morris	1,336	1985
7.	Tiki Barber	1,216	2003
8.	Ron Johnson	1,182	1972

	Name	Yards	Season
8.	Rodney Hampton	1,182	1995
10.	Rodney Hampton	1,141	1992

Rushing Touchdowns

	Name	TD	Season
1.	Joe Morris	21	1985
2.	Brandon Jacobs	15	2008
3.	Joe Morris	14	1986
3.	Ottis Anderson	14	1989
3.	Rodney Hampton	14	1992

Single-Season Leaders: Receiving

Receptions

	Name	Total	Season
1.	Amani Toomer	82	2002
2.	Amani Toomer	79	1999
3.	Earnest Gray	78	1983
3.	Amani Toomer	78	2000
5.	Plaxico Burress	76	2005

Receiving Yards

	Name	Yards	Season
1.	Amani Toomer	1,343	2002
2.	Plaxico Burress	1,214	2005
3.	Homer Jones	1,209	1967
4.	Amani Toomer	1,183	1999
5.	Del Shofner	1,181	1963

Receiving Touchdowns

	Name	TD	Season
1.	Homer Jones	13	1967
2.	Plaxico Burress	12	2007
2.	Del Shofner	12	1962
4.	Del Shofner	11	1961